The Good That We Do

ALSO BY JOHN LUCAS

CRITICISM ETC
Tradition & Tolerance in 19th Century Fiction (with John Goode &
  David Howard)
The Melancholy Man: A Study of Dickens' Novels
Literature & Politics in the 19th Century (with Goode, Howard and Wm
  Myers)
Arnold Bennett
The Literature of Change
The 1930s: A Challenge to Orthodoxy (ed)
Romantic to Modern
Moderns and Contemporaries
Modern English Poetry from Hardy to Hughes
England and Englishness
Dickens: The Major Novels
John Clare
The Radical Twenties
Writing and Radicalism (ed)
William Blake (ed)
Ivor Gurney

POETRY
About Nottingham
Egil's Saga
Studying Grosz on the Bus
One for the Piano
On the Track

BIOGRAPHY
The Trent Bridge Battery: The Story of the Sporting Gunns (with Basil
  Haynes)

EDITIONS
George Crabbe: Poems
Jane Austen: Mansfield Park
W.H. Mallock: The New Republic
G.S. Fraser: Poems (with Ian Fletcher)
Oliver Goldsmith: Poems
D.H. Lawrence: Poems and Selected Prose
Robert Bloomfield: Poems (with John Goodridge)
Stanley Middleton at Eighty (with David Belbin)

The Good That We Do

John Lucas

GREENWICH EXCHANGE
LONDON

Printed and bound by Quorn Selective Repro, Loughborough
Tel: 01509 213456
Typeset by the Midlands Book Typesetting Company, Loughborough
Tel: 01509 210920

Greenwich Exchange Website: www.greenex.co.uk

ISBN 1-871551-54-4

To the memory of my grandfather

H. W. S. Kelly, 1880-1940

Prefatory Note

The following book blends fiction, biography and social history in order to tell the story of a man who, while in no sense famous, seems to me to have led an exemplary life. In saying this, however, I am not so much trying to redeem him from what E.P. Thompson famously called the enormous condescension of posterity as to endorse Thompson's conviction that "history from below" is both valid and valuable. H.W.S. Kelly ("Hod") wasn't a saint of humanity, not as George Eliot understood the term. On the other hand, the closing words of *Middlemarch* apply as fittingly to him as they do to those altruistic characters she so ardently admired. "For the growing good of the world is partly dependent on unhistoric acts," she wrote, "and that things are not so ill with you and me as they might have been, is half owing to the number who lived faithfully a hidden life, and rest in unvisited tombs." Her words apply equally well to innumerable others, of course. They no doubt deserve *their* biographers, *their* historians. But *The Good That We Do* is the story I want to tell.

The good that we do, and the virtues that we show, and particularly the children that we rear, survive us through the long and unknown perspectives of time.

Charles Dickens, *Commercial Travellers' Schools.*

Contents

PART 1

ROSE FARM LONGWICK, 6 FEBRUARY, 1940

He wrote "It has been very cold in the hall. The thermometer recorded 29 at 9 a.m. The boys were given P.T. and then games until 11 a.m. Then stories from Robin Hood were read to them. No written work was attempted this morning. Temperature at 1.30 p.m. 46. This afternoon Mrs Brown, foster parent of Edgar Bousfield, reported that he was badly in need of trousers." He had given instructions, as a result of which Bousfield had been taken to Princes Risborough and bought his much-needed trousers. Cost 2/11d.

There was more. Nothing must be hidden from the inspectors. "Mr. Baker, foster parent of John Coventry (8), called to see me this evening. He told me his wife had caught John Coventry interfering with his daughter (6). I reported the matter to Mrs Walker (building officer) who has promised to billet him elsewhere." Had she done so? He realised he did not know and at the same moment became aware of a terrible fatigue spreading up from his legs and sending wave after wave of heavy lassitude through his whole body, as though his veins were being slowly filled with threads of mercury. He was tired, more tired than he had ever been in his life, and the pen had difficulty pushing across the page. The nib was dry, it made useless scratches on the paper, and he would have to locate the silver-cased bottle he always kept topped up with Stephens' blue-black ink.

"Snowing heavily. Mrs Kelly has taken my place at school today." He must have written that. But why? Where was he if not in school? The question disturbed. If he concentrated on looking steadily in front of him he would surely see the rows of boys he had brought with him from Fulham: Barry Tibbles, John Gray, David Lockett, Fred Munday, George and Fred Murtagh, Leslie Noble, John Reed – no, not John, he'd gone back to London with his parents – George Owen, though, he was still here, or rather had come back to Princes Risborough after spending Christmas in Fulham, as had William Taylor; and there was Cyril Shankster who always sat beside Jack Dent, Bousfield in his new trousers, which weren't warm enough to keep out the cold, and if it came to that all the boys were more or less poorly dressed, shivering in the cold he himself could not feel, blowing on their hands or rubbing them vigorously up and down the calves of legs, many of which bore scabs and some of which were unmistakably bowed. He *must* tell the Assistance Board that as well as clothes the boys needed ample supplies of Vitamin D. Despite his tiredness he knew he would have to write to the Board, but where was his pen? There was something he wanted to write to Joano, something he wanted her to pass onto Billy and Jillian when they were old enough to understand.

Harry Kelly, suddenly alert beside his brother's bed, watched the fingers that made scarcely discernible movements as they lay on the turned-down sheet, then reached across and tucked them back under the thick, woollen blanket. As he did so, he once more caught the smell, that sweet, rotting stench of gangrenous flesh. Carefully he straightened Hod's pillow. Hod did not open his eyes. His usually pale face was now waxily white, the eyelids, thin-veined, sealed down by an even line of lash, the bald dome of his head, with its wispy frieze of grey hair, cold to the touch of Harry's lips.

He turned away. A fire burned low in the grate, the few coals sighing into ash. There was no other sound. The silent, freezing February night, lit by clusters of stars and a staring bombers' moon, was shut away behind heavy blackout curtains. Ought he to call Cissie? But he'd not long since ordered her to take some rest, worn out as she all-too plainly was from the long hours spent by the sick bed. He leant over Hod, his ear as near to his brother's mouth as he could bring it without touching him. Again, that smell. Hod's breathing was fainter now, no doubt about it. He'd better rouse her.

But by the time Cissie stumbled through the bedroom door, wrapping her dressing-gown round her heavy body, it was already too late.

ST MARYCHURCH, 12 JUNE, 1887.

Although the church clock had only just struck ten the sun was already hot on his back The day would be fine, just as his parents had promised.

Emerging from Albert Square into the high street, on either side of which were two-storied buildings, shops below, living quarters above, he glanced up at the lines of red-white-and-blue bunting stretched across the street. The union jack hung from windows, many of the shop fronts were decorated with large cardboard, gold-painted crowns with the lion and unicorn poised above, and above *them* were pictures of the queen's head in profile. He looked past the bunting to where the sky's blue was momentarily disturbed by a fat cloud disappearing over a thick line of oak trees that jutted over the houses and shops to his right. The oaks were on the edge of a park where he and Fred played, and where he'd found the stag beetle that was now stowed in a tin in his trouser pocket. As he walked he took the tin out of his pocket and inspected his beetle, its two-inch long, ox-blood coloured body topped by gleaming black horns that looked as though they could give a fearful nip, although by daring to brush his fingers against them he'd discovered they did nothing of the sort. "Snuff boxes ain't no use," Fred had told him. "Too small. Bet your ma has one of they pastille tins. Look, like this." And he'd held out a round, blue-painted metal box, about three inches across, its top punctured by a number of holes like those you saw on sugar casters. "Made these with a nail," he said. "Gives the beetle a chance to breathe." Then he'd prised off the lid and there, almost filling the space, was a stag-beetle.

Hod had seen them before, of course, clinging to oak leaves or feeling their way slowly along garden hedges, had even experienced a moment of panic when one bumped him in the face as he wandered with Fred through the park in early evening – "they fly about a bit at this time" his friend had said, laughing, "like ghosties" – but he'd never thought of catching one. "Don't they bite" he wondered aloud, and for answer Fred shook the beetle into his open hand and told Hod to touch it. Hod put out a finger, ready to leap back, but when he felt the beetle's horns it was no more frightening than rubbing his fingers along the teeth of one of his mother's combs that lay scattered about her dressing table.

Now he had his own beetle, "Arthur", nestling inside an empty tin box he'd found tucked away in his father's bureau. The box smelled strongly of pipe tobacco, but Hod had washed it and put in an oak leaf on which the beetle could rest. Later in the day he'd show Fred. For the moment, dressed in his Sunday best even though it wasn't Sunday, he had other responsibilities.

Outside his father's shop he paused for a moment and, as he always did, read the sign which said in foot-high, red-painted letters that twisted and turned like barley sugar.

WILLIAM S. KELLY FAMILY BUTCHER AND FINE MEATS

The blinds were down to show there'd be no business that day, but the door was ajar and through it he could hear his father's voice, deep and as usual muffled, because, so his mother said, "he do never have that dratted pipe out of his mouth", although Hod secretly thought his father's huge beard, that more or less hid his lips, made a kind of hedge inside which words could easily hide. Or a stag-beetle, he thought suddenly, wanting to laugh.

"That's as maybe. All I'm sayin' is, Churchill brought it on hisself." His father's voice was raised, not in anger but to emphasise a point as Hod often heard him do at the dinner table, to correct one of the children, perhaps, or explain a right and wrong. "I don't care what anyone says. Too big for his boots, that mester."

"Surprised you care, William, seein' as how you don't stand that side of the fence." Mr Coulter's laugh. He owned the next-door haberdashery.

"Don't 'ee now?" Hod thought he knew that voice, too. He pushed open the door and went in, his boots clumping on the wooden floor which had for today been swept clean of sawdust, and, yes, he'd guessed right, it *was* Mr Pannel. "Well, names do tell us a good deal, I'm sure," Mr Pannel now added, letting his gaze wander indifferently over Hod, before he turned back to the others.

"Meanin'"? William Kelly took the pipe from his mouth and

peered into the bowl, then pushed his fore-finger into it before looking across at the clean-shaven Mr. Pannel. Like the other men, Hod's father was dressed in a dark-grey three-piece suit, thumb of his left hand jammed into a waistcoat pocket from which a gold watch chain dangled. He had his back to the long, marble counter, covered by a white sheet, and Hod saw that the wooden chopping block, as deep as a kettle-drum, had been pushed to the back of the shop, below a line of polished knives, cleavers, a bow saw. After the sun, his father's shop, darkened because of the drawn down-blinds, felt cool and for once was almost free of the drone of fat meat-flies which would circle lazily around the heads of customers and animal carcasses, although Hod noticed a fly feel its way down one of the steel hooks that hung like inverted-question marks from rails running round the walls, empty of the sides of beef, of pork and lamb, that usually hung from them and dripped their slow blood into matted sawdust.

"Kelly", Mr. Pannel said, watching as Hod's father returned the pipe to his scarcely-visible mouth. "A touch of the Irish there, I fancy."

Hod went over to his father, who reached out and placed his free hand on his son's shoulder. Hod felt the fingers tremble slightly as Willliam Kelly noisily cleared his throat before saying "'Tis true the family come over from Ireland but that were more'n a century past, and we ain't been catholic these fifty years. Though sayin' that ain't to say I'm against Home Rule, because I ain't."

"Well, I say Gladstone's a fool as deserved to be turfed out. The Irish ain't fit to govern theirselves" Mr. Pannel said. Even in the gloom Hod could see his face begin to flush above his stiff white collar and the low-knotted shiny black tie. "Especially not arter what they done in Phoenix Park."

"Ah, I know what you mean," Mr. Coulter said reasonably, "still, I suppose if they'd had Home Rule there wouldn't have been no need for murder."

"Ain't no use arguin' with you two," Mr Pannel said, who seemed thoroughly angry. "I'd best be off. I'll no doubt be seein' you at the Green?" He made it sound a challenge.

"Oh, ah, we'll be there right enough" Hod's father said, and Mr.

Coulter added, "wouldn't not want to pay our respects as humble servants of her majesty."

Mr. Pannel looked at him as though wondering whether to reply, but changed his mind and went out, pulling the door shut behind him.

Mr. Coulter stared solemnly at Hod and his father, then suddenly winked as his face relaxed into a smile. "Ironmongery perhaps not doin' too well," he said.

Hod's father laughed. "Oh, he ain't so bad," he said, "just a mite too keen on bein' on the right side." And he cleared his throat again, making a noise which Hod thought sounded like brook water scuttering over pebbles.

"You orter do somethin' about that throat o' yourn", Mr Coulter said.

* * *

The church clock chimed three-quarters of eleven when Hod turned into Carey Grove to deliver the last of the packages his father had given him. Lamb chops for the widow Bullivant. "And mind you don't give 'em over wi'out seein' her money," his father had said, "she's a bit of a fly old bird, that one. Never has her purse when 'tis needed."

Hod went up the passage beside the house, opened the back-garden wooden gate, beyond which was a riot of hollyhocks, lupins and tall white flowers he didn't recognise, and followed the brick path to the back door. Just as he reached up to grasp the black knocker the door opened and Mrs. Bullivant, in creaking rusty black dress, peered out. Perched on top of her head was a black straw hat, looking somehow like a charred pork pie. Her dim eyes focussed on the bundle Hod was carrying. "Chops be they?"

"Two," Hod said, "fourpence three-farthen each, and father says can he have the money, please?"

"Two at fourpence three-farthen" Mrs Bullivant repeated. "I'll have to find my purse." She was holding it in her hand.

Hod pointed at it. "Nine and a half-pence, please" he said.

Mrs Bullivant stared at him. "You'm sharp for a seven-year old," she said, "sharp enough to come from Sheffield. Did you work that out for yourself or did your father tell 'ee?"

"Polly's been teachin' me sums," Hod said, "and I won't be seven until November."

"Oh, ah, clever Polly," Mrs Bullivant said, nodding her head slowly up and down. "How is your sister? Still at her school, where is it..."

"Truro," Hod told her, "but she's come home for today. We're all goin' to the Green. Everyone in the town's goin'," he added, feeling the excitement catch hold of him.

"Not me," Mrs Bullivant said, "I can't stand crowds, or the heat. Anyway, there are widders who need more care and attention than *she* does. Or deserves. I don't hold with marryin' foreigners. And now they say she's got this Scotch man so he b'aint much better." She counted the coins into Hod's outstretched hand. "You be sure to shut the gate behind you," she said, preparing to close the door. "I know you lads and I don't want no stray dogs in here, diggin' up plants and vegetables I've took the care to nurtur'."

On his way back to the shop, left-hand trouser pocket heavy with coins, right-hand cosseting the box in which Arthur lay content – at several moments during his errands he'd peered inside just to be sure – Hod's thoughts drifted to the coming afternoon. There was to be a pageant to celebrate the queen's fifty years on the throne, and while his father wrapped the meat parcels he'd to deliver, Mr. Coulter had told Hod what to expect. "It'll be a gurt big 'un, St. Marychurch's pageant," Mr. Coulter assured him. "A mite of the town 'll be in it, from big wig to tiddle pisky, all of 'un dressin' up as historical characters. An' accordin to what I hear they'll be actin' out" he paused, and then pronounced, "Events of Historical Significance in Our Island Story." "Come more natural to some than to others, I reckon," Hod's father said, and Mr. Coulter replied, laughing, "Ah, I shouldn't wonder at that, neither,"

What events, Hod wanted to know. Oh, King Alfred's victory over the Danes, for a start, the defeat of the Armada, the battle of Blenheim, victory at Waterloo. "Wi' Sol Pannel as Boney," Hod's father said, and this time both men laughed.

"How about the great pudding fight?" Hod asked. But Mr. Coulter shook his head. "I don't reckon that'd do," he said, to Hod's regret. Mr. Coulter had first told him about the fight one Saturday afternoon when the Coulter and Kelly families had all been for one of their picnics on Babbacombe Heights.

Hod loved those shared picnics. His father was always in a jolly mood, having shut up shop by midday – "them as haven't bought by now will have to go wi' out," he'd tell the family as he came in the front door, bearing a warm meat and potato pie "big as a cart-wheel, but then it's got to feed two fam'lies, my dear." And he'd kiss his wife on each cheek before turning to wink at Hod and Harry, who'd be with her in the kitchen, helping to pack the hamper.

"But look at all these sandwiches I've prepared," Sarah would wail, "*and* there's the lardy cake you wanted so special. How ever are we to eat it all?"

"It'll all go down the same way, don't you fret, Mrs K." And William Kelly would rub his stomach, groan and roll his eyes, his way of demonstrating hunger. "Let's be on our way, then. The sooner we're there the sooner we can eat. 'Sides, if we don't hurry, they Coulters will have packed up and traipsed back home."

In fact, the Kellys usually arrived at the grassy cliff-top first, and would have a table-cloth spread out and pegged down by stones some time before the Coulter family appeared, puffing up the slope, the youngest Coulter riding on his father's shoulders.

"'Bout time too," William Kelly would growl with exaggerated weakness from behind his pipe. "I've fainted dead away twice from hunger. One more time and I'd ha' been a goner."

"Don't look too weak to my way of thinking," Mr. Coulter said, on one such occasion. "Look more like you made off with the Paignton pudden."

"What's that?" Hod asked as Mr. Coulter knelt to set down his own baby son. "What's the Paignton", he paused, trying to pronounce the word as he'd been taught, "the pudding?" he said, feeling himself flush.

"Go on, tell 'un" his father said.

So Mr Coulter told him and the others, too.

It happened in eighteen fifty nine, he announced, a whole twenty one years before Hod was born. "That were the year when the railway first come all the way through Torquay and on to Paignton.

10

Took a sight longer than they reckoned, what wi rock falls and floodin', but once the line were complete, it seems the railway company as 'ad built it thought they'd have a bit of a celebration. So they hit on the idea of a feast and 'cos they wanted to invite a lot of folk they decided to 'old it on that there open ground near Paignton station. Hunderds, they 'ad. Bigwigs, o' course, but they also considered they orter invite all the poor from the parishes of Paignton, Marldon and Stoke Gabriel, as well as the navvies as'd worked on the line, and all *their* wives and families. Mighty nice on 'em, that was."

"Must have been like tryin' to feed an army," Sarah Kelly said.

"Wuss by many a long mile," Mr. Coulter said, grinning amiably round at his own four children and the four of William's who still lived at home and who were here now with their parents. But why, he wondered, had Sarah Kelly chosen to wear her crimmer this fine July afternoon. Hair stuck to her reddening cheeks, dabbing at beads of sweat as they salted her eyes, she looked liked roast mutton compared to his Emmalina in her straw hat and muslin. Muslin might not be fashionable but it kept you cool. Still, Sara was known for her odd ways, a matter he and Em had often discussed in private.

"So," he said resuming his tale, "arter a bit o' scratchin' of their 'eads, they thought they'd feed everyone wi' a pudden!"

"A pudden?" the children chorused, "why?" Because, Mr. Coulter said, every fifty years or so the folks – he pronounced the word "vokes" – of Paignton took it on themselves to make a whopper of a pudden'.

"How big?" someone wanted to know, and Mr. Coulter first tugged thoughtfully at his ample moustache, then raked it away from his red upper lip. "Accordin' to custom it were always enough for fifty or more," he told them, "ever since the time Rob'n Hood were a lad. But this time it were a real whopper. Nigh on a ton and a half. Five feet high it were, and gettin' on for fourteen feet across." As to ingredients, well, there was flour by the hundredweight, raisins, currents, suet, lemons, nutmegs, sugar, eggs – he ticked them off on his fingers – plus enough milk to sink a fleet of Brixham trawlers. "And when it were all ready to go, havin' been baked the previous night in sections, it were put on a waggon as took eight 'osses to pull'un up to the green, along of waggons piled mountain high wi' bread, meat and cider."

"You'd have thought that'd be enough to satisfy the nation," Sarah remarked, and Hod said, "the whole world."

"Ah, *you* might think so, young Horace," Mr. Coulter said, "but that warn't how others thought. See, a big crowd'd come along, just to look at the pudden', but when they clapped eyes on it while it were on the back of that there waggon, they reckoned they'd like to taste it for theirselves. That were when the trouble started."

Mr. Coulter paused, took off his jacket, and set about rolling up his shirt sleeves. "'Tis warm weather," he said to his wife, "I'll have a glass of cider, m'dear, if you'd be so good."

"C'mon, Jed, finish the story." Hod's father winked at his wife. "He spins this'n out to kingdom come, just so he's got an excuse to swaller more drink."

Mr. Coulter tasted his cider, then placed the pewter tankard carefully on the grass beside him. After that he reached for a beef sandwich, took a large bite from one corner and chewed, slowly, looking from face to face as he did so. Then he felt for his tankard, raised it to his mouth and took another mouthful of cider, brushed his moustache with the back of his hand, once more lowered the tankard, and finally said, "there were five policemen guardin' the waggon, been brought along in the expectation summat might be brewin', but o' course they warn't no use when it come to taken' on thousands. The navvies didn't like the look o'things when they seed outsiders clamberin' on the waggon, so they joined in. Then", another pause for cider, "then all the rest of the invited guests took a hand, and soon there warn't no pudden' left at all. Nor nothin' else, neither. All swallered."

"I can't believe folks from Stoke Gabriel would behave so," Sarah Kelly said, who came from that village.

"Wust of all," Mr. Coulter assured her, staring round at the others, "wust of all. Wouldn't lay off until every last scrap was a goner," and he finished his sandwich.

On later occasions Hod had asked Mr. Coulter to repeat the story of the great pudden' fight until he knew it by heart and could tell it to Fred. He also told his friend the story in which both Mr. Coulter

12

and his father shared the telling, of the storm of '65, when, so both men agreed, over fifty vessels sank in Torbay and nearly a hundred men drowned. Hod was as familiar with the heroes of that night as he was with his own name. There was the man at Brixham called Mills who pulled fourteen men from the water. Another, Christopher Bartlett, had been lowered over the cliff at Open Cove by rope and as a result had helped save some forty men whose boat had smashed onto rocks at the foot of the cliff. Above all there was Mary Butt.

"She got a reward," Hod explained to Fred. "She held a lantern over the cliff so's Mr. Bartlett could see where he was goin'."

He and Fred had once tried to act out the events of that night. Hod had been Mary, lying on the churchyard wall, and dangling the lamp – a half-brick tied with string – while Fred crawled along the bottom of the wall through long grass to where Harry obligingly lay crying out for help. Unfortunately his cries brought the sexton lumbering up from the other end of the churchyard, where, unnoticed by the boys, he'd been at work preparing a new grave, and they had to scramble up and over the wall before dropping into the deep, rutted lane that led to home. Harry got a scolding for tearing holes in his trousers' knees but the others made it up to him by handing him the reward intended for Mary alias Hod. It was a dead ladybird in a twist of sugarpaper.

* * *

Back at the shop he found Mr. Coulter had left but that his mother, dressed as usual for public events in her crimmer, together with his sisters Laura and Annie as well as Harry, stood ready and waiting for him.

"Where you bin?" Harry, a year younger than Hod and dressed in his old sailor-suit, was tugging at Laura's hand, impatient to be gone.

"I'm not late, am I?" he asked, and his father shook his head. "Right on time," he said, without taking his pipe from his mouth. "All safely gathered in?"

"I think so," Hod told him, and counted the money into his father's open hand.

"Five shillin and eightpence," William Kelly said. "I'll stow the shillins and seein' as this is a red-letter day you children can share the rest between you."

"What about me, pa?"

Polly. She stood in the shop doorway in a cool grey dress, button-up boots just visible below its hem, dark hair neatly braided, her face with its faint smile, large brown eyes fixed affectionately on her father's.

"More like I'll come a borrowin' off you," William Kelly said, "seein' as you're drawin' up a tidy salary, I'd not wonder." And he gazed back with an equal affection.

Hod went over and stood beside her.

At twenty-five Polly was old enough to be his mother, and he loved her even more than he loved his mother, who was fussing over Annie's lace collar, claiming that she ought not to have let it get crumpled, that people would notice and blame her for letting her children go out in public "all mithered and stogged."

"Can I walk with you?" he asked, looking up into Polly's calm face, the smile that seemed to shape her lips, and Polly said "alright, mister, and you can tell me your seven times' table as we go." Hod didn't mind, he knew all his tables up to eleven, and he knew, too, that for reciting them he could expect something in return, one of her nature drawings, perhaps. She'd already given him several, which he'd carefully pinned to the wall behind his bed. His favourite was a mouse, its tail longer than its body, clinging to a wheat stalk, and so light in weight that the stalk wasn't in the least bent. Underneath the drawing, in formal uncials, Polly had written "Harvest Mouse: Mary Parkes Kelly, 1 June, 1879," and then, beneath those words, in familiar cursive, "for Hod, from his sister Polly, Summer 1886." Polly could draw anything, Hod thought, and as he did so he stretched up to her and said softly, not wanting the others to hear, "I've got a stag beetle to show you."

"Let me guess" Polly whispered back, "it's in a box in your trouser pocket." Clever Polly.

A few moments later his father shooed them out of the shop, locked the door after him and bent his arm for his wife to slot her hand into it.

"Ready?" he called, the word emerging wrapped in tobacco smoke. "Ready" Hod and Harry shouted, and in twos and threes the family Kelly set off for St. Marychurch Green.

UPTON, 12 FEBRUARY, 1894

The funeral had been set for 3 o'clock. An hour earlier the Kelly family assembled in the front parlour, clear now of the coffin which two of the undertaker's men had removed the previous evening. Up in his bedroom over the parlour Hod had listened to them nail down the coffin lid. Then came scufflings and a single heavy bump before boots felt their way along the hall passage, a pause, the soft squeal as the front-door opened, and then the men emerged under his window. They swung the coffin up onto their shoulders and as they did so Mr. Coulter appeared at the front gate which he held open, bowler hat under his arm, eyes averted as the men manoeuvred their burden along the short slabbed path towards him. He must have said something to them when they passed because one of the men opened and closed his mouth several times while the other shook his head. Mr. Coulter shut the gate behind them and watched them slide the coffin into the back of the hearse. A moment later the two black-plumed horses pulled away down Buckland Terrace.

Hod listened to Mr. Coulter carefully close the front door. That measured tread on the staircase told him that his father's great friend was coming to see him. Sure enough there was a soft knocking at his bedroom door. Mr. Coulter stood there; "How are you bearin' up?" he whispered, peering round the room and seeing Harry's sleeping body in the other bed.

"Alright" Hod whispered back. He wondered whether to ask Mr. Coulter to come into the stuffy little bedroom but the big man showed no signs of wanting to advance.

"Good lad," Mr. Coulter said, speaking normally now as he smiled and nodded and looked steadily into Hod's eyes. "You'll be needing to keep strong." He lowered his voice again. "I'm afraid your ma's none too good, is she."

"Polly's with her," Hod said. Until now he had not wanted to cry.

"Right and proper she should be, at a time like this." Mr. Coulter nodded then dropped his gaze and stared into his upturned bowler hat, which he was grasping with both hands.

"Ah, but she can't stay for long," Hod said, "what with the baby and all."

"She didn't bring it with her?"

Hod shook his head. "Her husband's got permission for two days off, so's he can look after Frank and Doris. But Polly'll have to go straight back to Truro after the funeral."

"Be up to you, then, Hod", Mr. Coulter said. He seemed to have more to say, although for several seconds nothing came. Then, "you'll no doubt be sayin' a prayer for your ma," he mumbled, "these'll be difficult times. Your dad would've wanted you to take responsibility Hod, now there's only you and young Harry left at home. Well, only you two of use, if you know what I mean, as I dessay you do."

It was Hod's turn to nod at what seemed like a prepared speech. "I know," he said, and stopped there.

Mr. Coulter reached out a black-coated arm as though to touch Hod, but in the end he left it suspended awkwardly in the gap between them. "Well," he said, "you'd best be gettin' your sleep. It'll be a long day tomorrow. I'll just go and say goodnight to your ma."

Closing the door as quietly as he could – Harry stirred, mumbled something about boots, or was it books, but did not wake – Hod crawled into bed. Lying there in the dark, he tried to remember exactly how his father used to look, in the old days, but all he could see was that unfamiliar face with its hollowed, frightened eyes staring up at him from the hospital bed. William Kelly's beard had been shaved off for his operation, and his cheeks and chin, which Hod realised he'd never before seen, showed yellow-white, like chicken flesh, unnatural, untouchable, as repulsive, almost, as the thick bandages which swathed his throat. As only two of the family was allowed at the sick man's bed at any one time, Hod had gone in with his mother, while Jack and Lydia waited outside with Harry. Sarah Kelly sat by her husband's bed, sobbing quietly. Hod stood beside her, his arm round her shoulders; and his father looked from his wife's to his son's face, and back again. Denied speech, for in cutting out the tumour the surgeon had needed to remove the larynx, his father was forced to communicate by written message, and he was plainly too weak to be able to write much. Suddenly he fixed his eyes on Hod and, with much effort, tried, almost successfully, to raise his head. Hod understood and at the same time felt a surge of panic. "I don't want to touch him," he thought as he bent over his father.

William Kelly reached up a bunched hand from beneath the blankets and by a movement of his eyes indicated that Hod was to grasp it. As Hod did so he felt a small scrap of paper being released into the palm of his own hand. His father nodded, looked towards Sarah and then faintly shook his head. His eyes said, "understand?" Hod smiled briefly and nodded. Yes, he understood.

In the bare, green-painted hospital corridor, light filtering dimly through the glazed and barred windows – like a prison, Hod thought – he sat on the rickety chair vacated by his older brother Jack, who had now gone in with Laura to see their father. Sarah Kelly had wandered off somewhere in the hope of finding a doctor, or even matron, who could tell her the truth about her husband's condition, but she had done this before and all they ever told her was "Mr. Kelly is doing quite as well as can be expected," although once, when Jack as eldest son had tried to assert authority by enquiring how soon his father might be permitted to smoke again, he had been startled into silence by the matron's severe reply, "never," her long, starched skirt that crackled at her slightest motion, grey hair pinned-up beneath the severe white head piece, making her the very image of unopposable authority.

Hod was pulled from his thoughts by the sound of Harry's voice. "What's going to happen?" The words came as little more than a whisper. "We'll go as soon as Jack and Laura come out," Hod said. "No, I mean what's going to *happen*? You know...." Harry's dark eyes stared into Hod's. Hod looked at his brother, his new school uniform, grey trousers, grey jacket, white shirt with red and black striped tie. Harry liked to be seen in the uniform, Hod didn't, but that apart they were close in more than years, close enough for Hod to know what his brother meant, the fears he couldn't bring himself to put into words. "No need to worry" Hod said, "we'll be alright," speaking with more confidence than he felt. He knew what lay behind the fretful question. If his father died what would happen to the shop? And would they be able to keep the house they'd only recently moved to, its rooms and garden so much larger than those of Albert Square, its address a sure sign of his father's improved business? Who was there to take the business over? Not his mother for sure, it was man's work, and there was only Harry and him at home. He knew his mother had hopes he'd eventually succeed to the shop, she'd said so often enough, but that couldn't be for years yet. And meanwhile?

Meanwhile, there was Jack. But that was out of the question. Jack was still at home, always *would* be, but he didn't count, not with his weak heart. He could never be allowed to work, would always have to live an invalid's life, so the doctor had told Sarah, though as to that, the amount he ate and the way he expected everyone to wait on him without thanks but as if it was a responsibility they should feel honoured to have placed on them, suggested not so much illness as "a life of Riley", to use Polly's phrase. She'd once scandalised her mother by announcing that she was no longer prepared to take Jack his breakfast in bed. That had been when they'd still lived in Albert Square, Annie and Edie and Hod and Harry dividing one bedroom between them while Jack had the back parlour to himself. "He can get his own breakfast," Polly said, briefly home from her school in Truro, "he's got nothing else to do all day." "My poor Jack," Sarah wailed. "Poor my foot," Polly said, "he's as fat as a pig from being waited on, hand, foot and finger. Tell him to make himself useful for a change." But Jack never had agreed to make himself useful. And now what was to happen to him? And what was to happen to Harry, and to himself, if it came to that?

* * *

The questions recurred as he looked round the front parlour while the Kelly family waited for other mourners to arrive. On every available surface were photographs of his father. William Kelly as a young married man, his beard already full and curly, standing beside his wife who sat on a bayonet-legged chair holding their first-born, Polly, her long, crocheted shawl reaching to the ground, tiny fists clenched tight shut, face scarcely visible under the large, full-brimmed bonnet. Behind the family group a palm leaning tipsily from a large brass pot was outlined against heavily-swagged curtains. Another photograph, this one propped on top of the piano, showed William Kelly in front of his shop, in striped apron with straw hat pressed down onto his wide head, in the double windows behind him rows of unplucked pheasants and larger birds, all hanging head down, price tags pinned to their breasts. William Kelly in white flannels, a hooped cap several sizes too small atop his smoothed-down hair, arms folded across his broad chest, sitting straight-backed on a bench with four other cricketers, all of them solemn, unsmiling, behind them five more standing, also arms folded, flanked by two older men in bowler hats and three-piece suits, while at the feet of the seated men a further three cricketers sat cross-legged, the middle one, Mr Coulter, smiling beneath his moustache, the others staring severely towards the camera. Babbacombe Cricket Club, that was, where Hod had gone regularly to watch his father bat and, occasionally, bowl his slinging round arm, and whose junior team he himself now played for.

On the mantelpiece, draped in black, stood another group photograph, but very different in kind, taken, as Hod knew, because he'd often studied the printed legend on the back, by *J.C. DINHAM, Lower Union Street, TORQUAY.* It was of William Kelly and his wife with all eight living children. The photograph had been taken not long after Polly's graduation from Truro College. She was in black gown, standing beside her father, his arm around her shoulders, an expression of undisguised pride in the confident beam of pleasure which he directed at the photographer. Jack, Lydia, Laura, Annie and Edie were posed on either side of their mother, Sarah Kelly sat in front of her husband and eldest daughter, with Hod himself on her knee and the infant Harry in a cradle at her feet.

As he studied that photograph in particular, Hod thought yet again of the two words scrawled in uncertain pencil on the scrap of paper his father had managed to smuggle into his hand the day before he'd died. "Like Polly" he had written, and Hod understood exactly what he meant. William Kelly wanted Hod to become a teacher. He was intensely proud of his daughter, proud that the love of books which he'd tried to pass onto his children had led, by Polly's own admission, to her insistence on a professional career. Hod understood, too, his father's disappointment when the married Polly had had to give up school teaching, remembered a moment of real fury in William Kelly's voice in his reply to Sarah's remark that motherhood was a woman's true calling. "Not for all women, not for our Polly," he'd grated out. Yet when his first grandson, Frank, was born he wept for joy, and he'd taken into hospital a recent photograph of Polly with both Frank and the baby, Doris, a photograph that was now pushed to one end of the black-draped mantelpiece.

Almost the last thing Hod recalled his father saying, before that journey to hospital, was "When I get out o' theer I s'll venture down to Truro to do zum readin' wi' Frankie", although by then his voice was little more than a hoarse whisper. William Kelly had always read to his children, *The Ingoldsby Legends*, *Phantases*, *The Water Babies*, *The King of the Golden River*, *The Pickwick Papers* and *A Christmas Carol* – he loved telling them how in 1858 he had gone to hear Dickens himself read at Exeter and then the following night made the journey over to Plymouth where the great man was to appear. "'Twas blowin' fit to shove the Armada straight back to Spain" he told them, "a terrible time to be out, so 'twas, but Jed and me, we took the early coach and we wuz there in good time, so we walked about a bit and saw some of the sights. A fine gurt city, Plymouth. Then, when we'd arranged for a bed, we thought as we'd like sommat to eat afore the Event. We counted up our money and reckoned we'd enough for a morsel. So we chose an 'otel, and we'd just sat down to dinner and guess what? In comes Dickens hisself. We zeed 'im good and proper, large as life and twice as 'andsome. Ah, and weren't his readin' tremendous. Nothin' like it, nothin'! 'E could make that voice carry to the very back rows, up to the gods, too". And he would imitate Dickens's version of Sam Weller and "your uncle Scro-o-o-oge", Hod shivering with delight as his father drew out the miser's surname.

He looked now at a photograph which showed William Kelly in profile, at his desk, head leaning on his hand as he concentrated on the act of reading a book which was, Hod knew, *David Copperfield*. That was the last book he'd read to them, his voice sometimes so hoarse as to make the words indistinguishable.

Hod blinked and stared towards other photographs. They were all there, in metal or heavy wooden frames, to remind the rapidly assembling company of the man whose body they would shortly be following to the parish church. Through the whisperings and mutterings that grew as more people crammed into the parlour, Hod heard the church bell tolling, its deadening, hollow sound like a stone dropped into a pail, and in the dim, filtered light of the room, for the blinds were down, he was free to look about him, to see Mrs. Coulter's hands clasping a white lace handkerchief which from time to time she dabbed at her eyes, to watch neighbours staring at their feet and occasionally eyeing each other or casting a glance at the framed card his mother had placed on the centre of the table where, until last night, the coffin had stood. The card, which a well-meaning relative had sent to his parents on the occasion of one of their wedding anniversaries, was bordered by roses that framed some lines picked out in gold lettering.

> May you long each other love
> With benediction from above,
> And your faithful hearts when olden
> Celebrate the wedding golden.

His father had laughed at the trite verse. "I don't recollect that as bein' by Shakespeare," he said.

BABBACOMBE, 30 JULY, 1899

The grass where he and Fred lay stretched out was long, coarse to the touch, and splashed with the sunlight that fell irregularly through thick-leaved elms bordering the cricket ground. Fred, propped up on his elbows, hands cupped to his eyes as though they were field-glasses, studied the pavilion opposite. Groups of white-flannelled men, of women and children, lounged in deck chairs on the turf in front of it or sat on verandah benches or the pavilion steps, surrounded by hampers to which the women were returning carefully folded squares of grease-proof paper or handing out last pieces of cake while smaller children watched anxiously, or were distracted by men freed on a Saturday in July to demonstrate that fatherly care amounted to more than a weekday habit of stern refusal. One was helping his young daughter to tie a skipping-rope between two chairs so she and various of her friends could try their skills at jumping over the sagging line. The first to attempt the leap mis-timed her lolloping run and became entangled in the rope. After a long moment she slowly collapsed and a wailing sound rose thinly into the warm afternoon air.

"Don't reckon much on this marriage lark. Do you?" Fred asked Hod.

"We-ell." Hod was on his back now, knees bent, wriggling his shoulders deeper into the grass, contentedly breathing in the warm, sweet scents given off by crushed blades and darker, mustier earth smells. Above him the shoaling leaves of a tall elm looked black against blue sky. He thought of how, as a small boy, he'd loved to scare himself by bending to peer through his parted legs at air he might fall upwards into for ever and ever. The blue sky. Cerulean blue. From the Latin "caeruleus". "Caelum" sky. He rolled over and looked across at Fred. "If there wasn't marriage there'd not be any children – or not many. And if there weren't children we'd both be out of a job. Q.E D."

Fred went on studying the pavilion. "See all they kiddies," he said. "All to be fed and seed grow up proper. Don't seem right. You're Ma, now. Eight she's got, bain't it? And all on 'er own."

"But most out in the world, making something of themselves," Hod said. He felt called on to defend the family's honour. "We're not paupers, you know."

"Ah, well, right enough." Fred was in no mood to argue.

"Reckon we've got five minutes more," he said, "afore Teignmouth try to get at us. Where you battin'. I'm down for number eight."

"Six", Hod said.

"You never are?" Fred asked in mild astonishment. "They ought to give you three or four. What with you bein' top of the averages, an' all. Ain't nobody done better'n you all season.?"

"Suits me," Hod said, not prepared to admit his disgruntlement at Sol Pannel's decision. "Gives me time to look at the bowling. Anyway, it's only fair for Pannel to let others have a go."

"Dunno what they made him captain for," Fred remarked, sitting up suddenly, and tucking his hands under his thighs. "Bloody old pompous walrus. What do you mean about us bein' out of a job if there warn't no children? I mean, I can see why you'd be, but why me?"

Hod held up to inspection a finger on the tip of which a ladybird balanced. He blew gently and the ladybird wandered off into air.

"Because men who drink in pubs were once children. No children, no adults. No adults, no pubs. No pubs, no coopers."

Fred thought about it. "Well, anyway," he said finally, "I'd rather have my job than yourn, any long day. Dunno why you stick it, given all as you say agin it. You'd have been better off in your dad's shop."

"I doubt it," Hod said. "Anyway, I'm glad mother sold it."

But he wasn't sure about teaching, either. For the past few months, on those Saturdays when they found themselves both playing for Babbacombe's cricket team, Hod had given Fred progress reports on the miserable time he was having at school, especially this year, when he ought to have found it less difficult. Three years before, when he'd first started as a pupil teacher, Polly had warned him that it wouldn't always be easy. "There'll be the ones who know you don't have real authority," she'd said, "and they're the ones to watch out for. They'll try to make you lose your rag but, Hod, whatever else you do, don't let them. Lose your temper and you've lost everything, believe me."

For his benefit she'd recalled the tricks of some of the more difficult children she'd had to deal with: those who deliberately knocked over stools and who apologised before you could rebuke them, those who repeatedly asked to go "outside", those who surreptitiously kicked or pinched or prodded anyone beside or in front of them in order to make them cry out, the girl who, when Polly had made her stand facing the corner for some repeated infringement of the rules, just as repeatedly turned to the class and pulled faces to make them giggle, and then finally slid down into a sitting position, moaning she felt unwell and needed to be taken to the doctor's. "What did you do?" "Told her I'd take her to the Infirmary as soon as school was over," Polly said. "That scared her. It's sometimes a battle of wills, Hod, and you have to make sure that your will is the stronger."

Which might be true, in fact *was* true, but still didn't help him on those occasions when he had to face children in whose eyes he read not so much a challenge as a real threat to destroy his hold on himself. Upton Elementary might not be the best of schools, but he couldn't believe it was the worst, either. An easy walk from the small house where his mother now lived in mournful widowhood, the school had six full-time teachers and two pupil teachers. Each schoolday morning Hod would tiptoe down from the pokey bedroom – scarcely big enough to take his bed, a mahogany chest of drawers and bookcase, all brought from Buckland Terrace, together with a desk he'd chosen with money his father had bequeathed him, and on which he stood his cased collection of lepidoptera – and find that as always his mother had come down at some hour of the night to lay breakfast for Harry and him. (Jack's would be carried into the front parlour where he'd taken up quarters, at a later hour.) Harry, who had just begun as a pupil teacher at a school even nearer to their house, could afford to sleep on for a few more savoured minutes, although before leaving Hod would place a mug of tea outside the back bedroom where his brother slept and rap gently on the door to let Harry know what time it was.

A wash in the scullery, a quick scraping of his chin with one of his father's several razors, kept as William Kelly would have wished well stropped on the thick leather strap that hung beside the scullery sink, and then, having chewed and hastily swallowed a piece of thickly buttered bread with, if there was cream in the larder, some of that dolloped over, he'd leave the house just as the church clock struck half-past seven. The sound of the clock, its strange, deadening clunk, was farther off now than in the old days, although still audible through air that even on mornings which promised days of pure heat held traces of moisture, of salt spray – was it? – so that he imagined he could taste on his lips the tang of waves clawing at the pebbled beach invisible below a screen of houses and hotels that now stretched from Babbacombe Heights down towards Torquay.

Such mornings bred hope. Maybe this day won't be so bad, he'd think. And sometimes, perhaps even more often than not, he'd be proved right. Mr. Collins, the teacher assigned to oversee his efforts, would approve his work, the classes would follow his instructions, his questions would produce the correct answers, he'd see attentiveness, interest, even more than that in their eyes. But then there were the days when they wriggled or sighed in boredom, or, worse still, when they looked at him with the kind of silent indifference which made him feel wretched, desperate to do something, *anything*, that would bring them back from the huddled withdrawal of approval he registered in their faces.

Worst of all were the occasions when Chas Connolly came to school. Those were the days he'd told Fred about, days, and they'd been more frequent this last year, when Connolly tried tactic after tactic to plunge Hod into a chasm of white-hot anger, so that no matter how much he told himself he must stay calm, some final and usually minor dodge – a word out of place, a behind-hand snigger, even a blank look – would set Hod's heart thumping, sweat beading his forehead, his whole body atremble as, voice thick with rage, he'd yell uncontrollably at Connolly. And Connolly would look imperturbably back at him.

There was something deeply wrong with Connolly. Mr. Collins admitted as much, so did the other teachers. "Several bricks short of a load," according to Mr. Goodwin, the oldest of them, although not within hearing of the head, Mr Phillips. In his dark, buttoned-up suits, sallow, pock marked face, and with a cheesy smell about him that suggested something terminally rotten, Phillips was a terrifying figure.

However difficult or stupid he might be, Connolly never misbehaved in Phillips' presence.

But this didn't prevent him from public canings. Few days went by – certainly never a week – without the headmaster calling Connolly out at the end of assembly. And if he was there, which was by no means always the case, Connolly would slouch up to the dais behind which Phillips stood, cane already half-raised, be commanded to hold out each hand in turn, and would receive as many as six cuts on each of his open palms, the cane brought down from well above Phillips' head. For talking out of turn. For damaging books or slates. For misconduct in the lavatories. For bullying. For late arrival. For repeated failure to learn multiplication tables. For rudeness in class to Mr. Collins or to Mr. Goodwin or to Miss Lake or to pupil-teacher Kelly. The reasons for punishment might vary, the punishment never. And after the caning Connolly would slouch back to his place, dark eyes staring straight ahead, only occasionally flawed by tears, mouth set in a grimace less of pain than determination – though determination of what except to continue his war against school Hod couldn't imagine.

The pupil teachers weren't allowed to stand at the front with the full-time teachers during assembly. Each morning, therefore, Hod took up position halfway down one side of the hall, while the other pupil-teacher, Clarence Bebb, stood facing him on the opposite side. It was their responsibility to keep a look-out for misbehaviour during prayers and the singing of hymns. Hod couldn't help but notice that on mornings when Connolly was being caned the children seemed equally divided between those who stared down at their feet, or even shut their eyes, and those who craned to catch a glimpse of the flailing cane, from which small pieces occasionally broke away, and who more often than not winced at what they heard and who would sometimes stare at each other, teeth gritted, as though they themselves were undergoing the punishment Connolly endured. Not alone. Not always. From time to time others might be called to the front. But Connolly nearly always was.

"Poor little sod."

"So you might think," Hod said in reply to Fred's protest that he couldn't see the point of those regular thrashings his friend had told him about. "But you haven't had to deal with him."

"No, I haven't," Fred agreed, "but I know about that there family of 'is. Well, as much of a family as you can reckon, and that ain't much. 'Is dad's up to the *Rose and Crown* regular like, badgerin' for drink or toutin' for some job or t'other, and there's a round dozen of 'em to feed. My old dad reckons as they're always on the fly side of the law. A bit o' scrumpin', occasional poachin' down to Mister Carey's land – old man Connolly got caught by Carey's gamekeeper some six months since wi' a rabbit as he couldn't rightly explain about – anyways to put sommat on the table."

"I heard about the poaching," Hod said. "The school had a report on the family. Connolly was lucky to get off with a fine. I don't like Phillips, but he's right. You need to teach proper respect for the law and those who won't learn one way have to learn another."

"Knows a lot about that, does 'e?" Fred asked. "Respect for law don't seem to me to mean much if you've no food inside you. I reckon as Phillips orter be old enough to recall what happened to they bakers' shops in Torre when people weren't feelin' belly tight some years ago. Wing, Easterbrook, Mugford, Evans", he counted off the names as though repeating a mnemonic – "they all got broke into and they all got their bread took."

"I know, I know," Hod said, who had inevitably heard the story as told by Jed Coulter at a picnic years before. "But that was thirty years ago. You make it seem like yesterday."

"Ah, well, p'raps 'tis the way my dad tells it. 'E makes it *sound* like yesterday."

"Was he involved, then?"

"'is dad were, and his ma, my old gran. She reckons it was 'er stone what put a dent in March Phillips' face. Hey," Fred levered himself up onto his elbows and looked into Hod's eyes. "Phillips .... Phillips ... Don't reckon it's the same cove, do you?"

"No." Hod shook his head. "The Head's not that old, and he isn't disfigured, not more than usual, anyway. Besides, he isn't from round these parts. He comes from up north somewhere."

"Well, from what you tell me a taste of cobble-stone wouldn' do 'im no harm."

"The way you talk," Hod said, "anyone 'ld think you were a socialist. A lot of innocent people got hurt that night, you know."

The night of that riot was still talked about in the town, and Hod had often heard his father tell of the tar barrels which men had rolled across the streets in an attempt to set the centre of Torquay on fire, about others who'd marched to Livermead and, before the police got to them, had made a start on digging up the road in order to sever the gas main and drown the whole town in darkness. Then there had been the women who'd brought up supplies of stone and rocks from Ellacombe which they and their menfolk hurled at the special constables who'd been recruited to deal with the riot.

"'Course a lot got dinged," William Kelly had remarked, sucking on his pipe. "Broken bones, sore 'eads, and more'n a few ended up as 'ospital cases. Took a good many days to clear the streets and do up the shops, too. So arter that the magistrates swore in three hundred more specials. They 'ad nigh on eighty volunteers from round these streets."

"Were you one?"

"Not likely." His father shook his head and laughed. "Nor Jed Coulter. 'Course, Sol Pannel, 'e were new to town and 'e signed up. Always likes to be seen doin' the right thing, does Sol." And William Kelly laughed again, that familiar, gurgling laugh.

Whose side would he have been on? Hod wondered, chewing on a piece of meadowgrass as he watched Babbacombe's opening batsmen walk slowly out to the middle, portly men both of them. The run-stealers flicker to and fro. Perhaps, like his father, he'd have kept out of trouble, chosen not to take sides, although he suspected the old man was secretly more in sympathy with those who stole the bread than those who tried to prevent them. Would William Kelly have felt the same way if they'd been after meat? As for himself, he couldn't imagine wanting to be a special constable, but on the other hand if he'd been with the rioters he'd have had to line up on the side of people like Chas Connolly. What a thought! Yes, he knew that in describing the boy's many beatings to Fred he'd made him seem a pathetic victim. But Fred hadn't had to cope with his endless insolence, the way, whenever he was called to Hod's desk in front of the class,

28

he pressed up as close as possible, stinking of sweat and, it had to be admitted, of shit, his nose as often as not rimmed with scabs of grey-white mucus, the purple stains showing through his part-shaven head where ring-worm was being treated. "All things bright and beautiful," the school sang most mornings, shrill voices accompanying Miss Lake's attempts to coax notes from the arthritic piano, "All creatures great and small, All things wise and wonderful, the Lord God ma-a-ade them all." Connolly never sang, although occasionally he'd open his mouth and whisper to the boy or girl next to him. No doubt what he whispered was something crude or obscene. He might even be telling them that the Lord God hadn't made Chas Connolly

Fred interrupted this fancy by suddenly sitting upright and saying, "Well, like as not this'll be our last summer together. You'm off to Exeter and I'm thinking about the Queen's shillin'. No more church choir for us, Hod, and no more cricket, neither".

Hod spat out his piece of grass, looked at his friend in amazement. "What on earth do you want to volunteer for. I thought you liked coopering. And the army? You'd not fancy the discipline, would you?"

"I might not mind. 'Ello, first wicket down. We'd best be gettin' back to the others. Give us yer plier". Fred stood up, grasped Hod's outstretched hand, hauling him to his feet as he did so, and Hod, not for the first time, was made aware of his friend's easy strength. "This place is growin' a bit small for me. Time for a change. Twelve years to see the world, then I can settle down and produce some o' they children you reckon so important. I was talkin' to a friend o' dad's, back from Africa, 'e was, and 'e reckons it's alright, the army. Easy enough to get a stripe or two if you play your cards accordin'. Bit of alright, too, in your full regimentals. 'Ave to fight the tabbies off." Fred winked cheerfully at Hod. "Wouldn't mind that, Hod, wouldn't mind that one little bit."

EXETER DIOCESAN TRAINING COLLEGE, 8 JANUARY 1900

My Dear Mother,

Well, here we are at the start of the new century and here I am back at College and back in the routine, although not entirely so. The oppo. cried off football for this afternoon, because half of their side has gone down with some tummy bug, which is why I am sitting in the warmth of our library writing to you. This a.m. we had to make our customary march down to the Volunteers' H.Q. in order to be "put through our paces". It all seems *very* silly: forming fours so as to march and counter-march about a scrap of muddy ground is of far less use as a means to keeping fit than a game of football would be, as I know most of our tutors agree. However, now the government directive insists that we acquire a drill "certificate" we have to comply, even though nobody thinks that this thumping up and down in army boots and becoming in the process "mud crushers" will be of any use in teaching. Dr. Dangar has told us that we will be issued with our certificates at the end of term, so that will be an end to playing soldiers! I only hope Fred had better training before he went off to South Africa. I don't think the Boers would be over worried by the sight of tommies striding in orderly rows towards their gun emplacements.

Talking of Dr. Dangar, he called me into his study yesterday evening and informed me that he was prepared to give Harry's application "sympathetic consideration." From which I gather I have done nothing so far to displease him! This is more of an achievement than you might realise as he is *very* easily displeased. I told you at Christmas about how he'd once "gated" the entire junior year because two of them had pushed a desk over while he was showing some guests round the college, even though the two men responsible for the "affray" had owned up. On Thursday he handed out similar punishment to Jack Berry. Apparently the Vice-Principal had seen Jack shaking his football shirt out of a window! Danger, as we call him, has now gated poor Jack for a week. As my friend Charles

Simpson said at breakfast, it's probably just as well the football match was called off, given that Jack is our star player. He's even played for Bury – in the First Division! Without him I wouldn't fancy our chances against the City, though the College did apparently beat them last year.

I will write to Harry with the good news just as soon as I close this letter. Then I plan to spend the rest of the afternoon reading *Richard II,* which is our play for this term. And – guess what? – we are strongly advised to buy "Characters In Richard II and Other Shakespearian Plays" by "William Weeks, Senior Tutor, Exeter Training College"! Each shilling we pay no doubt goes to swell his coffers, *and* he wants us to buy his "Exercises in Euclid" for 3/-. As I have already bought Dangar's "Treatise on Mental Arithmetic" – none of us dared be seen without it – you will appreciate Charles' remark that "we must be keeping our tutors in beer and baccy"!

This library is a fine place to study in. I wish father was alive to see it, although I'm not sure he would approve of the choice in fiction. All of Scott, none of Dickens. When I plucked up courage to ask the librarian why this was, he showed me the Directors' report which recommended that "The young men should read such novels as Sir Walter Scott's, for culture, because our distinct ideas of chivalry, nobility of character, etc. are mainly to be attributed to the influence of Sir Walter Scott's writings." I wrote the words down there and then and wished I could have sent them to father for his comment. You *will* come to see the college, won't you? We are allowed visitors on a Saturday if not involved in sport, and on Sundays, if you don't mind seeing me in frock coat and silk hat, which Danger makes us wear for that day. (Did I tell you that the locals refer to us as "Danger's black lambs"?)

I hope Jack is as well as can be expected and that life at Barnshill continues agreeable.

Your affectionate son,

Hod.

EXETER, 8 JAN 1900

Dear Harry,

By the time I get used to writing 1900 it will probably be 1901, which is of course when some people think the new century begins. It feels odd by not feeling odder, don't you agree? I half-expected something truly extraordinary to happen: comets flashing across the sky, a lioness whelping in the streets, strong men miscarrying, victory over "the pestilential Boers", as Weeks – the Major (he really is one) – calls them. I told you, didn't I, that not long after I'd arrived here he was trying to get us all to volunteer for armed service? I gather he offered the entire intake to the Devon Rifle Volunteers, with whom we have to do some silly training every Saturday a.m. Fortunately it came to nothing, they turned his offer down. Just as well, because quite a few of us were planning to say "no", which would have raised Weeks' temperature to boiling point! As it is he keeps muttering about how "we" ought to show the rest of society an example, by which I suppose he means we ought to volunteer to be killed! But I don't mean to joke about this awful war. Have you seen or heard anything from Fred's parents since he went? I worry about him being out there, although everyone says "Oh Redvers Buller is an awfully good general." What's *that* supposed to mean? That he comes from Devon and won't let Devon men down? Well, we'll see.

Anyway, the good news is that old Danger called me into his study the other night – I entered in fear and trembling – and told me he'd had your application and that he'd give it "sympathetic consideration". I'm pretty certain that means he'll accept you. I don't *like* him, but I respect him. "I'm a despot" he tells us, and he is. He means what he says and he never goes back on his word. I've heard horror stories about chaps being expelled for minor offences, and of course anyone seen going into or coming out of a city pub is for the high jump. You have to go three miles out if you want a drink! Not that I think of you as a toper, but it's as well to know the worst.

Father wouldn't have liked Danger at all. He's got no sense of humour and he's a dreadful old Tory to boot. One of the fellows has a copy of a poster made for the opposition during the '95 election, and old Danger is kneeling right at the front worshipping the "Golden Calf" of the sitting Tory MP. I've made my copy of his copy and enclose it with this. Don't lose it! He's also a snob. I couldn't pluck up the courage to tell him the truth when he asked me what father did for a living. I said "farmer". Not *quite* a lie, of course, given that father would sometimes help out at Uncle Edward's farm and that he got his meat from there, but I couldn't have stood to see the look on Danger's face if I'd told him the truth. (By the way, I think father had probably read more than quite a few of the tutors here.)

I was hoping to take a leaf out of Polly's book and sign up for the French class. No luck, I'm afraid. M. Joel was full, so I've settled for more Nature Study and will begin the French next term. At least my early interest in creepy-crawlies has paid off! We also get a chance to work outside in the gardens. You'll like these. (You see, I'm assuming you'll be a student at Exeter next year.) And there's an orchard where we learn about grafting trees, and fields enough to practice crop rotation. Of course we don't do *all* the hard work ourselves. There are boys from our own training school who help out with manuring the soil and tending the poultry, and they often, no, *usually*, know more about farmyard ways than we do. Our gardener and stockman, "Dewdrop" Carpenter, says "bain't nowt they varmints be needin' from oi", and he's right. The fact is that the boys mostly come from farms around here, so they're well on the way to being farmers.

You'll also enjoy the sport. There are two big fields for football and rugger, and we are all required to play cricket in the summer, which, as you can imagine, I find no hardship. Oh, and there's a bicycling club you'll probably want to join. It's not for the likes of yours truly, be it noted, I prefer walking as you know, but *do* bring your bicycle with you. (Incidentally, when we're on teaching practice the Vice-Principal often rides out to see us on his tricycle, although Danger comes in a horse and trap. Very grand!) You can't bicycle round the track on Sports Day, however. You need Shanks's pony for that. It's the biggest day in the sporting calendar, when we're allowed to invite guests – girls, even! I'm going to chance my arm and invite Charlotte White, that young lady I met through church, remember? The one who's a seamstress at "Model Gowns." She'll probably turn me down, but it can't do any harm to write to her, especially as she did give me her address. Wish me luck! Of course I want mother to come to see the college, but not on that occasion, although if Miss White says no, as I suppose she will, then I may ask the mater. (No, it's alright, I don't *really* talk like that.)

I'm so glad she's made the move to Barnshill, aren't you? It means that when you leave home she won't be alone with Jack. She and our aunts seem to get on pretty well together, and the three of them can divide the day perfectly between them. One to take up his breakfast, one his dinner, and one his tea! I can hear mother protest that I ought not to be cynical, but as Polly says, if he can smoke that dreadful pipe all day and walk out each and every evening for his pint of beer, then why can't he do at least *something* about the house? I enjoyed Lyd's refusal to lift a finger for him, even though it was because she considered herself too grand. Becoming companion to that Lady Phillimore has rather given her airs and graces, don't you think? We'll soon be calling her Lady Lydia! Do you remember how father used to read that piece from *Great Expectations* about Trabb's Boy. "Don't know ya! Don't know ya!" And I thought she might have stayed more than the one night. However, Lady P. no doubt required her services!

And now I must turn my thoughts to study and to piano practice. Because of my skills at the "pianoforte", ever so 'umble though they are, I find I'm quite in demand for evening sing-songs. Thanks be to Polly for that. I'd never have stuck at it without her. I *did* have a lovely Christmas, and the few days you and I spent at Polly's were the icing on the cake. The station house is rather fine, I think, and Ernest – or Ernie – looks, as you say, "proud as a peacock" in his station-master's uniform. (It's just occured to me: do you think he's hit on everyone calling him Ernie because of the O.W. trial? After all, he used not to object to us calling him Ernest?) And although I understand father's sadness that Polly had to give up her teaching career, there's no doubt she loves being a mother. Frank is going to be a genius, I can tell, and Doris is a sharp little thing. Perhaps they'll someday follow us to college? If so, I hope by then the students will have grown out of the silly "rules" which have been created to separate "seniors" from "juniors". Do you know that if we travel to away games by train we aren't allowed to sit in the same carriage as the second years? And every dinner-time we have to serve them before we're allowed to eat our own food, which means that by the time we do get to sit down our dinner is cold. Men were created equal. Then let them *be* equal, even at Exeter Training College.

And with that happy thought I bid you farewell.

Your affectionate brother,

Hod

EXETER DIOCESAN TRAINING COLLEGE, 9 JANUARY, 1900

Dear Miss White,

I hope you are well and still enjoying work. You may recall that on one of our talks together I mentioned the College Sports Day, to be held this year on the second Saturday in May. I would be greatly honoured if you were able to be my guest on that occasion. I quite understand that there may be many reasons why you cannot accept this invitation, but it would make me *very* happy were you able, and willing, to do so.

I very much look forward to hearing from you.

With most sincere regards,

Yours,

Horace Kelly.

HEAVITREE ROAD P.O. EXETER 10. 1. 1900 TO MRS. W. KELLY, BARNSHILL, TORQUAY.

TELEGRAM RECD STOP AM WRITING AT ONCE TO POLLY STOP HAVE PERMISSION TO BE AT FUNERAL STOP ALL LOVE HOD

EXETER TRAINING COLLEGE, 10. 1. 1900

Dearest of dear sisters,

Mother telegrammed the appalling news. Poor little fellow, I only hope he didn't suffer. Meningitis moves so rapidly, as I know from a recent case at our training school, that doctors rarely detect it in time. How *you* must be suffering I can imagine. I won't write any more, words seem useless at a moment like this. But I'm thinking of you and praying for Frank's soul and of course for you and Ernie and Doris.

Your grieving brother,

Hod

PS. I *do* want to say that your love and example have meant more to me than anything else in my life.

Annie, Polly, Lydia Kelly.

Hod as a student.

North front of Saint Luke's College, 1885.

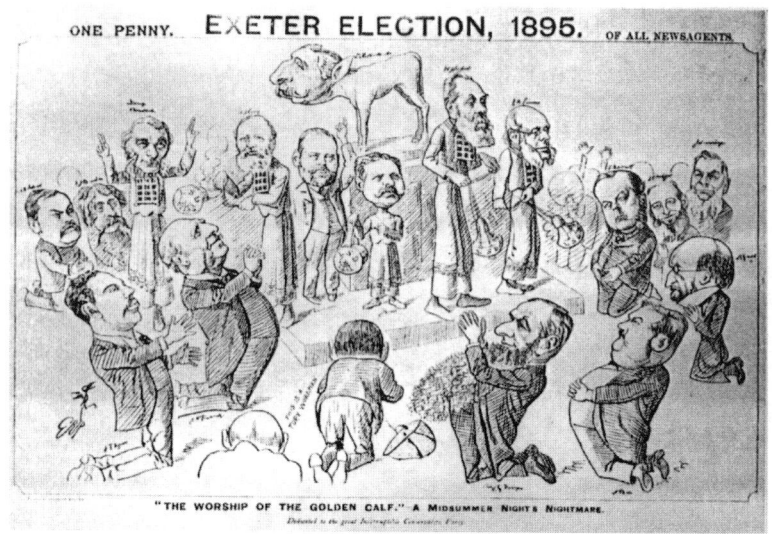

A poster published in 1895 against the Conservative Party. Dr. Danger, the College Principal, is conspicuously shown in the front (kneeling, with bushy beard). Second from left, kneeling in front, is John Stocker, a leading figure in Exeter Education. Behind him, both arms raised in Bishop Bickersteth of Exeter. The rest are prominent Exeter citizens. The 'Golden Calf' is Sir Henry Stafford Northcote who was elected M.P.

The Granville Theatre of Varieties, c. 1907.

LONDON, 20 APRIL 1905

"Looks as though the weather's set fair", Henry Morant remarked, as he and Hod strolled together the short distance down Hope Walk and out onto the King's Road. Hod glanced up from beneath his bowler at the late afternoon sky, plump white clouds moving slowly above the chimney tops, reddened undersides that dipped below the further roofs as though they'd been snagged on gable ends and now were drifting earthwards. He stood still, gazing up and down the wide street, thronged at this hour with omnibuses, horse-drawn carriages, an occasional motor-car. "How will you spend Easter?" he asked, not much interested. The other man shrugged. "One or two of us were thinking of a day on the river. And then there's the chance of some net practice on Monday. In the normal run of things I expect you'd want to be in on that ..." He smiled briefly. "Well," he said, "enjoy your last weekend as a bachelor." He extended his hand and Hod shook it, briefly. "I will," he said, and walked away, leaving Morant on the kerbside.

The walk down the King's Road took him some twenty minutes. He tried at first to keep to the brisk pace he preferred but soon gave up, slowed by thick crowds of shoppers, by strollers in the late-April sunshine, faces turned upwards as though in anticipation of a blessing, by groups of men concentrated in talk, their breathy, beery laughter tangled with the clatter of electric tram-wheels, the loud pleadings of flower-sellers, and of motor horns sounding raucously off – like a pod of land whales looking for mates, Hod thought, relishing his absurd fancy. The noises, the crowds, all seemed to announce the clamorous excitement of spring.

He turned off to the right, and now he was among narrower streets of back-to-backs, fetid smells of boiled cabbage, starch, wet cloth, all coming from open doorways where the kind of raggedy children he taught squatted on front steps, some chewing crusts, others, girls mostly, holding babies as if in apprenticeship to their future trade. A few boys played street cricket against a house-wall on which three stumps were shakily chalked. One bowled and the batsman, using a cut-down piece of fence planking, hit the ball high in Hod's direction. As fielders came in pursuit Hod caught the pocky, rubber ball expertly and tossed it to the nearest boy, who dropped it and looked hopefully at Hod. "Got a penny mister". Hod shook his head and continued his walk. "Stingy sod," the boy said. Hod stopped, but the boy was already half-way up a cobbled side-alley, scabby heels carrying him well out of Hod's reach.

Once out onto the Fulham Road, he dodged to the far side between the usual lines of horse-drawn cabs, buses, drays, and a few minutes later, having cut through more back streets, his whistling growing louder and increasingly flamboyant as though to match his increased pace, arrived at Fulham Palace Road. "One more river to cross" he said to himself, then chose his moment to sprint over the crowded road and into the top of Harbord Street.

The street had only recently been built, and on either side were new, raw-looking grey-brick town villas and continuous rows of two-storey houses. At the gate leading to the door numbered 55 of one such house Hod stopped, pulled out a bunch of keys from his waistcoat pocket and then, unable to prevent himself, looked round to see whether anyone was aware that he was about to enter his kingdom. The street was empty.

Feeling disappointed – cheated even – he let himself in. Harry was in the front sitting room, long legs dangling over the side of an easy chair, reading.

"Any good?" Hod asked.

By way of reply, Harry held the book up for Hod to read its title, *The Riddle of the Sands.*

"Ah, one of mine."

"I've only just started it." Harry smiled up at Hod. "I'm not sure it's my cup of tea but as you and other fellows keep on about the German scare I thought I'd better find out what you mean."

"Not me." Hod dropped into the matching chair on the other side of the fire-place and began to unlace his boots. "Childers tells a good story but this stuff about invasion plans is all my eye and grandmother."

"That's not what the *Daily Mail* thinks."

"The *Daily Mail* doesn't think," Hod said, free now of his boots and beginning to massage his toes.

The two brothers sat for a few moments in friendly silence. Then Hod picked up his boots and levered himself out of his armchair.

"Now," he said, "I'm going to change and after that it'll be time to go. So look smartish, brother mine."

Harry let the book fall to the floor beside his chair, swung his legs round and stood. The taller and leaner of the two, with a carefully-waxed moustache which gave him what he hoped was a sporting air although Hod privately thought it a great mistake, his hair was thinning as fast as his brother's.

"How was your meeting?" he asked, making for the door.

"Necessary," Hod answered. "I'll be sorry to give up Cook's Ground but Hope Walk's a better school, no doubt about it. There's a proper playground, the rooms are lighter and there's a half-way decent heating-system. They want me to teach some shorthand – for special evening classes." He followed Harry out into the hallway, feeling the lino's chill smoothness through his socks.

"And will you?" Harry asked over his shoulder as he began to climb the stairs.

"Might as well. It'll mean a bit more money, which I can always do with. One way or another, most of us who are transferring will stand to gain. Morant's been put in charge of games."

Harry paused at the top of the stairs, turned to look down at his brother. "And you mind?"

"Oh, no," Hod said, who did.

He went out into the kitchen, removed a used cup and plate from the plain deal table and carried them through into the scullery, where he ran cold water over them. Peering out of the small window above the sink, he stared at the garden.

"Mine, all mine," he said to himself, "a poor thing but mine own. And not so poor, either, Hod my lad." He allowed himself a moment to relish the pride of ownership, then shook his head like a dog emerging from water. "Come on," he fluted, "time for your best bib and tucker. Tonight the Granville must see you at your best."

The Granville Theatre of Varieties at Walham Green had been opened four years before Hod, in 1902, first took up the post of Assistant Master at Cook's Ground School, salary £95 p.a. Not much more than thirty bob a week, scarcely enough to pay for lodgings, a few books, and the suit required to "maintain appearances", which the head of Cook's Ground told the new assistant was expected of his staff. Hod had also to send back occasional hand-outs to Barnshill, it being understood by all members of the Kelly family who were in what Polly satirically called gainful employment that between them they would have to pay for Jack's upkeep. All of which outlays left very little over for him to enjoy even the most innocent forms of entertainment. An occasional visit to the Oval, Saturday rambles into the surrounding countryside with fellow teachers which might include sinking a couple of glasses of beer, and that – apart from the train journeys down to Torquay at two-monthly intervals to see his mother and of course Miss Charlotte White – was that.

Except for the Granville Theatre of Varieties. That was Hod's one indulgence, source of delights which never failed him. He had first been taken there by Henry Morant. The two young men, who lodged near to each other, established an easy-going relationship through a shared passion for cricket, although Hod knew they could never be especially friendly. He wasn't bothered by Morant's faintly raffish air, the bloodshot eyes into which left-over threads of colour seemed to have strayed from his glistening, beefy face, nor was he particularly shocked by the man's claim to know all the best "girl shops" in the area; but once, when he had tried to talk to Morant about a novel he was reading, *The Secret Agent* it was called, Morant had said, "a book's like a nun, Kelly – best left unopened, if you catch the wind of the word."

That had been on a Monday. The following Friday Morant came up to Hod at the end of the school day. "Still reading your old novel?" he asked, full lips parted in a friendly enough grin.

"I finished it last night," Hod told him, dismissing as out of the question the possibility that Morant might want to borrow it.

"Then that leaves you free for tonight."

"Free for what?"

"No need to be suspicious, Kelly." Morant put an arm round Hod's shoulders. "I'm not going to lead you into sin, unless Little Tich is your idea of sin. He's topping the bill at the Granville. Now, don't tell me you've never heard of Little Tich".

"Of course I've heard of him." Hod began to move off. "But I can't afford a night .... well, the fact is I've not much money," he said, fearing the words sounded more apologetic than they need. Lack of funds wasn't a crime, dammit.

But Morant waved his words away. "Don't need a full purse," he said. "Threepence for a seat in the gallery, add in a couple of beers, maybe a saveloy and chips, and what are you looking at? No more than a bob all told – cheapest way of having fun that I know. Now, if you've no other objections, and if you can't think of a better way of spending the evening, I suggest we meet outside the Granville at a quarter-past six. That'll give me time to call in at uncle's for my watch, change into my glad rags, and be all ready for the fray. Out by ten, a bite to eat and *you* can be tucked up in bed with an improving book before the watchman comes to call. How's that?"

Hod looked at Morant, was caught up by his anticipation of pleasure. "Alright," he said.

And that was how he came to discover the joys of the Granville. That first evening he waited for Morant at the minaret-style turreted main entrance and so almost missed him, because the gallery entrance was round the corner, "out of sight of the nobs," Morant said, when he found him, though once inside everyone could share in the splendour of the glazed tiles with which the theatre was lined throughout. Dan Leno, when he first saw the theatre's interior, had called it "these sanitary varieties", Morant chortled as Hod stared at the steeply raked tiers of seating, all red-plush lined except for the gallery itself, and which, together with the gold-gleaming brass rails, and proscenium arch with its ornamentation of masks and acanthus, gave the theatre an exotic air.

Morant registered Hod's amazement. "Never been in a theatre before?" he asked, as they struggled to find seats for themselves on one of the benches running the full length of the gallery.

"Never one like this," Hod said.

Morant finally located a small gap on one bench, sat on it, wriggled from side to side and gestured to Hod to sit. Hod squeezed himself in. Beside him, a man munched chips from a packet stuffed inside his shirt. Looking about him, he saw that others were doing the same, while still others chewed on sausages, pies, whole loaves, some with bottles clamped between their knees, everyone seeming to call out to friends or simply because they wanted not to be excluded from the hubbub that grew more intense as the minutes passed and, far below them, musicians began to emerge from a door beneath the front of the stage and fill the orchestra pit, stray notes from trombone, trumpet, violin, drifting upwards to join the fester of voices that congregated under the Granville's smokey roof.

Morant had brought two bottles of Bass, their corks drawn and loosely replaced. "Easier than fighting your way to the bar", he explained, handing Hod one of the bottles before using his teeth to pull the cork free of his own. "Well, here's mud in your eye "

Afterwards, Hod could barely recall the walk home. Which route had he taken? He didn't know. The excitement – no, the *joy* – of Friday night at the Granville so bewildered his senses that only when he was tucked up in bed did it occur to him that he'd forgotten to thank Morant for the new world he'd been introduced to. He closed his eyes, which smarted still from the cigarette and cigar-smoke, the smells in which sweat, the reek of cloth and the pungency of vinegar were predominant, and saw again the packed house, heard himself shout, as Morant had instructed, "I Ain't Barmy", which the entire audience had bellowed as the curtain rose to reveal a man in cap and muffler, Joe Elvin he was called, most of whose patter Hod didn't understand but which Morant told him was sporting slang, and which, to judge by the laughter and whistles that accompanied most of Elvin's remarks, was perfectly well understood by everyone else. He tried to hum the tune of one song which the gallery obviously knew by heart, about "the 'ouses in between," and then laughed out loud as the image of Little Tich came back to him, feet encased in vastly elongated boots, leaning stony-faced at impossible angles as the audience roared its laughter and applause.

Thinking about the previous evening as he lingered over his porridge and toast on Saturday morning, Hod was glad he'd rejected Morant's suggestion that they should make a night of it – "a bit to eat, a little to drink and who knows what we might pick up?" Morant had shouted in Hod's ear as the two young men fought their way down the balcony stairs at the end of the show, pressed into the sweating, jovially raucous crowd, "and keep your hands over your pockets. There'll be buzz-fakers about." Hod could at least guess the meaning of *that* term.

He could also guess that had he gone with Morant he'd almost certainly have ended the evening as cleaned out as if he'd been a buzz faker's victim. Still, he remained grateful to the other for opening up to him the glittering, red-gold riches of the music-hall world, and by the time Harry joined him in London – he'd been appointed assistant master at the Fulham Palace Road School – Hod was familiar with and an habitué of many of the London halls or theatres of varieties as they were known.

The experiment with Morant was however never repeated. Hod preferred to make his visits alone. On a Friday or Saturday night he'd take himself off to the Pavilion at Piccadilly Circus, or, for a change, Leicester Square's Alhambra, or he'd try the Oxford or perhaps Weston's in Holborn, especially if Harry Tate was billed to appear. He never failed to laugh at the sketch in which Tate pretended to be a gentleman taking fishing lessons and was utterly baffled and bewildered by the man appointed to teach him, who spoke throughout in cockney slang: "Hold that in your Dook." "My what?" "Your German Band." Or he'd cross London in order to applaud Kate Carney "the coster queen" at the Hackney Empire or to be convulsed by the antics of Fred Karno and his troupe at Hoxton's Brittania.

He loved the Brittania more than any other hall. Once inside its vast auditorium, he was in a foreign land, a world away from the London he inhabited by day. Here, he was not so much a spectator as a performer. He could join in the badinage between stage and audience or add his own voice to the shouted conversations that passed from gallery to circle and back again, and it seemed that the women who danced and sang were here more vivacious, ought to be more *accessible* than elsewhere, so that he could imagine himself actually inviting them to champagne and supper, becoming in his way a "masher", whose every casual remark would be treated as a killing witticism. Ah well, fanatics have their dreams.

But he also loved that theatre for another reason. He remembered his father reading aloud Dickens's account of a visit to the Brittania, and the first time Hod went there he wondered where exactly the Inimitable had sat. Now, every time he returned, he would ask himself whether he was sitting on the very seat from which Dickens had gazed down at the Brittania's stage. He looked the account up in a battered copy of *The Uncommercial Traveller* he'd bought from a street barrow, and found that Dickens wrote of being among young men wearing caps and that "we who wore them, slouched, high-shouldered into our places with our hands in our pockets, and occasionally twisted our cravats about our necks like eels, and occasionally tied them down our breasts like links in sausages". The gallery then? Likening the tying of cravats to such foodstuff showed that Dickens knew all about life in the cheapest seats.

The Traveller also claimed that besides some prowlers and idlers ("buzz Fakers" he presumably meant) "we" were composed of "mechanics, dock labourers, costermongers, petty tradesmen, small clerks, milliners, stay-makers, shoe-binders, slop-workers, poor workers in a hundred highways and byways." And, the Traveller added, the majority of us "were not at all clean, and not at all choice in our lives or conversation." That *had* to be the gallery. And certainly, Hod thought, looking about him one Friday night as he sat crammed into a space scarcely big enough for a man half his size, nothing much had changed since Dickens's visits. Except, of course, that schoolmasters were now part of the gallery. Would Dickens have picked him out? Before setting off for one of the halls he always took good care to change out of his suit and into what poor Fred would have called mufti, aiming to look, in bowler or, if weather permitted, straw hat, and with a dark jacket pulled on over white flannel cricket shirt daringly worn without a tie, as anonymous as possible.

It worked. At all events, nobody questioned his right to be in the gallery of any theatre he visited, nobody cried out "Schoolmasters not welcome" or "I spy strangers" as he sometimes, no matter how irrationally, feared they might, and he was free to watch, applaud, laugh, sing and shout with the rest. But the nearer to home ground, the more he felt the need to hurry into and out of whichever theatre he'd chosen for an evening's entertainment, as though to be seen by any of his pupils, or, more likely, their parents, would be shameful.

Nevertheless, he took Harry to his favourite halls and Harry, while not as keen as Hod on these diversions, enjoyed their shared Friday nights. Sometimes they would be joined by others teachers. Mostly, though, they preferred each other's company. And on this last Thursday of Hod's bachelordom it was to be just the two of them who would pay a visit – "for old times' sake" Hod said, feeling sentimental – to the Granville Theatre of Varieties.

Hod bought tickets for the circle. Perhaps that was why the evening felt something of a let-down. The carefree atmosphere of the gallery, the noisy banter, the shared food and drink, didn't extend to the seats they now sat in. They laughed at Harry Champion, red-nosed, his waistcoat stained with evidence of spilt beer and gravy, they sang along to "Boiled Beef and Carrots" and stumbled rather over "With the End of me Old Cigar," they tried to like Queenie Lawrence, they persuaded themselves they were enthralled by the company that staged the tableau "March of the Martial Man", but they left before the appearance of "AHRENSMEYER THE WIZARD OF THE PLAINS, *Master of Wonderful psychic force*", even though the bill promised them his "Marvellous Stone Breaking Test."

Afterwards, sitting in the eel-pie shop opposite the theatre, Harry said, "Well, Hod, perhaps it was just as well you didn't much enjoy it. You won't be able to gallivant off to the halls once Charlotte's installed at Harbord Street."

Hod trapped the last piece of eel with his fork, smeared it with vinegar and popped it into his mouth, chewing determinedly. He drank some beer, relishing its faintly brackish taste as it slid over his tongue. "No," he said, "we'll have to make our own entertainment." And then, as though he'd said something improper, felt himself colour. "If you're finished I'll pay up," he said quickly, "we've got a busy few days ahead of us."

"Finished," Harry said, pushing back his chair and standing. "Lead on Macduff."

"Lay", Hod said. "Not *lead* on, *lay* on."

"Really?" Harry said. "Oh, well, you're the expert. Sounds a bit odd to me, though." And he led the way out of the shop.

23 APRIL 1905

Hod and Fred were in their choristers' robes, sat in their customary places side by side at St. Marychurch. Suddenly Hod realised that Fred was silently crying, could feel his friend's body shaking as it pressed against his own. He was guiltily aware that he didn't want to acknowledge Fred's grief, didn't want to turn to him, would rather keep his gaze fixed on the figure of the young woman who shared a pew with his mother and her two sisters half way up the aisle. In the dim yellow flare of the gas lamps he could not make out her face, but from the dark coat with its astrakhan fur collar he knew who she was, knew that he loved her. He concentrated on her face, determined not to turn back to Fred, and now he knew with appalled certainty that he was waiting for her to lift her head and show him the skull beneath her hat....

He woke sweating. The occasional rumble of a heavy cart came to him from the Fulham Palace Road and, drifting up from the opposite direction, a tug's bleat shook out across the river. He lay still in the wide bed and thought of his friend, buried somewhere in Africa. Fred's death had become a part of what Hod, in company with a few like souls at his college, had gradually come to see as the unholy mess of the war in South Africa. At the time of the relief of Mafeking he had joined in the celebrations which Danger permitted the students, paraded three abreast through Exeter's city centre behind the Union Jack, and with others even dared to visit one of the more obscure side-street taverns in defiance of college rules. "The only fly in the ointment", as Weeks had remarked, was that "Redvers Buller had to hang his tail while 'Bobs' could wag his all the way to Pretoria."

A letter from Polly had, however, cracked the surface of Hod's unthinking. "Perhaps it's because my poor Frank is barely cold in his grave that I feel such anger," she wrote. "But Hod, what is to be gained by this jingoism? 'Lord, what fools these mortals be.' Remember how father used to quote that? Well, I've had it constantly on my lips during the past weeks. All these vain, puffed-up old men whose only pleasure in life, as far as I can see, lies in killing their fellow men and then expecting to be praised for it. We need a parliament of women, Hod. I think I may well be turning into a suffragette!"

Some weeks later, when the news of Fred's death had come to him in a letter from Sarah Kelly, Hod no longer thought of himself as an ardent patriot. And when, later still, he discovered that the apparent saviour of Empire, as Roberts was known in the *Daily Mail*, in his haste to get to Pretoria had marched his men across the arid veldt without giving any thought to water supplies, so that at least *seventeen thousand* of them had died after drinking from polluted streams and water-holes, Fred among them, he became so angry in discussions with those who insisted that "the Boer had been taught a lesson," that they took to calling him "Kaffir Kelly."

"A kaffir isn't a Boer, you blithering idiots," he shouted, blood pounding in his ears as he and some fellow teachers argued about the war in the tap-room of their local. "A kaffir is a black man."

"All the same to you," Jim Cassidy said, "black or white, it doesn't matter as long as they're not British. Well, I'm proud to be British."

"You mean you're proud of whatever's done in the name of Britain?"

"Of course."

"Then you're an even bigger fool than I took you for."

Cassidy put his glass down. "I'd be willing to settle this, man to man, with fists," he said, looking round at the others. "Trouble is, Kelly isn't a man." He pushed his heavily-moustached face closer to Hod's and Hod smelled the beer, sour on his breath, as he looked into Cassidy's eyes which glinted with drink and anticipation of a scrap. Cassidy was a big man.

"Now, now," someone else – Morant – said. "Gentlemen, please. We are here to drink and enjoy our conversation. I suggest we change the topic. Have you heard that when Eddie mounts the throne he intends to keep no ladies in waiting?" He waited for the laughter that gradually broke the tension.

Hod was grateful to Morant for his well-meaning, clumsy jocularity. And one of the advantages of the move to Park Walk was that Cassidy wouldn't be going with them. He'd accepted a post at Marlborough Road.

Good riddance, he thought, hearing from over roof tops the hoarse, scratchy cries of the cockerel kept by the nearby urban dairy as it greeted the first glimmerings of dawn.

He thought of Fred's easy strength, of the muscled body lying now stripped of flesh thousands of miles from the home of his grieving family. Fred, not Harry, should have been his best man, though given Fred's views on marriage would he have accepted and, even if he'd done so, what might he have said? And thinking that, Hod knew a part of himself was relieved to be spared the possible embarrassment of Fred's broad Devon brogue, that becoming a schoolmaster meant speaking and encouraging others to speak in a way that marked him out from friends of his childhood. Such knowledge was inseparable from shame. Let him not be like Bradley Headstone. And with those uneasy thoughts for company, he fell back into brief sleep.

KENILWORTH, EASTER SUNDAY & MONDAY 23-4 APRIL 1905

> Every facility is afforded to the Cheltenham boys as far as their
> ground is concerned, as the turf is of the best, and high scoring is
> the rule; indeed so good is the ground that the county of
> Gloucestershire plays a week's cricket there every summer. The
> ground, it may be added, is flanked by the school gymnasium,
> racquet-courts, and workshops, so that many forms of recreation
> are to be found in a very small area.

Hod looks up from Ranji's *The Jubilee Book of Cricket.* Just like
Cook's Ground, I don't think. He allows himself an ironic smile.
Outside the third-class carriage window, green fields of Warwickshire
are screened by lines of willow and, now, a straggle of houses and
factory backs. He leans across and taps Harry on the knee. Harry
is still immersed in *The Riddle of the Sands.* "Next stop," Hod says,
and jerks his eyes up to the luggage rack above Harry's head.

The London and North Western Sunday Special from Euston begins
to slow. Others in the crowded compartment look briefly at the two
young men when they stand, reach for suitcases, push past knees as
they mutter excuses – "sorry, very sorry," – and fail to avoid treading
on at least some feet before they slide the compartment door open and
squeeze their way out to the corridor.

Harry takes off his boater, then wipes his face with a silk
handkerchief he carefully folds and tucks neatly back into the breast
pocket of his green and white college blazer. "Much more of that and
I'd have fried," he says. "You'd think it would be worth putting up
with a few smuts just to let some air in."

He is referring to a losing battle the brothers fought against fellow-
passengers in the hope of travelling with the window open. At each
stop one of them would rise, seize the heavy leather strap attached to
the bottom of the window, and let the window slide down until it was
half-open – never more – before securing the strap to the brass stud
fixed below the window frame. And each time, as the train answered
the guard's whistle by a series of groans and shudderings and then
began to ease itself into a fresh start, someone, usually but not always

51

a newcomer, would rise, haul on the strap and return the window to fully-closed. For the most part this would be managed in silence, although one man, heavily built and sweating in a dark serge suit, who with his lady companion joined the train at Fenny Compton, hoisted the window with especial vigour, then sat emphatically down, sighed, wiped his hands on his thighs while staring at each occupant of the compartment in turn, and finally announced to nobody in particular, but looking, so Hod felt, particularly in his direction, that for reasons of health his wife was under the doctor's clear instruction *always* to sit facing the engine – otherwise her palpitations would be uncontrollable – and that to sit facing the engine with the window open meant, as anyone of sense must know, that she would certainly end up covered in soot, "like a perishing blackamoor."

The train lurches to a standstill and the shriek of steam subsides to a prolonged hiss. Doors swing open and the brothers step down opposite a station sign that says KENILWORTH. Ahead of them, a few first-class passengers are being helped from carriages by porters who pile their trolleys with leather cases, wicker hampers, hatboxes, while the station-master, in peaked cap, brass buttons and more than a hint of braid to the lapels of his dark, well-pressed suit, shakes hands with some of the wealthier-looking travellers. Harry draws Hod's attention to this by nudging him in the ribs. "So that's what Ernie gets up to," he says. And Hod, lifting an eyebrow says, "I only hope he washes his hands afterwards."

An invalid chair is awkwardly manoeuvred from the door of the parcels' van as the brothers, in common with other third-class passengers, make their way from the far end of the platform and out to the ticket hall. Hod hands their cardboard tickets, a little grease-darkened, to an official in a small booth beside the heavy, iron-grille gate, who silently accepts them and gestures that they are free to go.

They stand on the station forecourt under an ornate glass and iron canopy through which the afternoon sun can barely force its way, and are studied by cab-drivers uncertain as to whether they represent a likely fare. One half-raises a whip as though to attract attention. Then, perhaps thinking better of it, he flicks it across his horse's back. The horse stamps a front foot and continues to snort into his nose-bag, tossing his head from side to side in the hope of dislodging from the hessian some last piece of chaff or grains of barley.

"Where now?" Harry asks.

"Not far from here," Hod says. He uses the heel of his hand to push his bowler hat back, and looks around him. But no, no member of the White family has come to meet the brothers. "We'll walk."

Harry nods and smiles in defeat. Of course they'll walk. Sorry chums, he says silently to the cab-drivers, but if you're hoping for trade from Horace Kelly you'll be waiting until judgement day.

Carrying their valises, the young men walk briskly away from the station along a curving, tree-lined avenue with open fields to their left and, on the right, a number of handsome, brick-built villas. At the end of the road they come out onto the town's main street, stretching away in both directions.

"Where's the castle?" Harry wants to know. "Shouldn't we be able to see it from here?"

With his free hand, Hod points to the right. "Castle Green and Abbey Fields are in that direction," he says, "where the gentry 'reside', and where the parish church is. Get Charlotte's father to tell you all about that. We go left."

"Naturally," Harry says, with satiric intent, but Hod does not respond.

They turn up a wide street, known here as Castle End, Hod tells Harry, pass several shops, two inns, *The Bear and Ragged Staff* and *Earl of Clarendon*, and after a few minutes of striding along the flagged, tree-lined pavement arrive outside a double-fronted shop.

Number 53. "Here we are," Hod says.

Harry looks at the writing that arcs across both windows. HENRY WHITE IRONMONGERY AND CHINA-WARE. Hod also looks, sees the blinds are down, and thinks of his father's shop at Babbacombe with its sugar-barley lettering. He feels a sudden pang of – no, not grief, but regret – that William Kelly knows nothing of his son's adult life. If the old man were alive he'd surely have come to Hod's wedding, and if he'd come then Sarah Kelly would have accompanied her husband to Kenilworth, rather than, as she has done, write forlornly from Barnshill that she feels too frail to make the journey northward. The letter, which is in Hod's valise, goes on to say that she sends her blessings for his new life and trusts to the Lord that he and Charlotte will be happy, and will he be sure to show Charlotte what she has written, and to extend her good wishes to Charlotte's parents.

"Well," Hod thinks, "I hope he'd be pleased." Startled, he looks at Harry, but Harry's face reassures him that he can't have spoken aloud. He tugs on a metal chain beside the green-painted door and deep within the shop they hear a bell's clangour eddying into silence. After a few moments comes the muffled, but unmistakable sound of footsteps. The blind on the shop door shoots up, and at the sound of bolts being drawn back Harry turns from looking at the saddlery across the street to see a large, affable man with ruddy face and white spade beard framed in the doorway.

"Good afternoon, Horace," the man says, his voice burly with promised laughter, "and this no doubt is Harry."

He extends a broad hand into which Harry's disappears.

"So," he says, nodding at each brother in turn and smiling his welcome, "come in, come in," and he does his best to stand aside while the brothers edge past his dark-suited figure and into the shop's dim interior.

Harry has a general impression of copper-ware hung from hooks or glowing dimly on shelves, of delicate-looking china figurines within glass cases, of crockery set out on tables, and then they are through the shop and Henry White is leading the way up a flight of steps.

"The women are somewhere out the back" he says without turning his head, "but we'll be more comfortable in the parlour."

As Harry steps into the room in question, he judges it must run the entire length of the shop. There are two tall bay windows, framed by heavy-draped dark-blue patterned curtains which reach to the floor, and at a glance he can see that what Henry White calls as if dismissively "the parlour" is in fact a handsomely furnished, even elegant, drawing room.

Charlotte's father studies Harry's look as the young man gazes about him at the red-patterned carpet in which deep armchairs wallow, and then at the oval table covered by a green velvet cloth which takes up perhaps half the floor space. Around the table are arranged padded rose-wood dining chairs, and on the plum-coloured walls, covered in floral wallpaper, hang oleographs and water-colours, while an ebony-cased clock stands on the wide marble mantel-piece, to either side of it tall vases decorated with Japanese figures.

"All my wife's doing, isn't it, Horace?", Henry White says, meeting Harry's look of abashed admiration. "Myself, I'd settle for tin plates and horse-hair."

"Stuff and nonsense, Henry, and I'll thank you not to speak so." The woman who enters wears a long, white apron over her black dress, and her greying hair is pinned up on top of her head. "Good afternoon, Horace." Her voice is light, issues from thin lips, and lacks any suggestion of her husband's local accent.

Hod moves towards her, kisses her a little awkwardly on her cheek, and then introduces Harry. "No mistaking that you're brothers," she says coolly enough.

"Even though Hod's clean shaven," Harry says, smiling, wanting to be friendly.

"And Harry's got a broken nose," Hod tells her, also smiling.

"I'm sure I hadn't noticed." Emily White speaks as if to suggest that Hod has introduced an improper word.

"Happened at college," Harry says briskly, "in a rugger match."

"Rugger," Emily White says vaguely, "I don't think either George or Percy play 'rugger', do they, Henry?" Rugger also seems a less than proper word.

"Not any longer," Henry says, "but they still run about on the soccer field. And they play a bit of cricket when work allows. They're good lads. You'll meet them tomorrow, Harry. Now then, mother, when'll food be ready, these two here must be peckish after their journey an' all."

Without bothering to answer, Emily White goes over to the large sideboard, pulls from a drawer a white table-cloth together with a small brass-backed brush and pan, and, having swept some invisible crumbs from the velvet cover into the pan, spreads the cloth and says to her husband as she leaves the room, "Perhaps I can ask you to lay the table, Henry?"

"And I might even agree." He winks at the two young men, but she is gone.

By the time the three of them have prepared the table – all good quality cutlery, crockery and glassware, Harry notices – Emily White has returned, this time carrying a tray laden with a large pork pie, slices of ham and beef, a bowl of quartered tomatoes, one of chutney, slices of current loaf, muffins, jam, and a silver dish on which are arranged iced curls of butter.

"Must be something special going off," Henry says, gravely, "don't usually get this much of a spread for supper."

"Now," his wife says, ignoring him, "there's the tea to fetch, and then we're ready."

"Tea! I should think beer would answer better to our needs."

"*You* can drink what you like," Emily White says, "but I imagine that the others will prefer tea."

But the others indicate that beer will suit them very well, although in doing so they are made all-too aware that as far as Charlotte's mother is concerned they have failed an important test.

And then Charlotte enters.

For a moment nobody speaks. Henry White looks from his daughter to his wife, then to Horace, then back to his daughter. His wife, having glanced at Charlotte, fixes her eyes on Hod. Harry smiles at his sister-in-law to be, then realises she isn't looking at him and so begins to study an oleograph of what he assumes to be the ruins of Kenilworth castle, its grey stonework over which rooks hover outlined against a late – or is it early? – sun. Beside it, he notices a plain-wood framed photograph of a group of firemen in uniform, arranged in front of their fire-engine, several of them holding the horse-shafts, and, alone on the engine's platform, Henry White.

Hod meanwhile looks at Charlotte who looks smilingly at him. He wants to speak but finds he can't.

"Hallo, Horace," Charlotte says simply. She wears a plain grey, high-buttoned dress which outlines her full body, a thin line of white lace at neck and wrist, and a brooch, made of silver with coloured glass beads in the shape of a butterfly, pinned above her heart. Hod recognises the brooch, because he gave it her last Christmas.

Charlotte is broad-faced, like her father, and she has violet-blue eyes in which innocence and candour blend, her nose, with its wide-arching nostrils, is modelled on her father's, and she shares his generous mouth. She is not beautiful, but when she smiles, as now, her attractiveness is very real, and very dear to Hod. She comes over to him and Hod, aware that they are being watched, kisses her formally on her lips. He is, as always, stirred by the discreet, hovering scent of her hair, of her skin, of eau-de-cologne and violets. "How are you, Cis?" he says at last, and is surprised at how steady his voice sounds.

"Not as ready for tea as you must be," Henry White breaks in. "I vote for a belly full of tack. Harry, you sit there, Hod, you draw up a chair beside Cissie ..." And he expertly marshals them into position before drawing corks from several bottles of beer while his wife, at the opposite end of the table, cuts into the pie.

For the next half-hour of increasingly easy talk the five of them eat, drink, eat some more.

"This pie is simply *excellent*," Hod says enthusiastically, and Harry adds, "As good as any father ever made, I reckon."

Emily White smiles discouragingly. Talk of trade is not for high tea. There is a moment of silence, saved by Henry White who says, "Shame I never knew him. A tinman and a pieman. If you ask me, we'd have got on like a house on fire."

"Nobody asked you to call yourself a tinman," Emily White says emphatically. "You know perfectly well you're a coppersmith."

"Tinman and gasfitter's good enough for me," Henry says, laughing.

"Well, it shouldn't be" his wife says, and a faint chill falls on the company.

Soon afterwards, Emily White rings a small brass bell at her elbow, and a scullery maid who has been hired for this evening and tomorrow appears to help her carry out the plates.

Harry tactfully offers to carry his and Hod's bags to the house where the brothers have been billeted for the night, and Henry White insists on accompanying him. Hod and Charlotte are to take a turn round a town Hod scarcely knows, because his one previous visit was to ask Henry White for his daughter's hand in marriage, and

57

with that accomplished his only journeys out of London have been down to Torquay to visit his family and, of course, his fiancée, still working in the dress shop. But what with having to send money home for Jack, as well as the need to buy furnishings for the flat in Harbord Street and arrange for his piano and desk to be brought up from Barnshill, Hod hasn't often been able to raise the wind for the train journey to Torquay, with the result that much of his courtship has been managed by letter.

Now, as the couple saunter up Castle End, Charlotte's gloved hand resting lightly in his crooked arm, he realises that future visits to Devon will be a matter of duty rather than pleasure. For Cissie – he has become used to calling her by her family name – will from tomorrow be with him in Fulham. His heart lurches, steadies itself.

There are not many people about this Easter Sunday evening, although as the two of them turn up Abbey Hill they notice a few well-dressed families lolling in carriages, and an occasional top-hatted man canters past on horse-back.

"Coming from St. Nicholas's," Charlotte explains, her voice so light Hod has to strain to catch her words. "That's where mother hoped we'd be married of course."

"Of course," Hod says. "Well, St. John's will do well enough for us, Cissie, toilers and labourers in the vineyard that we are."

"Yes, Horace, *of course.*" Cissie says, entirely missing his intended witticism.

They cross a bridge over a shallow stream and pass on their left the parish church of St. Nicholas's. The last of the dispersing congregation from evensong stand outside in talk or move slowly away. Hod wonders whether Cissie recognises anyone there but Cissie says no, it's the wrong end of town, and anyway she's been away from Kenilworth in recent years and wouldn't know a soul. "What about friends?" Hod says. "What's happened to them? Don't you still correspond?"

"Mother didn't much like my friends," Cissie tells him. "She said they were 'common'. When I was young I used to play with some of the girls I was at school with. We used to make up games in the humpty-tumps."

"The *what*?"

"The humpty-tumps," Cissie repeats as she guides Hod around to the left behind the church and towards the castle, which they can see ahead of them, spread grandly on its mound.

"There's more to that than meets the eye," Hod says, and Cissie replies, "we used to spend a long time exploring all the ruins, you know."

"Are these the humpty-tumps, then?"

"No, of course not." Cissie speaks without emphasis. "Humpty-tumps are fields with ups and downs, that's all. They're near where we live. All the town children played there. They still do. In winter, when there was snow, we'd use them for sledge rides and in summer we'd roll down them, all of us, that is all the children I played with, we all went to the church school – St. John's, I mean. But then mother said it wasn't lady-like and so after that I had to stop." Her voice is wistful.

"But why humpty-tumps, I wonder?" Hod has paused in front of thick curtain walls beyond and above which the castle looms against a darkening sky.

"Oh, that's easy," Charlotte says. "An oonty-tump is a mole hill – well, that's what the locals call them. We used to say 'oonty-tumps and arnt heaps' because there are lots of ant hills in the fields. I suppose people still do say that around here."

"But not the children you were supposed to know."

"No," Charlotte says as they move away downhill and curve back towards Castle End. "Mother tried to get me to meet children from the 'top end' of town, but it never worked out. I was back home 'in a pig's whisper', as Father says. The only children I ever really knew were at school with me. And I'm afraid some of them *were* very rough. Farm children, mostly, or ones whose fathers worked in the tannery. They weren't always polite and they'd sometimes use terrible language. Although I was sorry for them."

"Why?" Hod asks, gently. He pauses in his stride, looks at Cissie, sensing she wants to tell him.

"Because they were so badly beaten at our school. One master in particular was horrid, quite horrid." And Cissie gives a little shiver. "Mr. Badley he was called. Of course we all called him 'Baddie'. He

caned boys so they'd cry and there was an occasion when one even
...."

"One what?"

"Well," Charlotte says, looking away from Hod so he can scarcely
hear her words, "one soiled his trousers."

Hod wants to smile at the phrase, but a sudden, guilty memory of
Chas Connolly comes to mind. Connolly, the boy who'd enraged Hod
the pupil teacher, Connolly, who had been regularly beaten in front
of the entire school at Upton and who carried everywhere with him
the stink of shit.

"You wouldn't ever be violent to your boys, would you?" Charlotte
asks now, and Hod knows the question is important to her.

"No", he says, and means it.

"I'm so glad," she says softly. "I wouldn't like to think I was
marrying anyone who could behave like Mr. Badley'".

* * *

The following, breezily-clear morning, as the brothers, spruce in their
fresh-sponged and brushed dark suits, white carnations pinned to their
lapels, walk slowly up the Warwick Road, Harry says to Hod, "You
know, I clean forgot to ask Henry about the mystery of the parish
church you said he could clear up."

Hod shakes his head. "I didn't say it was a mystery," he says, "It's
Anglicanism. The rich man at his castle, the poor man at his gate."

"Don't follow." Touching his bowler, Harry steps aside to allow
a couple with three small children in tow to continue their slow
progress down Castle End. All are dressed in Easter finery, the
woman's large bonnet in particular an object of wonder, its high-piled
tiers of silk and artificial roses looking like an upended flower basket.
The family show no sign of acknowledging Harry's gesture, nor of the
brothers' existence.

"Looks as though it's them that's going to a wedding rather than
us," he says, when the party is well past.

"Not up our end, anyway," Hod says. "They'll be parish church
material." And he tells Harry all he's heard from Henry White about

how, some fifty years previously, the wealthier parishioners of St. Nicholas's had become increasingly dissatisfied with having to worship in the same church as the "great unwashed."

"Meaning?"

"Oh, you know, anyone in trade, anyone who didn't have the vote, the tanners, railwaymen, general rag-tag-and bobtail, piemen and tinmen. Apparently the nobs got together a sum of money – three thousand pounds, I think – and told the rest to shift moorings, go and build their own church as far away as possible from all true gents and ladies."

"And they did?"

"They did," Hod says. "Henry doesn't mind, or anyway he laughs it off. 'Got our own place to thank God for not being like others' he says. But Cissie's mother gets in a stew about it. I rather think she feels she ought to be up at St. Nicholas, not among the riff-raff of St. John's."

"She chants the poker, I'd say," Harry remarks.

Hod looks at his brother in mock astonishment. "And I'd say I don't know what you're talking about."

Harry laughs self-consciously. "A good phrase, though, isn't it? Picked it up at school. She wants to persuade us she was born to better things."

Hod nods briefly, forced to concede the reasonableness of this supposition. "From what Cissie tells me," he says, "I gather her mother doesn't like it one little bit when Henry calls himself 'tinman and gas fitter.' 'My husband is a skilled coppersmith'. And he is, you know. I've seen some of his work, it's first-class. She thinks he ought to spend more time on that and less with the fire-brigade."

"Yes, I saw the photograph of the brigade. He's there, proud as Punch, standing on the engine."

"Trouble is, being Punch isn't dignified enough for his wife."

"Not like being a general, eh?" Harry says. "Remember old Weeks? 'Gentlemen, note that teaching is akin to soldiering. It is a dignified profession, a *gentleman's* profession.'"

The brothers laugh together. "Yes," Hod says, "Weeks'd insist on marching us down to St. Nick's, wouldn't he. I can't imagine that either he or Danger would consent to marry at St. John's."

"And who do you think would consent to marry either of those dried prunes? Hello, this must be it." For the brothers have now arrived outside a stone-built church, set well back from the road behind a generous sweep of grass that continues round its south side. From the belfry, bells are not so much pealing as tinnily and, Harry now thinks, apologetically clunking.

"Yes, this is St. John's," Hod says, gazing up at the spire, "and apparently the foundations are none too secure. Still, I don't expect it'll collapse in the next hour or so."

And he leads the way up the curved path to the west door.

The right-hand side of the nave is empty because nobody else from the Kelly family is able to attend the wedding. A few of the pews to the left are occupied by men dressed in fireman's uniform, some with wives, and towards the front two thick-set young men whom Hod recognises sit shoulder to shoulder in brown serge suits. George and Percy.

Hod taps the one nearer the aisle on the shoulder as he and Harry pass, and Percy, jerking his head up, sees it's Hod and winks at him.

A few minutes later Mrs. White comes down the aisle, arm in arm with an older woman, elaborately grand in long coat with astrakhan fur collar and veiled hat. "Mrs. Bishop," Hod whispers to Harry, "Cissie's grandmother. This is foreign territory to her. She *does* go to the parish church. Let's everyone know that she thinks her daughter married beneath her."

"Must be catching," Harry whispers back, and the two brothers exchange a quick smile.

The organ, which has been at some colourless exercise, now breaks into a loud, sustained chord, Harry and Hod hear people shuffle to their feet, cough, and the vicar, in cassock and surplice, comes to the front of the choir steps. Hod sees Cissie and her father pass him and the vicar motions him and Harry forward.

He does not remember much about the next twenty minutes, except that he hears Cissie's quiet voice say "I do," that he himself repeats the words, and that the Reverend Harrington Clareless, clean-shaven, with wide, friendly mouth, and remarkably lacking in unction, then pronounces them man and wife. He is scarcely aware that he is led away to sign his name in the registry, although he has a vague recollection of shaking hands with several people and of walking back to Henry White's house, arm in arm with his bride.

Even in the drawing-room, as the family arrange themselves around the oval table, Mrs. Bishop being encouraged to sit where the light will least affect her eyes – "eyes very delicate" Henry White says to Hod straight-faced – Hod is still, as his father would have said, wool-gathering.

He comes to, or thinks he does, when his newly acquired father-in-law proposes a toast to the "young couple," but as he begins to rise Cissie on one side and Harry on the other pull him back down.

He turns to Cissie, who smiles gravely at him and shakes her head.

Then Harry rises to speak. He apologises for the fact that no other member of the Kelly family is able to be here on this very important occasion, but circumstances, which he will not bore the company by dwelling on, have combined to make it impossible for any but he himself to manage the journey to Kenilworth. Oh, and Horace, of course, without whose presence the wedding could hardly have been managed.

They laugh at the poor joke, although Mrs. Bishop looks as though she would not greatly have minded Hod's absence.

Harry then reads out messages of greetings and good wishes from Sarah Kelly, from Jack – "whose weak heart means he can only travel short distances" – as far as the *Rose and Crown* and back, Hod thinks – from Lydia, "whom Lady Phillimore regrets she is unable to spare" – Mrs. Bishop is suddenly attentive – and from Polly, nursing an indisposed husband. This is the absence Hod feels most, but he knows how death shadows Polly's existence now and he understands, though he grieves, for her almost desperate anxiety over any illness that affects either Doris or Ernie. Her anxiety is also, he suspects, something Ernie exploits to the full. Polly sends her dearest love to both Horace and Charlotte, and hopes to see them soon.

Having read out these messages, Harry raises his glass and proposes a toast to "Absent Friends."

With the exception of Mrs. Bishop, who looks as though she does not approve of friendship, all drink the toast; and Hod thinks of his father and of Fred, and wishes they could be here.

And now he has to speak. It is the moment he has been dreading.

For the past week he has been flicking through the pages of the Commonplace Book he began to keep at college, and which is now half-filled with quotations, *pensées*, epigrammatic remarks he has picked up in the course of his reading, not one of which seems useable on the present occasion. He has also consulted page after page of the copy of *The Works of Shakespeare* which he was awarded as "Prize for General Knowledge," signed *Midsummer, 1901, J. G. Dangar, D.D.*, but Harry has persuaded him that although he is in Shakespeare's county his present audience might not be a suitable one on which to try quotations from what Hod considered calling the local poet.

Now, looking round the table, Henry White smiling encouragement, George and Percy looking a little blank though friendly enough, Emily White not quite meeting his gaze and Mrs. Bishop staring candidly away, he is at a loss. Even the words he had earlier rehearsed have gone from him. Gesturing vaguely at the table, its plates of meats, of cheeses, the opened bottles of wine and beer, the as-yet uncut, single-tiered wedding cake encased in smooth white icing with a line of pink piping around it, *Charlotte and Horace* picked out in silver across its surface, he stumbles out his thanks for the hospitality of his parents-in-law, as he may now, he hopes, call them, says that each and all will always find a warm welcome at 55 Harbord Street, Fulham, regrets that the life of a schoolmaster means that he and Charlotte, Cissie, will not be able to take a honeymoon – Mrs. Bishop here smiles sourly, as though to indicate her clear understanding that her granddaughter has married into graceless poverty – but that he hopes, no, *knows*, that life with his dear wife will be its own reward.

Only then does he look at Cissie. Her violet-blue eyes study him and again he can hardly speak. Then, he doesn't know how or why the words come to him, he says, to her, not to the others, "In thy presence is the fullness of joy," and sits down.

As he does so it occurs to him that at least one person at the table will take the words as blasphemy, but he doesn't care. He's not marrying Mrs. Bishop. It's enough that Cissie puts her hand on his arm.

"Thank you, dear" she says simply, and smiles at him.

And again Hod cannot speak.

PART 2

Each morning when I go into my study, and before I sit down at my desk to start work, I pause to look at a photograph which hangs on the wall to the right of the door. More often than not I run a finger along the top of its plain brown wooden frame. Then, as always, I let my glance linger on faces which, although they have inevitably faded over the years, are almost as familiar to me as those of old friends. In some ways, indeed, they *are* old friends or, if not that, then acquaintances. There are sixteen of them. Who are they? OLD EXONIANS CRICKET CLUB the legend on the generous mounting over the photograph declares in Gothic script, and then, underneath and in bold italics, *1907*. Beneath the photograph itself are printed in small capitals the names of those pictured, and beneath the names, in lower-case italic, the name and provenance of the photographer: *C.F. Hands Barnsbury Hall, Islington N.*

The frame's dimensions are 20 inches x 15, and the photograph itself measures 12 inches x 8. Not large, but not small, either, and certainly not a casual snapshot. For all that the photograph has been taken *en plein air*, it's composed with considerable panache and an eye for telling detail. Even the setting, which is presumably a corner of the club's ground, has been put to good use. Behind the men, and acting as a half backdrop, is a wooden fence, beyond the fence what may be the top of a lush, well-groomed hedge, and then finally a screen of raggedy, full-leaved trees which look to be fruit-bearing. An orchard, a suburban garden? The grass on which the men variously stand or sit is thick, matted, and I can just make out a scatter of daisies as well as the occasional spike of meadow barley. As to the cricketers themselves, the photographer has taken great care over their grouping. They are in four rows. The three at the back must be standing on a bench or chairs, although their legs are obscured by the six in front of them who stand at ground level. Then comes a bench-full of five seated figures, and then, at the very front, two more cricketers, sitting not quite cross-legged on the grass.

Yet this formality doesn't at all take away from the men's individual qualities. The three who make up the back row are not dressed for cricket. They have on heavy-looking suits, two with fob watches, their shirts topped by stiff white collars, and all three sport ties as well as trim moustaches that follow the curve of their upper lips. H.D.L. Nancarrow is on the left as you look at the picture. Slim, youthful, with a lock of hair that falls – just – over his right temple, he stares above folded arms directly into the camera's lens. There may be a hint of truculence in that stare. Perhaps he's sore at having been omitted from the eleven picked for today's game?

No such problem for the man who stands next to him. L.A. Trollope is broader shouldered, has a generous jaw and mouth which could, you feel, easily lend itself to laughter. Arms hanging loosely by his side, he gives the impression of being entirely at his ease. The third of the trio, W.Z. Payne, gazes not at the camera but towards his right, as though suddenly alerted to movement beyond the hooded man with tripod. Older than the other two, he's stockier than either and, perhaps because he does not expect to command a regular place in the eleven, feels no compunction at looking about him. Or does the initial Z provide a clue to that look: Zephaniah? Zechariah? Minor Old Testament prophets. But theirs were tales of foreboding, and there's nothing to suggest coming distress in Payne's candid, untroubled gaze.

The second row of Old Exonians includes four men in their cricket whites, flanked by two in suits. At the far right, hands clasped behind his back, J. Ryall, in three-piece suit with watch-and-chain from which hangs a coin, or medallion it could be, gives at first glance the impression of being the very model of a club umpire. But this may be misleading. For all that he seems older than the others – or do I think this because he's nearly bald – there's a certain dapperness about him that suggests an *elan* not often met with in umpires. This is partly a matter of his splendid moustache, which must surely be waxed at its turned-up tips, partly a matter of the lower-than-usual collar with natty and fashionable white bow tie; and partly his gaze, in which geniality and the sardonic are nicely balanced. If he is, as I assume, the club's umpire, you can be sure that he will enjoy using his authority. Not that Ryall could for a moment be mistaken for a jobsworth. But bumptious batsmen and hectoring bowlers should beware.

Beside Ryall, E.H. Lintott is all youthful openness, his recent moustache a dubious attempt to assert maturity. But he looks determined enough, and has accordingly rolled up the sleeves of his open-necked shirt, which must be made of flannel and is almost certainly the one he recently wore as a schoolboy. H.T. Trew, on the other hand, has merely removed the collar of his workday white shirt. Taller than Lintott, possibly the tallest of them all, with his combed-back fair hair, high forehead, eyes half-closed as though used to scanning far horizons, long nose and fair moustache, he looks to be a Guards Officer let out for an afternoon's fun. Next to him, wearing a wide-collared jumper, F. Holland is surely keeping his distance from the others? Whenever I pause to study him I think of E.M. Forster's famous description of the Greek poet Cavafy as a man standing at a slight angle to the universe. Holland's smooth face, the long jaw-line and fleshy lips with their faint suggestion of a moué, all suggest an element of camp.

Then comes one of my favourites, G.E. Pepler. If Trew is the tallest cricketer on show, Pepler is undoubtedly the shortest. He also comes across as the essential county pro. Stocky, broad-faced almost to squareness, he is tanned, "leathery", his body all muscle and toughened flesh, and as soon as you look at him you know that he'll be good at just about any sport under the sun. In the many years during which I played club cricket I came across several men of Pepler's kind. Uncomplicated, quite without envy or rancour in their judgements of fellow sportsmen, making few demands on life, they're content to spend their days playing football, cricket, golf, tennis – whatever they are asked or choose to turn to – although they're as uncensorious of, as they're baffled by, those for whom sport is an occasional pleasure rather than a compulsion. Pepler wouldn't, I think, have much in common with J.P. Squire, who stands on the left-hand flank of the second row and who, hands thrust deep into his suit pocket, looks frankly cross at being excluded from the team. Like Payne, Squire stares towards his right, but this is because he's damned if he's going to do the photographer's bidding. Although not much taller than Pepler, he's even broader, and his large face is dominated by an expression which, while less than a scowl, is decidedly sullen.

Now, the five men who make up the third, seated row. Farthest to the left is C.H. Parr, his head at a level between Squire's and Pepler's shoulders, well-muscled arms crossed, his shirt sleeves, in common with most of the others, rolled up above the elbow. Parr's gaze, which doesn't quite meet the camera, is in no sense evasive. He's relaxed, even quietly amused, as though looking forward to a certain fifty or maybe an opening spell on a wicket perfect for his kind of bowling. And although the generous turn-ups to his tidily-pressed white trousers reveal dark socks, that doesn't to my eye make him any the less a complete club cricketer. In 1907 few cricketers, even those who played at the highest levels, bothered to kit themselves out with white socks. In the section of his *Jubilee Book of Cricket* devoted to correct dress, Prince Ranjitsinjhi recommends that anyone taking up the game should possess a white shirt, which "ought to be of canvas, wool or flannel", as well as white flannel trousers and boots which "ought always to be kept clean by the use of whitening or pipe clay." But he has nothing to say about socks. Socks didn't count.

Next to Parr is S. Nugent, identified as *Vice-Capt.* His wavy hair, which may well be ginger, together with his slim, athletic body, gives him an almost dashing appearance, as of one who has mastered the art of the late cut. F. J. Thompson, *Capt.*, on the other hand, sitting foursquare at the centre of the picture, is more of an avuncular type, a wise old head, open-featured, a man of wry humour, adept at consoling a failed batsman or of putting a reassuring arm around the shoulders of a fielder who's dropped a crucial catch. It must be a sign of his status, and perhaps background, that his trousers are secured by a tie. "Boys are in the habit of putting on belts," Ranjitsinjhi tartly observed. "This is a mistake, since the noise the belt makes may at times be mistaken for a catch at the wicket. I advise instead scarves or sashes, which also have a smarter appearance." Or of course the old school tie. Or, equally of course, the club tie. (W.G. Grace is usually pictured with his MCC tie strained round his ample middle.)

Now comes a face that intrigues and even disturbs me. It belongs to H.D. Powe, *Hon. Sec.* Below his thinning hair and high forehead, Powe's eyes stare in almost grief-stricken panic at the camera. As for his mouth: half-open but with no trace of a smile about its thin, taut lips, it seems determined to repress speech. One hand rests loosely in the other, not, however, as an indication of ease. On the contrary, it's as though Powe has no awareness of his hands, nor for that matter of his long, excessively-thin and awkward-looking arms. He's retreated wholly into whatever thoughts or fears lie behind the fixed stare of his haunted eyes. Squire may look as though he wants to detach himself from the club, but Powe is truly alone. Even his buttoned-up shirt collar suggests a man shut away from the rest.

In absolute contrast, G.E. Skinner, who completes the row, is normality personified. The knuckles of his half-open hands rest comfortably on his knees, his full moustache spells trustworthiness, and behind round spectacles his eyes seem to smile in the contented knowledge that this photograph is, like every other aspect of his life, business as usual. G *must* stand for George. George for England, George the dependable, Trooper George.

Finally, at the very front, two men sit on the thick grass, legs crossed at the ankles – more evidence of dark socks – and have been posed so that, turned slightly to one another, they appear in half profile. They alone do not seem to be looking at anything in particular, for the angle at which their bodies are turned requires each to cross the path of the other's gaze with an oddly abstracted or perhaps contemplative air. The man on picture right has a moustache to challenge Ryall's, the one on the left, with slightly fuller face, is clean shaven. The man on the right has centre-parted hair which is obviously thinning, although not so rapidly as the other's, whose hair has already receded to the crown of his head. Yet a similarity of nose, slightly aquiline, of firm-set mouth, and of rounded, shapely ear, suggests that they are related.

As indeed they are. The moustachioed cricketer is H.P. Kelly. Harry Kelly, great uncle Harry, who when I knew him was headteacher at the junior school in Sawtry, a then small village in Huntingdonshire, near Peterborough. The other man is his older brother, H.W.S., Horace William Scott Kelly, known to his family as Hod. By the time he achieved his first headship, nearly ten years after this photograph was taken, he'd become the father of a daughter from whom, some twenty years ago, I acquired the photograph. H.W.S. Kelly is my grandfather.

* * *

He died early in 1940, not long after the outbreak of the second world war. At that time I was two-and-a-half years old. His widow, Charlotte, "Cissie", my maternal grandmother, came to live with us after her husband's death, and I learnt from her over the years a number of things about him. Some of what she told me I put into a poem, "My Grandmother's Dream of Heaven," which I wrote some six or seven years ago. That was when I was beginning to become fascinated by the grandfather I never knew, a fascination sparked by my mother's casual remark (casual for her, for me it was a revelation) that he had been friendly with Ernie Bevin and had taken tea with the great Trades Union leader at the House of Commons. How on earth had this come about? Was my grandfather a socialist? Yes, it seems that he was on the left, or so she said. And what of his friendship with Bevin? Did they meet through party politics? No, she thought not, although politics had cemented a friendship begun in schooldays.

She was wrong about this, I later discovered, although there's no reason to doubt that in later life Bevin and Hod were, as my mother insists, friends. She was, however, able to tell me something of the men in the photograph which hangs on my study wall. I know that the Old Exonians were former students of Exeter Diocesan Training College, later St. Luke's, and that they were all practising teachers living and working in London. I don't know when the club came into existence, nor where its ground was, although I have a strong suspicion that my grandfather had a hand in helping to set the club up.

Leave speculation aside. What do I know of the photographed Old Exonians? Well, I know that S. Nugent was called "Sammy", that he did indeed have sandy hair, that he was a married man with a wife called Ivy and a daughter, Joyce, and that his family were friendly with Uncle Harry's. I know that F.J. "Tommy" Thompson, *Capt*, was a bachelor, kindly towards small children, someone who was a welcome weekend visitor to my grandfather's house in Fulham. I also know that he must have had money problems.

At about the time of the photograph, the Exonians formed a Lodge – my mother thinks it was my grandfather's idea, and she recalls that for several years he acted as the Lodge's secretary. He was certainly involved in helping to set up a joint fund into which, week by week, each Lodge member tipped whatever cash he could spare. The idea was to help members who might be in temporary financial difficulties and who, at the Lodge's discretion, were allowed to borrow from the "Library", as the fund was nicely called. Almost as soon as the "Library" was established, Tommy Thompson asked to borrow several "books". After a while he had borrowed so many that he was denied further access to the stock.

I'm sorry about *Capt*. Thompson's money difficulties, but I'm more struck by the fact that my long-held convictions about H.D. Powe's state of mind turn out to be correct. I now know that the poor chap – "a very witty man" who was "besotted" with cricket and who would take my mother when she was a girl to matches at Lord's and the Oval – became mentally unbalanced and while still comparatively young died in a "Home." Powe, known to his friends as "Curly", fought through the Great War, and on his return was thought by those friends to be "strange". This is hardly surprising. Anyone who went through that hell was entitled to be made "strange". Yet looking at

73

the photograph convinces me that Powe's condition wasn't so much caused by the war's horrors as exacerbated by them.

I look at the photograph and wonder how many of those men beside Powe, men who stare confidently at the camera or who are locked into their own thoughts, would have fought in the Great War? And of those who did how many survived? Would Pepler have proved to be "a man you'd want to have beside you in the trenches", as he seems set to become? Might Trew have turned into the guardsman of my imagination? Surely G.-for-George Skinner would have been an uncomplaining, resolutely cheerful soldier wherever he found himself? These and other questions about the men's subsequent lives come readily enough to mind but I shan't be going in search of answers to them. My concern is with the figure who sits at the left front of the photograph. H.W.S. Kelly. Hod. My grandfather.

Because he is in half-profile I can't see his eyes. Of all sixteen Exonians caught by the camera on that summer's day in 1907, he is by far the most elusive. There he sits, "gazing inward", evading my stare, the questions I want to ask. But I'm determined to ask them. I want to find out all I can about the grandfather I never knew.

* * *

The little I have discovered about his early years is contained in the opening section of this book. Inevitably, some of it is hearsay, some pure guesswork. I have also invented friends for both his father and himself. As far as I know, Jed Coulter, Fred, and Henry Morant never existed. Nor did Sol Pannel or Chas Connolly. On the other hand, Dickens gave public readings at Exeter and Plymouth in 1858, and the stories about the great pudding fight, the Torbay storm, and the bread riots are true enough. So is everything Hod says about Exeter Diocesan College, later to be St. Luke's. I found out about the former from J.T. White's 1878 *History of Torquay*, and the information about the training college is narrated in Frederick Fuller's 4 volume unpublished *History of St. Luke's College, Exeter*. Details of these and other books are listed in the bibliography at the end of this book. What follows is as factual as I can make it.

PART 3

1. MARRIAGE

By the time the photograph of OLD EXONIANS CRICKET CLUB was taken, Hod and Charlotte were two years into married life. The house in Harbord Street, where they were to live for nearly twenty years, would have been comfortably-sized for the two of them, small though it was. Unfortunately, they rarely had it to themselves. When Hod took his new wife there, Harry went with them. And when Harry married and left to set up with his wife in a similar house further along Harbord Street, his place was taken by brother Jack. This arrangement could have been of no financial benefit to my grandfather. Harry had paid his way, but Jack of the weak heart wasn't allowed to work. Hod was therefore faced with an extra mouth to feed out of his own pocket. Given his very modest salary, that pocket must often have been empty by the end of a month. And though, in the autumn of 1907, he moved from Hope Walk to another school at Store Rd., Hammersmith, his salary barely altered. Making ends meet remained, and for years to come was to remain, a problem.

Harry's wife, Ella, was also a schoolteacher. When I came to know her, she looked grandmotherly, but she retained a wonderful zest for devising and passing on mnemonics for spelling, for parts of speech, for arithmetic, in fact for all those educational basics she'd been trained to dispense. Tricks of the trade she called them. I learnt a great deal from her, although it never seemed like learning, and I loved the schoolhouse where she and Uncle Harry lived, in Sawtry, a small village near Peterborough, and where we – that is my mother, grandmother, my sister Jill, younger than me by sixteen months, and I – spent several summer holidays during the Second World War.

They always began the same way. Long before we were due to set off, my grandmother would be in the hall, placid beside her suitcase, while my mother rushed through the small semi-detached house we rented in the Leicestershire village of Burbage, making last-minute adjustments to furniture, luggage, our dress. Jill and I would be posted at the front-room window to watch out for the arrival of the taxi – a saloon car with cracked green-leather upholstery – in which we'd be driven to Hinckley station by either Mr or Mrs White, whose main line of business was a petrol station and repair service at the top of our road. From Hinckley a train would deliver us to Leicester, and at Leicester's large, important station we'd catch a stopping-train to Peterborough. For the last stage of our cross-country journey we transfered to a car driven by Mr Colman, a thin man with a moustache which I later realised was meant to make him look like his namesake, the 'thirties film-star, Ronald Colman. The Colmans owned a cafe on the A1 just by the Sawtry turn-off, and for them, as for the Whites, taxi-driving meant the chance to earn a bob or two on the side. Somewhere on the car journey we'd pass under two sets of steel hawsers strung across the road. Square buckets, suspended from the hawsers by what looked like closed hooks, moved slowly and with what seemed trembling uncertainty on their way to or from clay-pit and brick kiln. Soon after that we'd turn off the A1.

The road into Sawtry was really no more than a lane running between high hedges and wide, grassy verges tangled with flowers and cow parsley. Years later, I came across Edward Thomas's description in the *South Country* of wayside greens, those "no man's gardens, measuring a few feet wide but many miles in length .... as beautiful and cool and fresh as rivers." I've no idea if he invented that lovely phrase "no man's gardens" or whether it was common coinage for the kinds of green stretch that accompanied us into Sawtry. But when I was a boy there were still plenty of them about, although the gipsies whom Thomas refers to as regularly camping on them for a night had largely disappeared from view.

As to Sawtry itself, my memories of it are not surprisingly centred on the school and its immediate surroundings. The schoolhouse was separated by the width of an asphalt yard from the classrooms, and the bottom of the yard was sealed off by a brick wall in which was set a green-painted door. This door was kept locked – perhaps against schoolchildren's scrumping – but aunt or uncle would open it for us, and once through we were into a garden where, on most afternoons when the weather allowed, grandmother, mother and aunt carried deck-chairs and knitting, while Jill and I were allowed to make ourselves useful by shelling peas and broad beans into a battered metal colander. There must therefore have been a vegetable patch, although

I don't recall it, any more than I can remember flower beds. The garden was really an orchard. At all events, the grass was thick and tussocky, studded with bruised, fallen apples and gashed plums over whose gummy, yellow flesh, platoons of wasps slowly crawled. We were warned against picking up the windfalls - "you'll get stung".

Once indeed I was stung, although not in the orchard. It happened as I crossed a meadow opposite the school. I was as usual whistling – I was an inveterate whistler – and must have paused to draw breath. When I closed my mouth it was onto a wasp that had settled on my lower lip. The wasp did what a wasp has to do. The scream of pain brought my mother running and I was taken back into the schoolhouse where a blue-bag was applied to my swollen, throbbing lip, and the district nurse sent for. By the time she arrived I'd recovered, although my lip remained sore for several days.

As always, I'd gone into the meadow saying that I was on the look-out for mushrooms. But although when I returned from those expeditions I made sure to have some fungi with me, I was really after silver foil. And on nights when, lying awake, I'd hear overhead the rumbling pulse of enemy aeroplanes as they headed towards midlands cities, Leicester, Coventry, Birmingham, I'd know that, come the morning, there'd be a good chance of finding one or more tight rolls of foil among meadow grass, or stuck like improbable Christmas decorations in the hedges or dog-rose bushes that lined the meadow. The foil was, so we understood, lobbed from aeroplanes to mess up radar scanners, and in playground barter it was priceless stuff. You could trade one roll alone for half-a-dozen assorted marbles. So I wasn't bothered when the mushrooms I brought back to the schoolhouse were carefully inspected and then thrown away. "You can't be too careful," one or other of the adults would remark, and follow up with tales of so-and-so whose friend, father, cousin, had died agonizingly after eating a toadstool or some deadly boletus. "Sorry", I'd be told, as the fungi were taken out to the dustbin, and I'd pretend to sadness. But all the while I could feel the silver foil in my trousers' pocket. That was true riches.

Then, on one of my meadow hunts, I stumbled on even rarer trove. At school we were repeatedly told to be on the look out for metal canisters and the like. They might well be unexploded bombs, jettisoned by German bombers as they turned for home after their night raids. On this particular morning I was certain of foil, so many German aircraft had thumped the air as they headed inland the previous night, and I'd already collected two rolls, when, in the cattle-pond at the bottom of the meadow, I saw a rusty metal object, about the size of a kettle drum, sticking up out of the water.

I ran back to the school-house, burst into the kitchen where my mother, grandmother and Auntie Ella were still sitting at the breakfast table, and announced, "Quick, quick, I've seen a land-mine." I don't know why I'd decided that the object was a mine, but my breathless manner must at least have half convinced the grown-ups, because Uncle Harry was summoned and, when I'd repeated my story, he pedalled off to find the village policeman. Within minutes the two men returned and we all set off across the meadow, the policeman leading the way, Jill and I running to keep up with Uncle Harry, and, some way behind us, the three women, occasionally calling out a warning to take care.

They needn't have bothered. The land-mine turned out to be an upended "copper" – one of those metal tubs much used in pre-washing-machine days – which had obviously come to the end of its useful life and whose owner had carted it across the field before heaving it into the pond. I wasn't however rebuked. The policeman agreed that the object did look suspicious and even Uncle Harry nodded and remarked that in these days it paid to keep your eyes open.

I say "even" Uncle Harry, because I think of him as a peppery man. Or was that because he wore a ginger, hairy, and therefore to my mind stinging, sportscoat? Whatever, I wasn't entirely comfortable in his presence, although I can't recall any unkindness from him, and on occasions when the tin bath would be hauled in front of the fire and filled with hot water so that Jill and I could be bathed, he'd more often than not be somewhere in the room making conversation as he trimmed the oil lamps – Sawtry at that time still had no electricity, or – once – singing to us, in a dry, scratchy voice.

I owe him a considerable debt, too. From Uncle Harry as well as from Auntie Ella I learnt and even now can remember various of the tricks they taught me for what was then called "mental arithmetic".

Arithmetic played a crucial part in the examinations that determined who'd go on to grammar school. The intelligence tests that also featured in those examinations must, I think, have required some of the same skills. Thanks to my aunt and uncle, I've always taken pleasure in mental arithmetic, so much so that when years later I first read *David Copperfield,* and no matter how sympathetic I felt with David's panic over his step-father's terrorising methods – "I go into a cheesemonger's shop, and buy five thousand double-Gloucester cheeses at fourpence-halfpenny each, present payment" – I knew they were precisely the kind of sums I'd enjoyed trying to work out as a small boy.

I'm also pretty sure that Dickens enjoyed doing such work. In one of his journalistic pieces, on "Cheap Patriotism", he has a lordling of the Civil Service require his staff to know something "say, French ... and be up in their arithmetic – Rule of Three, Tare and Tret ... Decimals, or something or other", and you know that while the lordling himself won't have the first idea how to do Tare and Tret, Dickens most certainly *will*. (Deductions involved in calculating the net weight of goods to be sold retail, should you want to know.)

Aunt and uncle's skill at handling numbers may well have been partly native. But it must have been honed by their college training. Ella in particular was a dab hand at mental sums. I can remember playing games devised by her – that's how I think of them – in which she'd set me tasks of division, subtraction, multiplication, to see how fast I could complete them without have to write the numbers down. "You need to see them in your head," she'd say, and after a while I could. There were of course trick questions. If it takes 4 minutes to boil one egg, how long will it take to boil three eggs in the same water. If a boat's hull is two feet below the plimsoll line at low tide, how far below will it be at high tide, assuming the difference between low and high tide to be twelve feet. Those games took place in the schoolhouse kitchen-cum-dining room, the tiled floor half covered in a rag rug, on which stood a long, scrubbed wooden table and a scattering of chairs, some straight-backed, others sagging at their ease. Running half the length of one wall, so memory insists, was a black kitchen-range, on and in which all the cooking was done. The range also supplied the house's hot water. (You fetched water from a pump in the yard.) The kitchen was Ella's domain, and because I associate her so closely with this room, she's inseparable in my mind from the idea of domesticity: her broad figure in its blue-and-white spotted silk dress, grey hair done up in a bun, seems an image of domestic calm.

But it's a distorting image. My mother tells me that not only was Ella a formidably intelligent person, she was often vehement in arguing her case. Knowing this, I think now she must have been, like my grandfather's older sister, Polly, one of those women who, through experience of training college, glimpsed a future world they weren't in the end allowed to enter, or from which they were ejected. And this wasn't simply because once married they had to give up their teaching careers, but because going to college must have made them feel that it was perfectly proper for them to be interested in and committed to ideas and the arts, that they could justifiably think of themselves as intellectually and perhaps socially, even sexually, liberated, that they didn't have to be waiting for marriage to justify their existence; whereas nothing that came afterwards seemed to justify that interest, those commitments. A later generation of young women used art school as the quickest way out of Manchester. Evelyn Gibbs, Nan Youngman, Elizabeth Vellacott, Gertrude Hermes, Kathleen Hale and others, undoubtedly experienced frustrations in their later lives: nevertheless, they were able to practice their art. But women teachers of my great aunt's generation who married had no choice in the matter. They were made to exchange their profession for a life of domesticity, a "woman's life." Their plight, the plight of countless women of their generation, is evoked in Gwen Harwood's bitterly eloquent sonnet, "In The Park", about a woman who by chance meets an ex-lover as she watches over her children at play.

> They stand a while in flickering light, rehearsing
> the children's names and birthdays. "It's so sweet
> to hear their chatter, watch them grow and thrive,"
> she says to his departing smile. Then, nursing
> the younger child, sits staring at her feet.
> To the wind she says, "They have eaten me alive."

This isn't to say that either Polly or Ella thought their children had eaten them alive, but it is to suggest that in later years they must have felt that a door had banged shut on the vistas they'd glimpsed as college students.

And this will help to explain why Ella and my grandfather wrote each other long letters in which they argued about many things. I don't know what exactly. Politics, no doubt, world affairs, their ideas of what made for a good education, the merits or otherwise of the public school system (Ella and Harry's son was sent to one such school), authors, and, later perhaps, films. But what the letters above all testify to is Ella's refusal to give up her right to be considered a serious person. She apparently gave no quarter, took no hostages, as the saying is: like Dr. Johnson, she argued for victory, whether by letter or in conversation. On one occasion, my grandfather, exasperated at not being able to unpick a particular argument of his sister-in-law's, said to her in rueful despair, "If I were married to you, Ella, I'd either murder you or become prime minister."

I can't imagine him saying anything like that to his wife. I've no reason to doubt that they genuinely loved each other, and in his last, desperately ill months, she successfully took over a good many of his pastoral responsibilities, difficult and demanding though they often were; but she hadn't an independent mind. She took for granted that men were the breadwinners and therefore knew best, and with this unshakeable conviction went a kind of wise passiveness, an almost impregnable placidity. "I, a stranger and afraid, / In a world I never made," Housman wrote. My grandmother would have agreed with the second line but not the first. Let those who'd made the world take on the fear. This was in no sense heartlessness. It was merely that she saw the world as mysteriously beyond her understanding. She'd therefore concern herself with what she *did* understand. As a small boy I once tried to swallow some stringy cabbage which got stuck in my windpipe. My mother was out of the room at the time, but my grandmother, sitting opposite me at the dining table, watched with kindly interest as I spluttered, reddened, gagged, fought for breath, and with increased desperation tried to claw the cabbage from my throat. "I do believe he's choking," she finally and mildly said, and my mother, hearing her words, rushed in and banged me on the back until I coughed the cabbage up.

83

She must always have been like this. When Harry was still lodging with them he bought a labrador which my grandmother was supposed to keep shut into the flat while he and my grandfather were out schoolmastering. Sooner or later it was bound to escape, and one morning, when my grandmother answered the door to a tradesman, the dog bolted through the gap and made a dash for the bottom of Harbord Street where there was a small public garden featuring an ornamental pool. Into the pond went the labrador and began a wild and joyous swim. My grandmother arrived on the scene at the same moment as the official garden keeper, who began shouting at her and the dog to get out of there and wanting to know what was the point of all the notices that said it was forbidden for anyone to use the pond if nobody paid attention to them.

My grandmother broke off from asking the dog to come out of the water in order to explain to the keeper that it couldn't read.

"But *you* can" the keeper shouted.

"But it's not my dog."

The unassailably calm manner in which my grandmother will have spoken these words wouldn't have been meant to enrage the keeper. She was far too sweet-natured to be capable of sarcasm, let alone irony or satire. The dog *wasn't* hers, it belonged to her brother-in-law. But her matter-of-fact retort worked as well as the deadliest *coup-de-grâce*. The keeper was left gape-mouthed as she fished the dog out of the pond and walked him sedately home.

"Sedate", the OED says: "Calm, quiet, composed; cool, sober, collected, tranquil, equable, esp. excessively or tediously so." And then, a bit confusingly, "Motionless; smooth and steady in motion." Wordsworth's leech-gatherer, then. "Motionless as a cloud the old man stood, / That heareth not the loud winds when they call, / And moveth all together if it move at all". The garden keeper's windy indignation would no more have made my grandmother move at an awkward pace than would my grandfather's occasional squalls of ill-temper, to which he was apparently liable. And this wasn't because she possessed the steely indifference, let alone egotism, of a Rosamund Vincy, say, but because she was a truly sedate person.

I'm not sure this was a virtue, although it amounted to the same thing. It was at all events its own reward, and frequently entailed her being the victim of the world she never made. I don't think she ever got used to modern travel. In an attempt to cope with the hurry she associated with railway journeys she always arrived at the station far too early, and as a result invariably boarded the wrong train. She would then take some time to realise that she was being hauled in a direction other than the one intended, at which point she'd summon the guard, ask to be put off at the next station, and from there telephone my mother in a kind of placid bewilderment. "Joan, I am at High Wycombe. Why am I not at Coventry?"

As to bus journeys, she must have believed that driver and conductor naturally shared her knowledge of the particular stop where she planned to alight. Not to believe that would, perhaps, have seemed to her a slur on their professional, male, competence. On more than one occasion she therefore stepped from a bus that had made no attempt to slow, and would as a result topple haplessly into the road. Amazingly, these falls never caused her serious harm, although there were times when my mother would stand at our front window muttering in exasperation, "oh, no, she's done it again!" And there would be my grandmother, limping dustily up the road, on her face the customary look of uncomplaining bafflement – once more the world had let her down. And as she nearly always wore her fur coat when taking the bus to visit friends or for shopping expeditions, it became over the years increasingly matted and torn, although undoubtedly useful in cushioning her falls.

At least once, however, she insisted on being in control of those circumstances which more usually threatened to control her. As I've already said, when Harry left the flat, brother Jack took his place. I doubt this was my grandfather's idea. More likely his sisters at Barnshill had had enough of he-who-must-be-paid-for-doing-nothing. Unsurprisingly, therefore, they took the first chance they had to shoehorn him out of Torquay and into Fulham. Once installed in his brother's flat, Jack took up residence in the front room, which was Cissie's pride and joy. She kept spruce the furniture she and Hod had bought, lovingly polished the piano he'd had delivered from Barnshill and on which he loved to play, sweetened the atmosphere with fresh-cut flowers, and took great delight in the various pictures and decorative items the pair of them assembled with much thought for the overall look of the place.

Then Jack arrived. He brought with him his indolence, his assumption that he'd be waited on, and of course he paid nothing towards his upkeep, although for a man of reputedly delicate health he was a more than hearty feeder. He also brought with him a pipe which he stuffed with rank-smelling tobacco and smoked continuously.

It was the pipe that did for him. One evening my grandmother told Hod she could stand no more of it. Either Jack went or she did. Next day Jack was returned to Barnshill.

* * *

So now they had the place to themselves. In that sense at least they were better off, although regular supplies of money had still to find their way to Torquay, to help pay for Jack's upkeep. It meant that once they'd settled their bills and paid into my grandather's pension fund there was precious little left over for frivolities. They lived frugally, but then most of the people they knew did the same. On weekdays they'd rise early, and after a breakfast of porridge and, occasionally, an egg, my grandfather would set off to walk the mile or so to his school or, in wet weather, to catch the omnibus. My grandmother's routines were as unvarying. Monday was washday, Tuesday sewing and darning, Wednesdays were given over to polishing silver and plate (chiefly cutlery), house-cleaning occupied much of Thursday, (all wood had to be wax-polished,) and on Friday she'd bake and, in season, bottle (jams, pickles, chutneys). Besides these duties, there'd be shopping, food to prepare for evening meals. Cottage pie, steak-and-kidney pie, Lancashire hot-pot, tripe-and-onions, of which they were both passionately fond – I share their love of this dish but my grandmother could no doubt buy grey-seam tripe rather than the present-day's blanched, bleached rags smelling of ammonia – liver, chitterlings, hog's pudding when they could get it (although even then it wasn't often discoverable outside Devon), pasties, and fish for Fridays: whiting, cod, herring, sometimes plaice, boiled, baked, fried.

Plain food all of it, and cheap, too, but nourishing. I imagine the only area of cookery where my grandmother let herself go was in baking. A battered old recipe book of hers which I've inherited contains no recipes whatsoever for main courses. It does, however, mention several for cakes and scones, including "Cokernut (sic) pyramids", "Hot Scones quickly made", "Rock Cakes", (two recipes), "Irish Plum Cake", "Christmas Cake" and "Ginger Cake"(against both of which are written "Ella's Recipe"). There's also one called "Rich Cake", the recommended ingredients for which are 1 ½ breakfast cups of flour, 3 table spoonsful of raisins, 3 of currants, 3 eggs, ½ lb of butter, 1 ½ teacups of sugar, and peel. In addition there are instructions for making "Marrow Curd" and "Marrow Ginger", jams which no doubt featured along with the cakes at Saturday and Sunday's high tea.

Weekends provided a release from the routines that filled Mondays to Fridays. Most Saturdays during the summer my grandfather played cricket. Or, if he was without a game and could afford the entrance money, he might take himself to Lord's or the Oval. At other times of the year there would be visiting and being visited, even, on those rare occasions when funds allowed, a trip down to Torquay or up to Kenilworth. As for Sunday, that was probably closer to Mrs. Clennam's ideal than I care to think about. Matins or Evensong, or perhaps both, at St. Etheldreda's, their local church on the Fulham Palace Road. For the rest, "proper" Sunday best, quiet indoors and out, and a general sense of that deadliness which so blights Arthur Clennam's soul:

> "Maddening church bells of all degrees of dissonance, sharp and flat, cracked and clear, fast and slow, made the brick-and-mortar echoes hideous. Melancholy streets, in a penitential garb of soot, steeped the souls of the people who were condemned to look at them out of windows, in dire despondency .... Everything was bolted and barred that could possibly furnish relief to an over-worked people."

I doubt that much had altered between the mid-1850s, when Dickens was writing *Little Dorrit*, and the London my grandparents encountered in the early years of the twentieth century. Even if certain places of entertainment were no longer bolted and barred to all, they most certainly were off limits to "respectable" people. And as Eugene Wrayburn so devastatingly remarks to Bradley Headstone, schoolmastering is "a most respectable profession." Being respectable meant treating Sunday as a day of self-denial, of cancelled pleasure. It still did nearly half a century later. In the late 1940s we moved from the midland village where my mother, sister and I sat out much of the war, to the fringes of outer London, where my father, newly demobbed, had found work. Walking home from church one Sunday evening, I heard the sound of an accordion coming from a wooden community-hut at the bottom of our road. Not only that. People were clapping in time to the music, and the heavy, regular thump of feet meant they must be dancing, enjoying themselves! Who were they? Catholics. What's more they were almost certainly working class. Disreputable heathen.

I don't recall how I knew all this, but I certainly *did* know, just as I knew that I was leading my sister astray when, years before, in wartime, and with my father briefly home on leave, she and I were as usual packed off to Sunday school and something in me rebelled. Instead of trudging up through fields to the village, I got her to join me in trawling a favourite minnow stream. Hours later we returned home with wet, muddy shoes, and had to confess our truancy. Nothing bad happened. My father wasn't especially angry. He must have realised that a sunny afternoon held promises far more alluring for small children than any offered by Sunday school. But he also knew that sending your children to such a school was what respectable parents did.

I've no idea whether my grandparents were especially religious people. When she lived with us, my grandmother used to sing hymns about the house in a faint, quavery, but surprisingly sweet voice. Her favourite was "There is a green hill far away / Without a city wall," which always puzzled me. Why should a green hill *need* a city wall? She sang with equal fervour her favourite waltz, "Now that the ball is over". Her religious beliefs were almost certainly conventional rather than deeply personal. On the other hand, I don't believe she or her husband were hypocrites. And I'm sure they'd have felt uncomfortable with any solecism on what my grandmother invariably called "the Lord's day."

As to the rest of the week, they cultivated their patch of garden, and of an evening my grandfather, who was an inveterate and absorbed reader, got through books apace, or whiled away an hour or two at the piano, playing favourite songs from the music halls, a few sedate ballads for his wife, and rather more taxing pieces for his own pleasure, while my grandmother, although she'd sometimes undertake a little light reading, for the most part knitted. She was a prodigious knitter. Even in old age I rarely saw her without knitting needles in her hands, balls of wool on her lap (powder-blue and pink were her favourite colours, although she sometimes veered into green and rust-red), while ribbed bed-socks, scarves and tea-cosies accumulated in piles at her feet, all of them intended as Christmas or birthday presents for family and friends. She also, and as far as I know uniquely, knitted egg-cosies, although I don't think they were ever sent out. Instead, you'd find what looked like woollen thumb-stalls at the bottom of kitchen drawers or shoved into far recesses of the airing cupboard.

One Friday in every month, on pay-day more likely than not, they'd make tracks for the Granville Theatre of Varieties or the Shepherd's Bush Empire, where they'd queue for tickets to the balcony. On one of these occasions my grandmother, who found queuing difficult at the best of times, fainted. My grandfather meanwhile went on reading his newspaper, unaware that his wife had collapsed at his feet. (Well, I did say he was an absorbed reader.) I don't know when that was, but it may well have been late in 1909. For by then she was pregnant.

2. A DAUGHTER

In January, 1910, the nation, or as much of it as could vote, went to the polls. In his classic study of the period which he calls *The Strange Death of Liberal England 1910-1914*, George Dangerfield says that the result of the January election marked the beginning of the end for the kind of liberalism upheld by Asquith. The prime minister had been forced to dissolve parliament because of the Lords' refusal to pass Lloyd George's budget of the previous autumn, but January 1910 didn't bring him the vote of confidence he both needed and expected. According to Dangerfield, "After a month of very dull electioneering, the country went to the polls in small numbers and recorded a lethargic opinion. As a result, the Liberals were 60 reduced, and the Conservatives so swollen, as to be almost equal in numbers: the Irish and Labour Parties held the balance of power."

"The Lords may decree a revolution, but the people will direct it," Lloyd George had told their lordships late in 1909. For Dangerfield, the outcome of the January election was that there was no clear outcome. Asquith's gamble had failed. A low poll and no overall winner, so he says. I used to assume this was so. I now know it wasn't. Dangerfield fiddled the statistics to suit his argument. The turnout for the 1910 election was in fact the highest ever recorded: 86.6. Moreover, and as the Tory Austen Chamberlain remarked at the time, the result made plain that the people had "voted against the Lords, and, above all, against the landlords." Liberal and Labour candidates gained 51 per cent of votes cast, the opposition 46.9. Dangerfield is however right on one point: the Liberals lost their overall lead and had to rely on Labour votes to keep them in power.

I don't know how my grandfather cast his vote but I'm pretty sure it will have been in the Labour interest. Surmise and hearsay make me think that the Kellys traditionally supported the Liberal cause – always strong in and around Torbay – but in Fulham in 1910 Hod couldn't have voted Liberal because there were only two contestants for the seat, the Conservative W.H. Fisher and the Hon. F. Hemphill, Labour. The Liberals presumably chose not to put up a candidate because they didn't want to split the radical vote, and also because they could rely on a successful Labour candidate voting with them in the Commons. In the 1906 election the tactic had worked perfectly. The Labour candidate, T. Davies, triumphed over Fisher by 8,037 votes to 7,407. But in January 1910 the same tactic failed. Fisher's 9,690 votes put him almost two thousand ahead of Hemphill's 7,761. Later that year, in the December election, Fisher beat off a new Labour challenger by more or less the same margin, although on a lower turnout: 8,252 to 6,526.

Why do I think Hod voted Labour? It's possible though by no means certain that he wouldn't have baulked at the Conservative government's Education Act of 1902-3, which provided for church schools, including public schools, to be supported by public rates. (The Act prompted a Nonconformist campaign of refusal to pay such rates.) But without doubt he'd have been contemptuous of the welcome that same government gave to the infamous Taff Vale decision of 1903, which made trade unions liable to payments of damages to employers for strike action by union members.

The decision was prompted by events of August, 1900. In that month workers on the Taff Vale railway in south Wales went on strike after a signalman who'd led a campaign for a rise in wages was sacked. The strike, officially supported by the Amalgamated Society of Railway Servants, was settled after eleven days, but the Company's general manager, Ammon Beasley, decided to secure an injunction and damages against the Amalgamated Society for the picketing activity of its leaders. He was initially granted his injunction and awarded damages, but the Amalgamated Society went to the Court of Appeal and got the Court to reverse the first court's decision. Beasley then took his case to the House of Lords and – would you believe? – the Lords found in his favour. The Railway Company was the richer by £23,000 and the Amalgamated Society, which had also to pay the court costs, lost overall some £30,000.

By the time the Taff Vale decision was announced Hod had been teaching in London for three years. Many of the children he taught came from back-to-back slums. They went to school bare-footed and ragged-arsed. They were undernourished and frequently ill. Rickets, ringworm, impetigo and, far worse, TB, were common among them.

From the log-books he was required to keep once he became a headmaster it's plain to see how deeply my grandfather was affected by the poverty of so many of his pupils, and of its consequences for their mental and physical well-being. He did what he could to help them and, in an England where the inequalities of wealth and deprivation were so pronounced, one of the things he'd have done was to vote against the party of wealth and privilege.

He wasn't alone. In April, 1906, the Conservatives' own *Quarterly Review* decided it had better enquire into the party's poor showing at the then recent election. The *Review* points to the Taff Vale judgement as forming part of "an accusation of plutocratic conspiracy"; and, it goes on, "Even the Education Act was presented as a victory for privilege, and so fell in with the general charge that the Unionists were the party of the rich and the selfish ... [ready] to keep the public schools of the nation as the preserve for their friends, and to put workmen under the heel of the capitalist by overthrowing the trade-unions."

* * *

A few months after the election which did much to curb the power of the Lords, Edward VII died. He'd set out in April for his customary Spring jaunt to Biarritz, but broke his journey at Paris, apparently because he wanted to see Lucien Guitry in *Chanticler*. The theatre was over-heated, Edward caught a cold, and when eventually he arrived in Biarritz the cold had become bronchitis. By the time he returned to London he was a stricken man. He died at 11.45 pm on 6 May. According to J.B. Priestley, in his entertaining account of *The Edwardians*, "it was one sign of a rapidly changing world that passengers on the larger liners, now equipped with wireless, knew of his death before people living in London suburbs."

Edward, most commentators agree, was a popular king. Hod's parents-in law had often seen one of his acknowledged mistresses, Daisy, Countess of Warwick, clattering in her landau along Kenilworth's main street, always attended by a troupe of outriders, sometimes with the king at her side. (Although it was another mistress, Mrs Keppel, who was called by Queen Alexandra to Edward's sickbed.) It seems that few were scandalised by the monarch's open infidelities, any more than they were troubled by his crass indifference to intellectual and artistic matters. He licensed philistinism and, we are to believe, was loved for it. Apart from women, his passions were directed to hunting, shooting, fishing, and "correct" dress. "Mornin', Harris," he once greeted an aquaintance who showed up at Ascot in a suit made of his own tweed, and then, sniffily, "Goin' rattin'?" He insisted that on a morning visit to an art gallery men should wear top hat but not tails; and he had a sharp eye for a misplaced decoration or the wrong ribbon. He sounds like a nightmare to me, but when news of his death reached New York, Broadway Theatre orchestras played the national anthem, flags flew at half mast, and the offices of Pierpoint Morgan were draped in black. Immense crowds turned out to see his coffin on its way to burial at Windsor, and at that summer's Ascot ladies going into the royal enclosure wore black feathers, ribbons and bows. "Black Ascot" it was called.

Would my grandfather have joined in the mourning? Perhaps, and yet part of me wants to think that he'd have felt at least some scepticism about the public response to Edward's death. It wasn't, after all, as though the king had died young. Nor had he done much beside enjoy himself. Besides, he not merely licensed philistinism, he made vulgar wealth respectable. "New commonness upon the throne," Yeats wrote contemptuously after Edward's accession. But such commonness went with wealth. The king and his court reeked of uncommon sums of money and of the things such money could buy. At the end of the nineteenth century Thorstein Veblen had identified conspicuous consumption as the chief characteristic of those with newly acquired riches; and Edward, that image of wheezy corpulence, was the most conspicuous consumer of them all. Champagne, cigars, women, motor cars, (of which he owned stables'-full), pheasant shoots, horses: he made no bones about wanting all he could get nor of getting all that he wanted. He was the very image of Sir Epicure Mammon, the embodiment of a crass materialism. I don't really see my grandfather shedding tears over his death.

* * *

On July 4th, 1910, two months after Edward's demise, Hod became a father. He and Charlotte named their daughter Phyllis Joan. "Joan" was Harry's suggestion and they themselves chose the then-fashionable "Phyllis". They took her the short step along the Fulham Palace Road to their parish church, St. Etheldreda's, for her baptism. Judging from photographs, the church, which had been built as recently as 1897, was about as unlovely as any church can be. No spire or tower (a vast central tower was planned but never built), gaunt, unrelieved walls, narrow windows, squat entrances. In photographs at least it looks for all the world like an overblown version one of those non-conformist chapels that were until quite recently soul-numbing features of most northern towns, though they're nearly all gone now, or have been converted into warehouses or small covered markets.

St. Etheldreda's has also gone. On the night of September 24/5, 1940, a clutch of the Luftwaffe's incendiary bombs landed on its roof and set the church on fire. It was declared unsafe and abandoned to nesting birds and a gathering wilderness of flowers and grasses. Then, in 1954, after the Bishop of Kensington had deconsecrated St. Etheldreda's, it was demolished. A new church, incorporating the former parishes of St. Etheldreda's and its companion, St. Clement's, now stands on the spot, unprepossessing if not obviously ugly.

But however graceless the original church must have looked, it succeeded in attracting more than its share of worshippers. Its first vicar, the Revd. John Sadler Phillips, incumbent 1897-1917, was, according to a *Brief Guide* put out to mark the church's centenary, "no mean preacher." Nor did he jealously guard against competitors. Quite the contrary. He regularly invited visiting preachers, whose names, the *Guide* rightly remarks, "read like a 'Who's Who' of the Church of England: the Archbishop of Canterbury (Temple), the Bishops of London (Creighton and Winnington-Ingram), Henry Scott Holland, W.H. Frere, Stewart Headlam, T.A.Lacey, W.C.E.Newbolt, Charles Gore, William Collins, J.Adderley, Robert Dolling, Lord Victor Seymour and Herbert Pollock were among those who preached in 1901 and 1902, for example. Not surprisingly, there were sometimes 2,000 in church at Evensong."

I'm not sure I believe those figures. St. Etheldreda's was certainly large, but I doubt it could hold a congregation of 2,000 people. On the other hand, some of these names, in particular, Temple, Creighton, Gore and Headlam, would have been certain to attract large congregations; and as all of them were on the liberal wing of the Anglican church, it seems reasonable to assume that Philips must have been sympathetic to their cause. Archbishop Temple, for example, had in younger days contributed to *Essays and Reviews*, a book which, on its appearance in 1860, caused such a storm of protest from more conservative church spokesmen that, when Temple became Bishop of Exeter nine years later, one High Church journal called his appointment "the darkest crime which has been perpetrated in the English Church."

The publication in 1889 of *Lux Mundi* was every bit as contentious. Described by its editor, Charles Gore, as "an attempt to put the faith into its right relation to modern intellectual and moral problems", its contributors, who included Scott Holland, were denounced by ritualists in the church as capitulating to secular trends. Creighton, whom an historian of the Anglican church in the nineteenth-century, T.Elliott-Binns, lauds as "one of the greatest and wisest of her bishops," while not as far as I know closely associated with contributors to either book, nevertheless held views broadly in sympathy with theirs. His conviction that "unintelligent acquiescence in opinions, though these might be true, was immoral and dangerous," chimed sweetly with the thoughts of Temple, Gore and the others. All these preached at St. Etheldreda's.

But perhaps the most interesting of the visiting preachers was Stewart Headlam. In 1875 Headlam had founded the Guild of St. Matthew, which was intended to "to promote the study of Social and Political questions in the light of the Incarnation." A ritualist – he stood bail for Oscar Wilde but wouldn't officiate at the marriage of Parnell and the divorced Kitty O'Shea – Headlam, who had written that "The best manual of Socialism is the Church Catechism", and that "the Church is bound by its nature to be communistic", was also on record as asking his brother clerics whether "it is not to a large degree their fault that so many men and women among the workers are alienated from the Church." Among the good causes for which he campaigned were land reform, an eight-hours bill, universal suffrage, and abolition of the Lords. This last campaign got him into trouble with his bishop, who for eleven years refused the turbulent priest a cure of his own, after Headlam had spoken at a public meeting in Trafalgar Square called to press the case for abolition of the upper House.

Official church disapproval notwithstanding, Headlam joined the Fabian Society. And as if this wasn't bad enough, he lectured to William Morris's Hammersmith Socialist Party in the spring of 1893. Not only that. David Rubenstein tells us in his fine study *Before the Suffragettes: Women's Emancipation in the 1890s*, that as a member of the London School Board in the late 1880s, Headlam combined with the socialist Annie Besant to force through "a number of resolutions in support of trade union wage rates, free schools, the provision of pianos in schools and an examination of the problem of malnutrition."

And he enjoyed the music hall. Edith Nesbitt put Headlam in her romance of 1909, *Salome and the Head*, where he's shown eagerly watching from the stalls the heroine dancer and "clapping his hands sore." Nesbitt, a Fabian herself, wasn't taking liberties. She'd have known that Headlam had founded the Church and Stage Guild, whose purpose was, so Ian Fletcher says, "to study theatrical dancing and publicize it as a moral and religious activity." And Fletcher, in his great essay, "Symons, Yeats and the Demonic Dance," refers us to a minor character in John Todhunter's *A Comedy of Sighs* (1894), a curate who says, "It's out of the Music Hall the drama of the future must come ... the drama of the working man."

I don't know whether the curate is based on Headlam. Nor do I know whether my grandfather would have been aware of the Church and Stage Guild or of Headlam's part in it, although I incline to think that in both cases the answer is yes. But beyond doubt he'd have known of and admired Headlam's work as a member of the London Education Board. It pleases me to think that he'd almost certainly have heard Headlam, who died in 1924, preach at St. Etheldreda's, just as it does to know that from the saint's name comes the word "tawdry", meaning cheap finery. (St. Audrey's lace used to be sold at the fair held on Etheldreda's feast day at Ely.) Cheap finery: a knowing parody of expensive ornamentation. A wink and a nudge at the la-de-dah. Pure music hall.

It also pleases me, greatly, to think that my mother was christened in a church sympathetic to Christian socialism. If there was ever a photograph of her in her christening robes it hasn't survived. I do however have an early photograph of her, taken in the garden of her grandparents' house at Kenilworth when she was perhaps two years old. She wears a white knee-length dress with frilled half-sleeves, her expression one of worry mingled with fretfulness. Hod himself is sitting on what looks to be the base of a rockery. He's in his dark three-piece suit, on his head the inevitable bowler hat. His head is tilted to study his small daughter, who's perched on his right knee. His hands look surprisingly large. The left one clasps his left leg, shin-high, the right holds his knee so that the arm forms a support for her. Bony wrists show below what seem short-cut coat sleeves, or has he unusually long arms? As for the fingers, they are long, supple-looking, at once sensitive and powerful. Such hands would be equally adept at spanning an octave or spinning a cricket ball. They might also be the hands of a writer or artist. But as far as I know Hod never drew or painted, and the only writings of his I possess are his Commonplace Book, which he's subtitled "A Collection of Reminders," one or two letters he pencilled to his wife, and the note-books he struggled to keep up in the autumn and winter of 1939-40. His most substantial writings are, however, to be found in the log-books he required to keep once he became a junior school headmaster, all of which I've read and reread in the Metropolitan Archive, where they are now housed. They are written in a clear, legible hand, but while painstakingly meticulous never veer into the kind of verbal flourishes that might imply frustrated authorship.

* * *

There were to be no further christenings. My mother was an only child. I once asked her why she thought this might have been. Well, she said, her mother had told her that she'd had such a difficult time giving birth that her doctor had cautioned her against having other children. My mother repeated the words with some scorn. She would have liked siblings and was plainly suspicious of her mother's motives for not supplying them. It wasn't so much that Charlotte was warned off having other children as that she couldn't be bothered.

I used to think my mother's suspicions well enough founded. Now, I'm not so sure. Her great friend during girlhood and adolescence was the daughter of friends of my grandparents. Like Hod, Arthur Reynolds was a teacher. The two men got to know each other while both were at Hope Walk, and acquaintance warmed into friendship. The Kellys and Reynolds even shared a love of music hall, although the Reynolds favoured the Shepherd's Bush Empire whereas Hod stayed faithful to the Granville. Soon enough, Hilda Reynolds and Joan Kelly became close friends. My mother was devastated when, at the age of seventeen, Hilda died suddenly of pneumonia. The Reynolds' grief was the more intense because Hilda, like my mother, was an only child.

Two families each with an only daughter. A coincidence, perhaps, but surely no more than that. Then, in early summer, 1999, I was in London for a family weekend. My son suggested a walk along the Thames from Tower Bridge, near where he and his wife live, to Rotherhithe. On our stroll we came to a metal sculpture of an elderly man seated on a park bench. Hand raised in salutation, he looks towards the figure of a small girl who gazes intensely back at him from the parapet above the river.

The story behind the two figures is at once noble and heart-breaking. The man is based on Dr Alfred Salter. He was born at Greenwich in 1873, and from 1898 began practising medicine where he chose to live, in Bermondsey, one of the poorest areas in the whole of London. He set up a scheme which encouraged people to pay into an "illness allowance", as a result of which – and to the anger of professional colleagues – he was able to charge only 6d (half an old shilling) for consultation. In June 1902 his wife, Ada, gave birth to a daughter, whom they called Joyce. That same year Salter became a JP and was elected Liberal whip for Bermondsey Council. A few years later, however, he resigned from the Liberals to join the I.L.P., and with fourteen others formed the Socialist Movement in Bermondsey. Later, in 1922, he became Bermondsey's Labour MP. (A year earlier, George Lansbury and 29 councillors of Poplar, on the other side of the river, had gone to jail rather than levy rates which they knew their constituents couldn't afford to pay.) When a Labour administration took office in 1924, Salter's plans for replacing high density housing in the public sector with lower density developments were put before parliament, but Ramsey MacDonald's minority government soon fell and the incoming Conservatives scrapped the proposal. Auden famously dubbed the 1930s a "low dishonest decade" but it strikes me that, taken all in all, the Tory administrations of the 1920s were about as low and dishonest as you can get.

But while Salter must have been disheartened by this reverse, it didn't stop him from going on with his good works. He campaigned for a solarium to be installed for the numerous sufferers from tuberculosis in the Bermondsey area, between 1911 and 1935 was much involved in attempts to bring down the district's infant mortality rate, and took great pleasure in the fact that in 1935, when 1487 babies were born, not one mother died in childbirth.

As for his wife, she became London's first woman mayor when she took on that office for Bermondsey – among her achievements was the planting of 1000 trees throughout Bermondsey's straight, drab streets; and she joined her husband in campaigning for – and getting – playground and park facilities for the local children.

The Salters' own daughter couldn't, however, take advantage of these. Her parents had Joyce educated locally, and partly as a result of this, or so the legend attached to the sculpture declares, she contracted scarlet fever not merely once, but three times. These successive illnesses must have weakened the little girl, with the result that the third attack of fever killed her. It's difficult to imagine the state of mind of her parents, whose entirely honourable decision over their loved daughter's education had, they must have felt, led, however indirectly, to her death. It may well be that the tireless, disinterested energy with which the Salters campaigned for better lives for the citizens of Bermondsey was at least partly prompted by a desire to assuage the agony of their loss. Diane Garvin, who executed the figures of Joyce and her father I saw that Saturday afternoon, calls her work "Daydream of an Old Man Waving to his Daughter." It isn't a great work, but it's a deeply moving one, above all because the doctor's raised arm, and the steady way his gaze is fixed on his young daughter, powerfully suggest that he's saluting a future which he and his wife worked so hard for, but which Joyce wasn't to see. Yet *her* absorbed gaze suggests that she is both acknowledging and encouraging her father's dreams of freeing the Londoners among whom he and his wife lived from the poverty and hardships about which others saw nothing to be done.

So here was yet another only daughter, and she, too, tragically dead before her time. Further coincidence or was a pattern beginning to emerge? If so, it surely lay not in the three deaths, nor in their being daughters. No, what struck me was the fact that all three were only-children. Back home, I pursued some enquires, as the police say. It didn't take long to discover that in 1907 Sidney Webb had issued a Fabian pamphlet (no. 131) entitled *The Decline in the Birth-Rate*. It begins:

> The falling-off in the birth-rate, which has during the last twenty years deprived England and Wales of some 200,000 babies a year, is the result of deliberate intention on the part of the parents. The persistence and universality of the fall in town and country alike; the total absence of any discoverable relation to unhealthy conditions, mental development, the strain of education, town life or physical deterioration of any kind; the remarkable fact that it has been greatest where it is known to be widely desired; the evidence that it accompanies not extreme poverty but a variety of conditions (among which social well-being is only one) leading to a positive wish not to have a large family; and that it is exceptionally marked where there is foresight and thrift – all this points in one and the same direction.

Webb concludes that "to the present writer, at any rate, it is the differential decline in the birth-rate, rather than the actual extent of the decline, which is of the gravest import." He means, although he's careful not to say as much, that the poor continue to breed in large numbers, but that the professional – middling – classes employ foresight and thrift, those eminently bourgeois virtues, to limit their families.

Behind Webb's argument is that *fin-de-siècle* fear of "impoverishment of the stock", which led to various proposed remedies, including the suggestion, put forward with entire seriousness by the Rev. A. Osborne Jay, that Penal Settlements for the criminal poor should be established in various isolated part of the country, where the inmates would be well treated "but actually sentenced to remain there for life, and will not under any circumstances be allowed to propagate their species and so perpetuate their type." Only the healthy should be allowed to breed.

But as Webb's pamphlet argues, the trouble was that the healthy were refusing to do so. The issue was not so much a decline in the overall birth rate as the spreading menace of the working-class, among whom, as Webb coyly admits, there was no sign of the birth rate slowing down. As I read Webb's pamphlet, I thought of *The Wind in the Willows*, and of how, in that exemplary fable of reactionary Edwardianism, the wild wooders, a fester of ill-bred stoats and weasels, threaten to engulf Toad Hall. For the novel's author and many like him, foresight and thrift might not be such virtues after all, not, anyway, when it came to replenishing "healthy" English stock.

But it's hardly surprising that they operated as powerful factors in limiting the size of families such as the Reynolds and the Kellys. Of course, one very simple way of wiping out the anxieties without which there'd be no need for foresight and thrift would have been to pay schoolteachers rather better. But that wasn't about to happen. And so when, in a leader of October 31, 1913, *The Times* tried to explain the decline in the birth-rate "amongst Western civilized nations", it listed among possible causes, "the high standard of living and greater love of pleasure, and the consequent shirking of parental responsibility; the higher education of women and their wider entrance into industrial and professional pursuits; even the fear of the pains of parturition have been pressed into the argument; our alleged moral degeneration has been frequently upon the lips of preachers, whilst the view that the most worthy desire to give the fewer children a better chance than the many had in earlier days is quoted with applause."

In the same year, "the National Birth-Rate Commission, instituted, with official recognition, by the National Council of Public Morals – for the Promotion of Race Regeneration – Spiritual, Moral and Physical" reported into the decline in the birth-rate, although the report wasn't published until 1916. It's by no means clear what the "official recognition" of this Commission amounted to, but in common with Webb and *The Times*, the report noted that the declining birth-rate "has been more marked in the more prosperous classes." The Commissioners therefore concluded that "Conscious limitation of fertility is widely practised among the middle and upper classes, and there is good reason to think that, in addition to other means of limitation, the illegal induction of abortion frequently occurs among the industrial population." The Commission further reported that "There is no reason to believe that the higher education of women (whatever its indirect results upon the birth rate may be) has any important effect in diminishing their physiological aptitude to bear children." Well, that's nice to know.

If my grandfather came across that report he'd have raised a hollow laugh at the idea of being among the more prosperous classes. He was undoubtedly well-off compared to many of the parents of children he taught. Large numbers of his pupils came from appallingly impoverished families; and it's one of the great and good things about him that in a variety of ways he tried to help those families. But he wasn't a man of means. I assume he and my grandmother used some form of contraception to avoid having further children. And it seems pretty obvious that contraception – as well as abstinence – must have been widely practised among those required to keep up a professional appearance on a salary scarcely more than that with which in *Howards End* Leonard Bast struggles to stay "above the abyss."

* * *

Some time after the birth of his daughter, Hod switched schools again. Among the teachers he met at his new school was James (Jimmy) Dawes, yet another parent with a daughter, Muriel, as only-child. She and my mother became friends, as did their parents. But a shadow hung over the friendship. Hod detested his colleague's bullying of the children in his charge. "There was something sadistic in it," he told his daughter. "He enjoyed caning those poor boys."

Dawes wasn't alone in the savagery with which he handed out corporal punishment. Violence in schools at the time seems to have been endemic and, as it were, licensed. In his *The Edwardians: The Remaking of British Society*, Paul Thompson, drawing heavily on recollections of those who lived through the period, remarks that

> Caning in school was ubiquitous .... Children were liable to be caned, not merely for talking in class, or for being late for school, or more serious offences, but for not getting their answers right ... even for coughing. Teachers would not only use the cane, and in Scotland the tawse, but would slap, pull hair, throw books and slates, tie children to radiators, or make them stand for hours holding their petticoats above their heads. Most of these teachers were simply acting within the educational conventions of the day, but the number who showed signs of definite imbalance was considerable.

Violence towards children sickened Hod. He was determined to outlaw it from any school of which he might become headmaster. But two years before he took charge of his own school, violence on a far larger scale began to shake the world.

3. TAKING COMMAND

On August 4th 1914 Britain and its allies entered "the war to end wars". I imagine that, like most people at the time, my grandfather assumed there would be a short conflict and that the soldiers would be home by harvest. A few of his friends, "Curly" Powe among them, volunteered for service. He may have done so himself, although if so he was rejected, as indeed were many who presented themselves at Recruitment Offices across the land during those early, heady days. More likely, though, he simply went on with his work as a schoolteacher, work to which he was devoted and for which he had an aptitude and skill in instruction that earnt him the love and admiration of successive generations of his pupils. He wanted them to do well, he took delight in their achievements, and in addition he often acted as a surrogate parent to them and to other members of their families.

He also yearned to turn into reality ideas for improving the school day that had been growing in him through the years he had put in as a teacher. New ways of arranging the time-table, more emphasis on outdoor pursuits – sporting, educational, cultural; and of course providing for a happier, warmer atmosphere by controlling, if he couldn't entirely do away with, the terrors of corporal punishment. In the winter of 1914 it looked as though his chance might have come. Among his surviving papers is a Testimonial written on 15 December by his old college head, James G. Dangar, who gives his address as St. Mary's Rectory, Washfield, Tiverton, Devon, and signs himself D.D. Prebendary of Exeter Cathedral. "Danger" must by then have been in his very late seventies, but his handwriting is firm enough, as is his wish to bid my grandfather "God speed & to recommend him for the post of Headmaster in a public Elementary School, to the managers in need of a genial and efficient co-worker." No school is specified, but Hod is unlikely to have asked for the testimonial unless he had one in mind, and he must have been pleased with Dangar's statement that as a student H.W.S. Kelly "gave abundant evidence of his fitness for his life-work; he was diligent, attentive, helpful, a good teacher & a man of the highest character." Coming from such a quarter, this was no small praise. It wasn't however enough to gain Hod a headship. Two years later, however, he had better luck.

St. Stephen's School for Boys, as it was called in 1916, stands back from the Uxbridge Road, on the opposite side from Shepherd's Bush station. If you go by train, as I did one early summer day in 1999, you cross the main road, pass the top of Lime Grove, and see ahead of you the parish church of St. Stephen. What you might not see is the short, narrow, railed-off path that leads at an angle to the school play ground. It was only when I'd made a tour of the church's exterior and found it to be walled off from the school, the roof of which I could make out between dusty sycamores, that I realised I'd missed the school entrance. I turned back onto the Uxbridge Road, came upon the path – a kind of aborted spinney – which I'd previously missed, went down it and suddenly came face to face with the school where my grandfather first became a head teacher.

It's no longer "for boys." It is however still a junior school, and although a new wing has been added, the original building must look much as it did in Hod's time. It was built in the 1870s out of bricks made from London's yellow-grey clay. Its two stories are generously proportioned and I would guess that the classrooms are and must always have been light and airy. And on that warm, summer's day at least, when I stood in the ashphalted playground while small children who'd been released for break milled about me and a kindly woman teacher rightly asked my business, St. Stephen's seemed to breathe an atmosphere that was itself warm, a kind of unemphatic happiness or contentment. Perhaps the fact that it's screened from the hectic noise and stir of the Uxbridge Road helps. From one of the Road's many shops I'd heard the thud of rock music as an over-magnified voice urged folk to "step inside for the buy of a lifetime". The sounds battered at my ears as soon as I emerged from the station, and went with me along the road and round by the church; but from the school playground I couldn't hear them.

St. Stephen's has always been a voluntary aided school, which means that the Anglican church helps to fund it and has some say in its educational policy. The church can't, however, have required all the boys to be members of the Anglican community, because my grandfather records in a Log-Book entry for September 17th 1919 "Attendance very poor this week owing to Jewish holidays." In the Spring of 1916 its then headteacher, Mr. Y. Vellacott, was appointed to take charge of a London Blue Coat school at a salary of £200 p. a. Like Hod, Vellacott had been a student at Exeter Diocesan College and no doubt James G. Dangar D.D. had written on his behalf. Now, courtesy of the appointment committee, Vellacott was to be succeeded by another of the college's former students.

The school's log-books, which were originally issued by the London County Council, are today housed in the Metropolitan Archive. At the front of the one which covers the years 1913-1927, Vellacott has signed his name in copybook script. Under it, I read the signature *H.W.S. Kelly*. The "y" is wonderfully assertive, a kind of swooping, exultant paraph which has forced the headteacher who followed Hod at the school to disrupt the signing of his own name, Rowell, so that *Row* appears to the left of y's tail and *ell* to its right. Impossible to miss the sense of achievement that bursts through my grandfather's signature as he takes possession of his first school.

There could also be a sense of relief implied in that flourish, for he might well not have made it. In the first months of the war the British army was composed of regular soldiers and, increasingly, volunteers. But by the end of 1915 Haig's murderous incompetence had caused so many deaths that he was in danger of running out of cannon-fodder. Early in 1916, therefore, the "Military Service Act" came into operation. Under it, all able-bodied men of the right age were to be conscripted into the armed forces. The Act was at first intended to apply only to single men, but it quickly became apparent that there weren't enough of them to feed the war machine, and in May the Act was extended to married men between the ages of 18-41. At 36 my grandfather qualified for active duty. Fortunately for him, he failed his medical examination. He was therefore free to continue his civilian career of schoolmastering.

Not that he could escape the consequences of war. By the time he took up his post at St. Stephen's two of its staff of six had left for the front, and though both Thomas Cook and Oswald Wardman (of whom more later) survived and rejoined the school in January, 1919, during their absence Hod had to make do with less gifted assistants. I know this because of various Log Book entries, and since I shall be drawing on the Log Books for much of what follows, I need to set down a brief description of their purposes.

Headteachers were required to keep accurate records of everything that might be said to matter in the day-to-day running of their school. Each was therefore issued with a ledger, or Log Book as it was called, which had to be kept up to date and available for inspection. Among the many sections were ones for reporting the comings and goings of staff (including all illnesses and other absences), for detailing visits of inspectors, church commissioners and other V.I.Ps. I'm therefore able to read that in 1924 the visiting church commissioners to St. Stephen's reported that "the little boys in the bottom class strangely confused the Transfiguration and the Ascension." Most importantly, every Log-Book provides a kind of diary of school events, the good, the bad, the unusual. And it's because of his meticulously kept records (of all the Log-Books I've looked at Hod's are undoubtedly the fullest) that I know so much about my grandfather, can share in his pleasures, taste his defeats, understand and sympathise with his passionate desire to do the best by his schools and the boys he taught.

Thus, to take an entry at random, he records that for the summer term of 1921 he will be teaching the following:

Physical Exercises	Standards II and TII
Arithmetic	Standard III
Music	Standards IV and V: II and III
Recitation	Standard VI
Old Testament and Prayer Bk.	Standards VI and VII

In addition, he will be responsible for classes in Reading, English, Scrip. (scripture), Comp. (composition), Literature, Mental Arithmetic, Handwork.

Hod was, of course, well equipped both by training and natural aptitude to be a fine teacher of all these curricular activities. He was a keen sportsman, good at numbers, loved playing the piano, and his passion for literature was strengthened by his keenly retentive memory.

He delighted in quoting from the English classics, above all Dickens, and at home he would mesmerise his daughter and her friends with his impassioned declaration of speeches from Shakespeare's plays. It isn't difficult to imagine how he'd have enthused the boys he taught with a relish for all he loved.

There were seven "Standards" or "classes" at St. Stephen's, and on October 31st. 1919 Hod recorded the average age of each standard, at a time when the total number of pupils in the school was "about 188". (The note of caution presumably covers long-term illness and truancy, plus, of course, religious occasions such as the Jewish Festivals). Standard I 8 yrs; Standard II 8 yrs. 4 mths.; Standard III 9 yrs. 11 mths; Standard IV 10 yrs. 9 mths; Standard V 11 yrs. 6 mths; Standard VI 12 yrs. 7 mths; Standard VII 12 yrs. 11 mths. 188 pupils and 6 staff might on the face of it seem to permit classes of not much more than 30. But I doubt matters worked out so simply. The Standards couldn't always or even often be put together, and they wouldn't necessarily have been of equal size. Still, it wasn't a bad ratio, and Hod never complains about class sizes.

Nor does he complain about work load. Indeed, studying the entries in his Log-Book for St. Stephen's I get the sure sense of a man coming into his own. St. Stephen's is a tidy distance from Harbord Street, and although he was a keen walker I can't imagine Hod often used Shanks' pony to get him from door to door. More likely he walked to Hammersmith Station (or in wet weather took a bus) and from there hopped on a tube that would carry him the two stops on the Bakerloo line to Shepherd's Bush. Once there, his working day began.

The very first Log Book entry in my grandfather's handwriting reads "August 28th 1916. Horace Wm. Scott Kelly commenced duties to-day as Head Master." As with the signature on the Log Book cover there is a forgiveable flourish about the way he writes his name, but he's soon down to business. The first clue as to his determination to introduce his own ideas comes in the entry for October 2nd. "New Time-Table to be tried for one month from today." A month later he writes, "New Time-Table to be continued for a further month". At the beginning of December he makes the same entry, and this goes on until on May 8th, 1917, when he can report triumphantly that "The new Time-Table has been approved by the District Inspector (Mr. Murray.)"

I don't know all the alterations and, to his mind at least, improvements Hod made to the school's time-table, but they certainly included the introduction of gardening. An entry for April 5th, 1917, notes that "The Observation Lesson 2.15 – 2. 45 pm will be replaced by School Gardening, and on Mondays 10. 25 – 11 a.m. Recreation and Physical Ex. will be occupied by Gardening." The benefits of gardening had been made much of during Hod's time at Exeter, and knowing that so many of his pupils came from terraced and gardenless back-to-backs, it isn't surprising that he should want them to learn about the natural world, nor that he welcomed the chance to let them spend at least some of the school day away from the class room. This was after all a period when the benefits of healthy out-of-doors pursuits were widely publicised, especially among the more radical.

Not all were as extreme as the Whiteway Colony, which had been set up as a kind of Tolstoyan agricultural settlement in the very early years of the century. The Colony was initiated by a group of "clerks and schoolmasters and shop assistants" in Croydon, who founded their first commune in Purleigh, Essex, then migrated to the Cotswolds, where Jimmy Dawes, a native of Cheltenham – he'd gone to college there – very likely came across it. The Cotswolds became home to many arts-and-crafts and guild-socialist groups at the time, whose doings made news among and often scandalised the locals. (Though not, I like to think, Hod's sister Polly, living with her station-master husband Ernie at Cirencester.) And nearer to home the allotment movement, greatly indebted to Octavia Hill's work in the later years of the nineteenth century, had ensured the safeguarding of common land for the poor, on which they could grow their own produce. In their study of *The Allotment, Its Landscape and Culture,* David Crouch and Colin Ward note that at the beginning of the nineteenth century "through Fulham, Parson's Green, Walham Green and Hammersmith the land was almost solid with gardens, much of it common land on which the gardeners rented strips." By the time St. Stephen's was built and Harbord Street developed, a good deal of that land had been lost. But much remained. My grandfather's decision to have gardening play a proper part in the time table he constructed for his school is one of enlightened good sense.

I suspect, though, that this counted for less than another innovation. On November 2nd he notes in the Log Book, "Have delegated to Mr. Turner the power to inflict slight corporal punishment." There's no doubt that Hod detested the regular, unwarrented use of violence by teachers on pupils which, as we have seen, was then so disfiguring an element in schools throughout the nation. I don't say all teachers were on a level with one whose sadistic beatings were reported to Paul Thompson – "one boy, he was the most poor, miserable boy, all cracks on his hands and they were all purple and bleeding and he had to go up to have slashes over his hands" – but there must have been plenty who were. When he delegated Mr. Turner to inflict "slight" corporal punishment, Hod was therefore making sure of two things. First, Turner wasn't to slap, punch or cane boys as he pleased. "Slight" means what it says. Second, no other teacher was to have the power to hit the boys. Hence, an entry for 2nd Feb. 1917. "I have today warned Mr. Fryer of the consequences of irregular corporal punishment & informed him that he must send for me if a child needs to be punished." Henry Fryer must have been many years senior to my grandfather, because the school records show that he joined St. Stephen's as an assistant teacher in 1886. Even if that was his first post it makes him getting on for twenty years Hod's senior. He probably took corporal punishment for granted. But from August 1916 all that changed. Perhaps that was why my grandfather was able to record in an entry of Dec. 21st, "Was presented with a silver cigarette case by the boys of Classes I and II with best wishes for Xmas."

Getting on for forty years later, when I was at a "posh" grammar school at Hampton, Middlesex, there were still teachers who would lash out at boys. Once, in my first year there, a history teacher called Garside chased a terrified class-mate of mine up and down the room where we were being taught, grabbing him by the ear, swung him round, slapped him across the face – I can still hear the *crack* of flesh on flesh – gave him a black eye and made his nose bleed. Garside was a rotten teacher, a snob, vainglorious and a racist. Looking back, and remembering some of the excellent teachers at the school, I can't believe they approved Garside's violent tantrums, his unprincipled bullying. But however such behaviour may have been frowned on in the staffroom, it was *permitted*. And from reminiscences of others I'm well aware that in the middle years of the 20th century most schools had their Garsides, often several at a time.

In the inter-war years corporal punishment was simply accepted as being normal to school-life. In *Are You Still Circumcised*, his memoirs of life as a Jewish schoolboy in London's East End in the 1930s, Harold Rosen recalls that the headmaster of his Myrdle Street School, who rejoiced under the name Margolis, kept canes "pickled in brine in an aquarium." Canings were regular and unvarying: Disobedience, 4 strokes; Lateness, 2 strokes; Impertinence, 4 strokes; Damage to school property, 6 strokes; Talking in class, 2 strokes; Foul Language, 6 strokes; Obscene Behaviour, 6 strokes. So it went. At my junior school in Burbage, I was caned by the headteacher, a foul-smelling bastard called Hyams, for not eating my school-dinner (a mess of swede and gristle).

It therefore says a good deal for my grandfather that he wouldn't tolerate such behaviour at St. Stephen's. There's only one further occasion when he has cause to mention it. An entry for July 9th, 1924, reads: "Mr. Guy was to-day guilty of inflicting irregular corporal punishment on Fred Smith. I have reported the matter to the Correspondent & Chairman of the Governors." Mr. Guy was taking a calculated risk. By the time of that entry the staff would have known that Hod was leaving to join another school. Mr. Guy may have been looking forward to a future, more illiberal regime.

One other innovation of my grandfather's deserves to be noted. At various times he took boys from the school to see productions of, among other plays, *Julius Caesar*, at the King's Theatre, Hammersmith, and, at the Hammersmith Palace, *As You Like It*, *Richard II* and *A Midsummer Night's Dream*. All these theatre trips belong to the post-war years, which is scarcely surprising. What may at first seem surprising is that Hod thought his boys would enjoy and benefit from watching Shakespeare. I can only say that I love and honour him for what he did. Not that he was alone in this, but searching through other log-books of the period has convinced me that he made much more than most of the opportunities to take his pupils to the theatre, especially so that they could be enthralled by the theatre's greatest dramatist.

Nowadays, of course, Hod's behaviour would be thought eccentric, or worse, elitist and reactionary. Educational orthodoxy dictates that Shakespeare is off-limits, is not, god help us, "relevant"; his plays ought to be allowed to rot among others manifestations of "elitist" culture. This means, of course, that Shakespeare is reserved for the toffs. Hod more wisely thought Shakespeare was for everyone, even boys from the backstreets of Hammersmith and Shepherd's Bush. He'd have been quick to agree with a remark R.H. Tawney makes in his great essay of 1914, "An Experiment in Democratic Education", that it is time to give the lie "to that smiling illusion which whispers that 'culture' is something that one class – 'the educated' – possess, that another – 'the uneducated' – are without, and that the former, when sufficiently warmed by sympathy or alarm, can transfer to the latter in pills made up for weak digestions."

No such placebos for Hod. When in February, 1919, a Mrs Goodge presented the school's lending library, "with many books, including novels by Scott and Dickens", my grandfather was genuinely delighted.

* * *

By then, with the war finally over and Tom Cooke and Oswald Wardman restored to their teaching posts, life at St. Stephen's must have been rather more comfortable than in the period immediately after Hod's taking over the headship. During his first two years, he had to cope with a number of difficulties, quite apart from those created by the loss of good teachers to the armed forces. The first was a coal shortage. After two-hundred thousand South Wales miners went on strike in the autumn of 1915, the government brought the mines under state control. Nevertheless, by early 1917 the supply of coal for any purpose other than the war effort often failed. On 8th April of that year *The Observer* sent one of its staff to report on a queue at a south London railway coal siding. The newspaper's readers were told that:

> The would-be purchasers assembled soon after seven o'clock in the morning and a queue of waiting women and children extended to a great length within an hour or so. Several policemen regulated the crowd, who had first to secure tickets at the coal merchant's office, and then make their way to the siding, where the coal was served out to them directly from the railway trucks.

On more than one occasion Hod joined such queues. Thus, on Feb. 6th, 1917, he notes in the Log Book that he has dismissed the boys "at 11.30 a.m. as temperature is below 40 and there is no coal whatever." He adds that he has been given permission "to purchase up to 2 tons of coal locally." Two days later he is able to report "Coal delivered this morning (through my own efforts) & for which I have had to pay. The Council have not yet succeeded in getting any delivered." A month later the boys are once again dismissed – he calls it suspending school – because there is no coal and the building is too cold for teaching to continue. After that, matters must have improved. At all events there are no further reports of such suspensions.

The shortage of coal was no doubt an irritation. But another consequence of the war threatened to be a good deal more than that. It, too, affected the civilian population at large and it did far more damage than could be done by cold. It nearly did for Arnold Bennett's wife, Marguerite, as she was returned to Liverpool Street by train from their house on the Essex coast, on the day of 13th June, 1916. According to Bennett, in a letter to his brother, Septimus, "the train came into the station at the exact moment, & the end of the train was bombed. Yet, although Marguerite was towards the end of the train she saw nothing of the bombing.... People took refuge in an underground urinal, very roomy." (*Letters* IV p 187.)

Bennett couldn't have known it at the time, but that particular air raid resulted in the deaths of 157 people, with 432 injured. One German aeroplane was brought down. Such raids – often conducted by zeppelins – had been a feature of the war more or less from its outset. 13 people were killed in Loughborough when a German bomb fell on the town in early 1915, and there were deaths in Hull at the end of the year when, so Bennett's *Journal* records "A Zep dropped fifteen bombs in the town." Bennett adds that as the Mayor of Hull had been assured that his city was "one of the most heavily defended places", officers who later came on the scene were mobbed by the population.

Whether the mobbing actually occurred I don't know. The war fostered many rumours, and Bennett's *Journal* is full of them. But his reports on various of the air-raids on London are accurate enough, and while the capital city wasn't the most heavily targeted place in England – that dubious distinction belonged to Dover, where dug-outs were constructed and local caves turned into shelters against the almost daily raids of autumn, 1917 – several hundred Londoners were killed in the zeppelin and aeroplane bombardments. A week of raids between 24th September and 1st October left nearly 50 dead. On December 9th five aeroplanes bombed London, causing 10 fatalities and wounding over 70. And on January 28th 1918, fifteen aeroplanes dropped bombs, causing the deaths of 67 and injuring 166. After that the raids faded out.

By comparison with the blitz which hit London and other British cities in the early 40s, the total number of dead and injured from air raids of the Great War seems small enough. According to official statistics, "between January 1915 and April 1918 there were 51 Zeppelin raids, causing 1,913 casualties, and between December 1914 and June 1918 there were 57 aeroplane raids, causing 2,907 casualties. Total civilian casualties were 5,611, including 1,570 fatalities, of whom 1,403 were killed in air attacks." But numbers cannot tell the whole story. The presence of enemy aircraft over England during the war years was deeply disturbing, and the panic and indeed destruction they caused are well evoked in Bennett's 1918 novel, *The Pretty Lady*. At one point, the novel's protagonist, G. J. Hoape, stumbling through the night-time streets of a London plunged into blackout, drops his walking cane.

> He turned back and, taking from his pocket the electric torch which had lately come into fashion, he examined the road for his stick. The sole object of interest which the torch revealed was a child's severed arm, with a fragment of brown frock on it and a tinsel ring on one of the fingers of the dirty little hand. The blood from the other end had stained the ground .... The arm lay there as if it had been thrown there. Whence had it come? No doubt it had come from over the rooftops.

He smelt gas, and then he felt cold water in his boots. Water was advancing in a flood along the street .... At the elbow of St. Martin's Street, where a new dim vista opened up, he saw policemen, then firemen; then he heard the beat of a fire-engine, upon whose brass glinted the reflection of flames that were flickering in a gap between two buildings. A huge pile of debris encumbered the middle of the road. (ch. XXX)

Bennett does well to set this as a night scene. Most of the German aircraft that hit London came by night. But there were some daylight raids. He himself records in his *Journal* for July 25th, 1917: "Great raid over Felixstowe and Harwich on Sunday morning about 8. 15. Heavier bombardment than we have ever heard before.... I was just beginning to shave, and so I did shave but the row was disturbing. It ceased in a few minutes (during which over 40 people had been killed or injured).... The 'air-raid warning' came through from the comic War Office about ½ an hour after the raid was over." (pp 201-2).

It was presumably the war office which instructed schools in the precautions they should take in case of an air-raid. In his Log-Book entry for 14 June 1917, Hod writes: "I have today given instructions to each class, that in the event of an air-raid, the children should at once be made to get under the desks. This has been practised today."

Further instructions followed. On 6 Sept. he records that "Boys are to be kept separate from Girls Infants in case of air-raid." Not only that. "All blinds to be drawn. All children to get under the desks and sing songs under the direction of the teacher. All outer doors to be locked on the inside."

However, there seems to have been only one occasion when the instructions might have been put into practice.

"Oct. 23. Air-raid warning received at 1.10. The number of boys present at 1.30 were 84. The all-clear signal was given at 2.15 and the children were sent home."

There is one other entry in the Log-Book directly connected with the war.

"Nov. 11th 1918. News was received today (11 am) that an armistice was signed. Cheers were given for the King & Queen, Soldiers and Sailors of the Empire. The boys sang the National Anthem and were dismissed."

4. THE HOME FRONT

The LCC Education Committee Minutes for 1916 which record the appointment of Mr H.W.S. Kelly to the headship of St. Stephen's School, "with accommodation for 175 pupils", also record his "Commencing salary of £197. 10s. a year in accordance with the scale." Hod the headmaster was therefore earning about £16. 10s (£16.50) a month. This puts him somewhere between the clerk on "thirty bob a week", whom John Davidson's poem had made famous some twenty years previously, and the Schlegel sisters of *Howards End*, who get by on £300 a year. Forster's novel, which is about life in Edwardian England, was published in 1910, when £300 p.a. could buy all the necessities of life and permit a good few luxuries into the bargain, including, even, a certain amount of foreign travel. Hod's pre-war salaries were decidedly modest, but they weren't crippling. This was largely because prices remained fairly stable throughout the years 1900-1914. But by 1916 prices had risen very considerably from their pre-war equivalents, and over the next two years they were to rise still further. In *The Deluge: British Society and the First World War*, Arthur Marwick notes that by the end of the war "wages had doubled, had, in other words, kept ten or twenty per cent ahead of the rise in the cost of living. At the same time wage rises often lagged well behind the most recent rise in the cost of living."

For all the caveat entered in that last sentence, Marwick's claims seem reassuring until we realise that he has in mind working-class wages. There were precious few salary increases for the teaching profession. Indeed, all professionals of the middle-rank were especially hard hit by war-time price rises. A government report of 1915 noted that because of these, "Many people in receipt of small fixed incomes necessarily ... feel the pressure ... and a family ... in which children are within school age may suffer exceptionally." With one school-age daughter, the Kellys could hardly be said to be among the worst affected by living costs. But Hod was required to be well-dressed for his work, and he and Charlotte belonged to that lower-middle class stratum which was always mindful of the need to keep up appearances. From 1916 the price of clothes rose steeply.

117

The price of food rose still more. By September, 1916, eggs were up by 82 per cent in towns, fish by 103 per cent, and sugar by a colossal 163 per cent. The cost of imported meats had also leapt to a point when many people could no longer afford to buy even the cheapest cuts. If nothing else did, this brought the reality of war home to many. In his *Small Talk at Wreyland*, published in 1922, Cecil Torr recalls conversations with locals he lived among in Lustleigh, Devon. "Not long ago one of the old inhabitants was talking to me about the war; and this was how it struck him. 'It be a terrible thing, this war: proper terrible it be. I never knowed bacon at such a price.'"

But if in 1916 prices felt troublingly steep, there was worse to come. During the following year, as the U boat campaign against merchant shipping intensified, so many boats were torpedoed that at one point there were fears that Britain might be starved into submission. According to Robert Clarke, from whose *Hope and Glory: Britain 1900-1990* I take the figures, "In 1917 over 6 million tons, 30 per cent of the British Merchant Fleet, were sunk." Lloyd George, acting on the advice of Sir Maurice Hankey and some younger naval officers, therefore introduced a system of convoy ships which effectively put an end to the U boat's supremacy. Marwick records laconically that "Admiral Sir John Jellicoe and the top naval brass said that the suggestion was out of the question." It wasn't merely army commanders who throughout the war gave flawless demonstrations of their unfitness for office. Fortunately, they were up against Lloyd George at what Clarke calls "his incomparable best...striding into the Admiralty and imposing the convoy system upon the barnacled Admirals."

And it worked. By the spring of 1918 most shipping was able to get through to British ports. But at that prolonged moment when the U-boat campaign was most devastatingly successful, and when Britain really did seem in danger of being cut off from the outside world, food rationing was introduced. No surprise there. That came with Lloyd George's choice of Lord Devonport as Food Controller. Devonport was a self-made man with little experience of government. Before his elevation to the peerage he had rejoiced under the name of H.E. Kearley and had come to Lloyd George's notice because he'd made a fortune in the retail trade. (Lloyd George was as famously fond of

self-made men as he was contemptuous of the landed aristocracy.)
Once installed as Food Controller, Devonport set about teaching the
nation to economise in matters of food and drink. He was
particularly hard on the consumption of crumpets and sugar-icing, and
issued instructions as to what could and could not be eaten in tea-
shops between 3 and 5.30 pm. He also issued a prohibition on the
feeding of game birds. Lloyd George must have liked that.

To the Controller's evident dismay, however, none of these decisions
was especially effective in lessening food shortages. Further action
was therefore needed, and early in 1917 Devonport decided to issue
an appeal for voluntary rationing. Each citizen was asked to restrict
himself to four pounds of bread a week, two and a half pounds of
meat, and three quarters of a pound of sugar. This proved no more
successful in mending food supplies than had the banishing from the
nation's tea tables of crumpets and icing sugar. Working-class people,
who by now couldn't afford much by way of meat, went on
consuming sugar and bread. The wealthier continued to eat or
anyway demand their usual meat intake. The Food Controller took
thought. In May a Royal Proclamation on the saving of grain was
read on successive Sundays in churches and chapels throughout the
land. Then came sugar "registration" and finally, in the autumn of
1917, by which time Devonport had left office, Food Control
Committees were set up across the country, which allowed local
authorities to go ahead with their own rationing schemes. This was
an entirely sensible decision. Lloyd George knew that a nation-wide
scheme of rationing would be unpopular. It might even harm the war-
effort, especially in those areas and trades where working-people were
supplying the much-needed munitions, shipping and machinery,
without which the war couldn't be fought. On the other hand, local
councils, simply because they were elected by and thus answerable to
their communities, could be trusted to devise schemes that would
work for the community good. That, at least, was the idea.

Unfortunately, not all councils made either sensible decisions or
managed to please their voters. A notice was sent out to farms in the
"Southern Division of Devon" stipulating that in 1918, 86,000 acres
of land must be given over to corn and potatoes. The notice

continued, "In order to get this quantity it is necessary for all farms to have 30 per cent of their total acreage into corn and potatoes. This percentage has been adopted by the Executive Committee for the Division, who have power to enforce it. You are expected to have [number inserted] acres into corn and potatoes in 1918." Cecil Torr, who quotes this in his *Small Talk at Wreyland,* comments, "I suppose the fools thought that an average of 30 per cent on all farms together was the same thing as 30 per cent on every single farm. But they had the power, and they used it with disastrous results. They ploughed their 30 per cent on dairy farms, destroying pasture that will not mature again for years; and on other farms with 60 per cent quite fit for ploughing, they ploughed no more than 30. On some moorland farms they only got their 30 per cent by ploughing such sterile ground that the crop was of less value than the seed that was put in." Not, it must be admitted, a distinguished example of planning, although presumably it did something to ease the food shortages.

In London those shortages bit deep. *The Times* of 10 December 1917 noted that the following were by then in short supply: sugar, tea, butter, margarine, lard, dripping, milk, bacon, pork, condensed milk, rice, currants, raisins, spirits, Australian wines. (Before it's assumed that the last item in particular wouldn't much affect the majority of Londoners, it needs to be remembered that one of the most popular drinks in working-class pubs was "white" Australian port – in truth a dirty yellow-brown colour – which to this day can still be found in Yates' Wine Lodges, and was, as it remains, a tipple especially favoured by navvies, for whom the Lodges were primarily built. They liked it because it was cheap. It was also strong.) From the autumn of 1917 food queues became a common sight. *The Times* estimated that the number of people queuing one morning for margarine on the Walworth Road was 3,000. There was talk of a meat famine. By the end of the war, meat, tea and butter were all rationed.

Not surprisingly, the shortages bred opportunities for some to tell others how to economise. The National Food Economy League published *Guides* as to what people should eat, depending of course on the class they came from.

Housekeeping on Twenty-Five Shillings a Week, or under, for a Family of Five.
(priced at a penny);
Patriotic Food Economy for the Well-to-Do
(priced at sixpence);
War-Time Recipes for Households where Servants are Employed
(also priced at sixpence).

The League advised those housekeeping on twenty-five shillings a week that breakfast for children should consist of porridge and milk, eaten with a crust or toast; and that adults should have tea, bread or toast with margarine. As for the mid-day dinner, that might comprise "Scotch Barley Broth (one large sheep's head makes enough for two days)" or "Meat Stew with Dumplings, Potatoes, Parsnips or Swedes, and Greens." Recommendations for supper, which was eaten only by the adults – the children had tea consisting of bread or toast, margarine or jam, and, every other day, scones – included "Lentil Soup with Toast" and "Haricot Beans with Dripping." Meanwhile for the Well-to-Do, breakfast could vary from "Egg Croquettes (two eggs between six people), Fried Sardines and Barley-Bread Croutes, bread and marmalade", to "Fish Kedgeree, Toast and Marmalade." And for lunch? "Chicken or Pheasant Braised with vegetables, Creamed Oatmeal Gingerbread Pudding, Cheese and Biscuits," or perhaps "Fish in Casserole, Braised Artichokes, Turnips or Parsnips, Pancakes (two eggs between six people)". The Well-to-Do were also provided with Dinner menus, eg. "Barley Soup (made with chicken or game stock), Risotto (made with tomato puree), Artichoke Chips, Chestnut Pudding (one egg), Lemon Sauce."

Hod's monthly salary translated into just over £4 a week. What did the money go on, I wonder? First, of course, housing and utilities. In addition to the rent on Harbord Street, there were bills for coal, light, and water, plus the ground rate. Then income tax (from 1916 every person earning more than £2.10 a week paid tax), after which came the money for clothes, insurance, Hod's pension scheme, (from which he was never to profit), beer and tobacco – he was a regular although not heavy smoker and he enjoyed an occasional drink, especially with cricketing companions, colleagues and friends from college days. Finally, money had to be found for occasional train journeys to Torquay and Kenilworth to see family; and there were one or two theatre trips.

And, as always, there was Idle Jack. At some time, and greatly to his siblings' surprise, Jack married. Since moving back to Barnshill from Fulham he'd resumed the habit of taking himself off to the nearest pub of an evening, in order to spend on beer and pipe-tobacco the money with which Hod and the others were required to provide him. Suddenly he let it be known that he proposed to marry a woman whom he'd met there, and whom the family privately considered to be a prostitute, although that probably says more about notions of lower middle-class respectability – "decent" single women simply didn't go into pubs – than it does about her true avocation. If they hoped his wife would keep him in the manner to which he thought himself entitled, they were to be disappointed. Jack installed himself and his new wife in a small flat but still required his monthly hand-outs. And he demanded prompt payment. Should Hod fall behind by so much as a day, he'd receive a letter, the unvarying contents of which ran in full: "Dear Boy, you haven't forgotten your obligation, have you?" It was always signed "Your affectionate brother, Jack."

The marriage was anyway short-lived. For whatever reason – the wife's death, a falling out between the pair of them? – Jack returned to Barnshill. Naturally his income was unaffected.

Add all these outgoings together and I estimate that the weekly amount my grandmother would have for herself and household provisions must have been somewhere in the region of £2. With that she could have fed the three of them reasonably well, although there'd have been little enough left over for luxuries, supposing they'd been available. But the rationing of some foods and shortages of others would have progressively restricted the family diet. My grandmother had no doubt to queue in company with other women through the autumn and winter of 1917 and the spring of the following year. She must also have queued for coal as my grandfather did when his school's supplies ran out.

For entertainment, they had, beside the books and newspaper my grandfather bought, music hall, films and, as I've already noted, an occasional theatre trip. Dancing was highly popular during the war but I've never heard that the Kellys went out dancing. That form of entertainment, which was mostly for wealthier people, became linked to the newly-favoured night clubs, and I don't really see my grandfather being attracted to such places. They were centres of supposedly "fast" living: gambling and drinking dens where the bands played "rag-time", while the fox-trot, which soon grew to be the most popular dance, was widely associated with decadent sexual behaviour – all that clasping of bodies, that interlocking of limbs; and the consumption of alcohol was reportedly prodigious. (It was served up as "tea" or "ginger ale" at grossly inflated prices.) Besides, going out at night was increasingly hazardous. Black-out made easier the work of pick-pockets, those "buzz-fakers", and who knew when the next zeppelin or aeroplane raid might not occur? When my grandfather ventured into the garden at night he always made sure to clap an inverted saucepan over his head, and his wife and daughter did the same.

Finally, Hod was careful to save money for medical expenses. Health, or rather ill-health, was a constant source of worry for most people in Britain and continued to be so before Aneurin Bevan's National Health Act came into being after the second world war, by which time my grandfather was in his grave. Doctor's fees were expensive; so, too, were the best medicines and hospital treatment. For those on fixed, none-too generous incomes, let alone those whose weekly wages had to go largely on feeding hungry mouths, any prospect of illness was therefore the cause of endless anxiety.

What to do about this? Discussions about the desirability of a Ministry of Health had begun under Asquith's administration, but little was accomplished until Lord Rhondda, who'd taken over as Food Controller from the hapless Devonport, submitted a memorandum to the War Cabinet pointing out that "Public opinion is now keenly aroused on the existing deficiency and inefficiency of our public medical services, especially for maternity and infant welfare." Rhondda went on to note that the working of the "Insurance Act has shown what can be achieved by a systematic provision of medical services". But that Act was still woefully inadequate, especially when it came to "the crucially important needs of women and children." The Act Rhondda here refers to governed men at work, but did not cover domestic circumstances. Hence, as he rightly noted, its inadequacy.

The idea of a Ministry of Health took time to come to fruition, and when a bill was finally introduced to the commons in 1919 it was far weaker than the one Rhondda had originally proposed. But Dr. Addison, who had the task of introducing it, made a powerful speech on the second reading, in which he reminded the House that "For years attention has been drawn to the fact that we have in children, in our elementary schools, armies who are physically defective or have defective vision, etc." Addison's use of the word "armies" was rhetorically astute. As he pointed out, at the outset of the war thousands of volunteers "were physically unfit and could not pass the very moderate standard of physical fitness which the army required." This is plain fact. In 1914 many would-be volunteers, for whom army service was an attractive alternative to the drudgery of badly-paid labour or, worse, the chronic unemployment of the immediate pre-war years, had to be turned away. Perfunctory medical examinations were enough to establish that the majority were either too short, too weak, too crippled, too poor-sighted, too nearly disabled (usually the effect of rickets), or quite simply unable to eat army food (a diet of sugar, condensed milk, poor quality margarine and soft white bread had rotted their teeth) to be of use in the armed forces. If you want a fit army for another war, Addison is saying to his fellow parliamentarians by way of making his modest proposal, you may as well vote for a Ministry of Health.

In common with other teachers in elementary schools, Hod knew all about the debilitating effects of endemic ill-health among the children he taught. Rickets, as the disease "Rachitis" became known, was especially common. It was caused by vitamin D deficiency – in plain terms, malnutrition – and it was characterised by softening and distortion of the bones, which frequently led to bow legs. Malnutrition caused other illnesses prevalent among working-class children, including weak sight. And tuberculosis, which was by no means uncommon, was usually a killer, and rightly feared. Hence the notices prohibiting spitting which were carried on buses and in trains, and in public places. (You can still occasionally come upon these notices in an unreconstructed café or pub.) The likelihood of such illnesses affecting boys who attended schools like St. Stephen's was increased by the cramped, ill-lit, poorly ventilated housing. No wonder Hod insisted on out-of-doors activities being built into the time-table he devised.

Fortunately for the Kellys, they kept healthy. Not even the flu' pandemic of 1919, which is estimated to have killed at least twenty-seven million people worldwide, affected them. And the Log Book records my grandfather as taking very little time off for sickness.

His own, at least. But soon after the war ended he had to go down to Torquay for his mother's funeral. Sarah Kelly had for some time been ailing and it came as no great surprise when she finally slipped out of life early in 1919. Among the few possessions she left behind her was a letter addressed "To the Family at Barnshill", which she must have written some years earlier in anticipation of her death. The undated letter reads as follows:

> My dear children all
>
> When I am no longer able to be with you, I
> Wish you all to know that I have [left] Laura Kate
> in charge of all my affairs. She knows my wishes and
> will respect them.
> Her sisters at home will help her and advise. I trust
> you will all agree together and be happy, and forgive
> all my faults and failings.
>
> With much love
> and may God bless you all
> Your mother
>
> S Kelly

5. MAKING A NEW WORLD?

Once America entered the war in 1917, and despite the collapse of the Tsarist regime and Russia's consequent withdrawal from the allied cause late that same year, there could be only one outcome. Not surprisingly, therefore, during this latter phase of the war Lloyd George's government began to consider the future. Hence the slogan "homes fit for heroes", although new houses and slum clearances were to be slow in coming. There was however a determination on the government's part to create an accountable Ministry of Health. During its passage through parliament, the bill drafted to create the Ministry was inevitably shorn of some of its most radical, innovatory features. Nevertheless, something was accomplished.

Education was also a matter of concern and had indeed been so since before the war. In 1913, and again the following year, Asquith's government argued that it made sense to increase expenditure on educational grants. But from August, 1914, the proposals were shunted into a sidings where they remained despite the Board of Education report for 1917-18, which declared that the war itself "has certainly brought a clearer and wider recognition of the value of education, and, while showing the defects and short-comings of our system, has produced the resolution to improve it."

One short-coming that especially bothered the Board was the habitual assumption, common to working-class parents and most teachers at junior schools, that "the juvenile [is] primarily a little wage earner." My grandfather regularly and laconically notes poor attendances at his schools when they re-open after summer holidays. Many of his pupils, he remarks, remained "on holiday". In fact, they were with their parents, working in the Kent hopfields. This practice of whole families decamping from London to Kent continued for some years after the Second War. From 1947, when my parents, re-united after my father's war service, moved to suburban Middlesex for the sake of his work, I was at school at Ashford, where we lived, and then Hampton. A number of my classmates at both schools spent every August with their families in Kent, hop-picking. And no doubt in other parts of the country children did as they'd always done, helped to bring in the harvest. But by the time I first attended school, autumn term began in early September, an adjustment of the calendar which must have been prompted by the realisation that it made precious little sense to re-open schools at a time when a sizeable proportion of pupils would have to be registered as absent "on holiday."

During the years 1914-18, "hopping" was merely one of many ways by which children could be used to eke out a family's finances. And the more that working men marched away to war, the greater the need for additional sources of income. For while a good number of those who volunteered in 1914 came from the ranks of the unemployed, from 1916 *all* fit men of eligible age were conscripted. The families of men in hitherto reasonably well-paid work suddenly found themselves living on a state pittance. In addition to "The King's Shilling" (it had been reduced from 2s 6d in October, 1914), family dependents of volunteers were, from the Spring of 1915, supposedly catered for, although Clive Hughes, in his contribution to *A Nation In Arms: A Social History of the British Army in the First World War*, points out that there were always "delays in tracing and paying those entitled." In such circumstances, and given the deeply-ingrained assumption among the working class that it was entirely legitimate to use children to bring in money, it's scarcely surprising that many kids were whisked out of school to do "war work."

This appalled educationalists. H.A.L. Fisher, historian and Vice-Chancellor of Sheffield University, who in December 1916 became President of the Board of Education, decided something had to be done. In the spring of 1917 Fisher put to the Commons his proposals for a major Education Act. He was keen, he said, that the Bill "should pass into law before peace is struck"; and he wanted it above all to put a prompt end "to an evil which has grown to alarming proportions in the past three years – I allude to the industrial pressure upon the child life of this country." There should be "State compulsion" for all to receive education up to the age of 14, and provision must be made for a greatly expanded system of state education.

Reasonable proposals, you might think. But farmers and industrialists – especially owners of coal-mines who looked forward to getting their mines back from the state control under which they'd been brought during the war years – were outraged. Fisher's Bill went against every right of the individual, and it took away parents' rights to do with their children as they thought fit. In short, it was an assault on hard-fought-for and long-cherished freedoms. If the shade of John Clare was hovering near parliament when the bill was debated, it would have understood only too well the stinking hypocrisies of those who in his words "barked of freedom": "It grows the cant terms of enslaving tools / To wrong another by the name of right," Clare had written in his great poem, "To A Fallen Elm", of an earlier generation of farmers and capitalists, those who "glut their vile unsatiated maws/ And freedoms birthright from the weak devours". But the barkers and the snufflers at the trough won. Fisher's original Bill was withdrawn and a much weaker one introduced.

Still, not all was lost. The war's terrible casualty lists included many teachers, who had volunteered in the early days or been later conscripted. Where were new teachers to come from? Arthur Marwick notes that Fisher proposed a doubling of the earnings of elementary school teachers. As a result, "elementary school teaching was now economically sufficiently attractive for it to become a middle-class rather than a working-class profession." Marwick is far from correct in claiming that in pre-war years elementary teachers mostly came from the working-class. My grandfather, for example, came from a lower-middle class background (like Hardy's Sue Bridehead), although his younger contemporary, D.H. Lawrence, was certainly working-class in origin. In contrast, women teachers were often recruited from the professional middle class. Teaching was, after all, one of the few professions open to women, and it continued to be so for many years. But Marwick's claim does some service in pointing to the fact that those who taught commonly aspired to a "profession", one which marked out its adherents as valued members of the community.

Such recognition exists independent of material value. That is its point, as virtue is its own reward. On the other hand, there's no doubt that my grandfather's salary greatly increased in post-war years.

So much so, that when he moved school in 1924 his new commencing salary was £535. Although this will have been an increase on what he was earning at St. Stephen's, his initial annual headteacher's salary of £197. 10 had more than doubled in the years since 1916. But if he hoped to be able to transfer pupils to secondary schools, he was to be disappointed. Fisher managed to get an acceptance for a certain number of what were called "continuation schools", but as C.L. Mowat points out in *Britain Between the Wars: 1918-1940*, while the number of these schools briefly increased, "and in London and several other places attendance at them was compulsory ... after 1921 compulsory attendance was abandoned (except in Rugby) and their numbers declined."

Yet for all the spoiling tactics of parliament, of those "indifferents and incapables", as Hod would have known that Dickens called them, there was a new hunger for education in the post-war years. Marwick quotes a report from the Committee on Adult Education which was set up at this time and which reported that an awakened interest "has been shown in the courses of lectures, study circles, and classes arranged by a large number of organizations. A large part of this activity has been directed towards the study of the historical background and causes of the war..." True enough, and of especial interest to me because in my grandfather's Commonplace Book are the notes he took from attending one such series of lectures.

In his customary neat hand, Hod has written and underlined *The World After the War*, and then, beneath that, "King's College, Oct. 1921, Mr. G. P. Gooch. M.A." Gooch, an historian whose study of early-twentieth century European history I used as an A level pupil in the 1950s, gave six lectures during that autumn on the world after the war. The first, so I learn from Hod's notes, was on expanding imperial ambitions up to 1914 with further information on how Germany's empire had been disposed of at Versailles. Hod remarks tersely: "G.S.W. [German South West Africa] passed completely into our hands and is now part of the South African Dominion. No commercial value whatever." As to the Cameroons: "Climate extremely hot and unhealthy. Conquered by the French with the help of some British troops. One tenth has come to England and the remainder to France."

Gooch provides a remorseless account of how the German Empire was
carved up, and he ends by telling his class that "One great result of the
war has been to make our colonies not daughters of the Empire but
more like Allied Nations within the British Empire – the transformation
from Mother & Daughters to a Family of Nations."

The second lecture was devoted to France, before, during and after
the war. Gooch concludes his on the whole sympathetic account with
the claim that "France will remain crippled for years. Her wealth is
not so great as ours and her debt far heavier." Then come lectures
on Germany's losses and the desperately uncertain state of her post-
war government, on the collapse of the Austro-Hungarian Empire, on
the Balkans, on Russia, and finally on the USA. Here, Gooch offers
a detailed resumé of what he calls the tragic failure of President
Wilson's attempts at Versailles to provide a fair peace settlement. He
also suggests that despite the terrible unemployment problem then
facing the USA, this must soon pass because of the nation's vast
resources. What he calls "the negro problem" is however more
intractable, and made the more so because black soldiers were
"treated exceptionally well by the French". As indeed they were.
Hence, of course, the numbers of black jazz musicians who made
France and above all Paris their home in the inter-war years.

Hod's notes make all these lectures seem both interesting and
politically sensitive. That's to say, Gooch clearly refuses to march to
the populist tune of "Blame Germany for Everything," and his
summing up of Wilson's failed mission, and indeed of his character,
comes across as a model of disinterested appraisal. But it's Hod's
notes to Gooch's the fifth lecture, devoted to Russia, which I find far
and away the most fascinating. *"Lenin and Trotsky"* – Hod
underlines the names – "both arch-devils." Then, again no doubt
reporting the lecturer's words, he goes on, "Bolshevism is the violent
reaction against the previous rule which ground down the under-dog
.... In 1917 the autocrats were over-ridden by the working class ....
cf. Lenin & Trotsky with Danton & Carnot." Yet for all he calls
them "arch-devils", Gooch does not entirely demonise Russia's new
leaders. The old regime, he tells his audience, was "wrong in theory
& utterly corrupt." Thus, "the present appalling condition of Russia

is not entirely due to the Bolsheviks & war but to generations of mis-rule. Both Austria & Russia were entirely unfit to enter a great war & the system under which they were ruled perished." The new Russian system, for all its cruelty, and despite its indifference to democracy as that is known in the West, ought to be left to find its own way. The ineffective Western blockade has simply made matters worse. Russia has become poorer and poorer, and the Bolsheviks as a result "wilder & wilder" with an army "larger & more powerful" than ever. As for the future. "Russia is bound to recover for they possess a vast tract of naturally productive land & will at some future date be one of the leading nations of Europe."

In reading Hod's notes to this lecture I've tried imagining myself back to the autumn of 1921. A year earlier the Communist Party of Great Britain had been formed. Tiny in numbers, its very existence was nevertheless seen as a threat, even to many on the left. The Labour party turned down its application for affiliation. Others saw it as a sign of the times. Labour, according to an article on "The Policy of Industrial Suicide", published in the *Fortnightly Review* in 1919, was "determined to challenge the whole existing structure of capitalist society." And in 1920 and 1921 that determination must have felt especially alarming or hopeful, depending on your point of view. In the spring of 1920 dockers refused to load arms onto ships bound for Poland, where they were intended to be used against the Red Army. On October 16th of the same year the miners went on strike. Two weeks later, after the railwaymen and transport workers threatened to join them, the government announced a temporary (six month) wage increase. In the same month came "The Battle of Downing Street", when a mass march of unemployed men was baton charged by the police.

Would Hod have been alarmed or hopeful? How would he have reacted to the prospect of strike action held out by the "triple alliance" in the Spring of 1921, when the government returned mines to private ownership from the state control they'd been under during the war years, and the owners at once lowered wages? The honest answer is, I can't be sure. I'm tempted to believe that he'd have agreed with the mass-circulation *Daily Herald* – Labour's newspaper – that the failure of railwaymen and transport workers to support the miners did indeed make for "Black Friday"; but then again, he might have breathed a sigh of relief at their failure, as so many English people did. I'm pretty certain, however, that he'd have been on the side of George Lansbury and those 29 councillors of Poplar who at the beginning of September 1921 chose to go to prison rather than levy the LCC rate on residents who very plainly couldn't pay it. Twenty-five percent of Poplar's workers were at the time unemployed and receiving outdoor relief which couldn't be met from the rates. "When the law is wrong, break it," Lansbury told his fellow councillors, "and thereby create a classless society." So off they went to prison. They were released on October 12th and, as a direct result of their action, a bill was passed which spread the cost of relief more equitably over London's boroughs. Hod, who was well aware of the desperate poverty of many of his schoolchildren, would have approved the stance taken by Lansbury, that epitome of Christian socialism.

In fact, it's as a Christian socialist that I think Hod is best understood, in later years at least. Meanwhile, at the end of Gooch's last lecture, he notes that America "Will be the greatest nation on earth – full of vitality – self-confidence & no worry for future. Great belief in education (a belief in the value of the common man) a much higher view taken than in this country." He may have been copying Gooch's words, but the flourish with which he sets them down suggests his own commitment to a belief in the value of the common man, and of education's role in strengthening that belief.

It was this belief which prompted the great socialist R.H. Tawney to urge so passionately the cause of adult education. Gooch's lectures seem a model example of the virtues of such education. Wonderfully clear, informative, and with a compelling narrative drive, they neither condescend to their audience nor flaunt unapproachable and remote donnishness. Hod's notes, which are themselves a model of lucidity, tell me as much. They summarise the main arguments of each lecture and add salient details. Hod also takes care to note down the lists of further reading Gooch supplies for his class. The notes thus amount to a superb precis of Gooch's lectures. From them you could, indeed, flesh out a book.

I don't say that the skills of this particular lecturer and student were out of the ordinary. What they testify to is rather the democratic decency of Tawney's great idea and the willing eagerness with which, all over the country, men and women came together to make the idea live. It wasn't only Tawney, of course. There were the Labour Colleges, later there would be the Communist Party educational weekends and summer schools. Together with other forms of adult education, these had been pre-dated by the Mechanics Institutes and various nineteenth-century as-it-might-seem hedge schools, all of them testifying to the hunger in themselves to be more serious which men and women are always surprising. Now, that great, prolonged surge of delight in education as a co-operative venture and the rightful pursuit of all seems very nearly collapsed, falling on the sands of accountability, of pettifogging officialdom, of those men in grey suits who require tutors to "specify Aims and Objectives", and who want students to complete "Evaluation" forms. From Gooch through to, let's say, E.P. Thompson, the aims and objectives were, as they have always been, clear. To empower ordinary people through awakening their thirst for knowledge and encouraging them to believe that culture is theirs *by right*. My grandfather's notes on Gooch's lectures are their own eloquent evaluation of the worth of the lecture course he attended for free. But nearly a century later, many of the museums and art galleries which Hod made sure his pupils visited charge admission, even though their holdings belong to the nation. And the Open University, which grew out of those Tawneyesque socialist ideals of bringing education to all who want it – for whom desire is the only needful qualification is my own way of putting it – labours under cost burdens it shouldn't have to bear. As for other forms of adult education, they have dwindled into a spectral shadow of that new world which seemed within reach in the years following 1918.

* * *

When I stood in the ashphalted playground of St. Stephen's School on that warm May morning of 1999, I was moved not merely by the thought that getting on for a hundred years earlier my grandfather must have stood so often on that same spot, but by the place's air of settled calm. I hadn't then so much as glanced at the Log Book which Hod was required to keep as headmaster of the school. A month later, however, as I sat down in the reading room of the Metropolitan Archive off the Clerkenwell Road to study those detailed entries for the period of his stewardship of St. Stephen's, from 1916-1924, a similar spirit lifted off the book's pages. For all the poverty, and despite the occasional doses of "irregular" corporal punishment which Hod punctiliously noted and clearly took action against, St. Stephen's must have been a good school to teach at and, more important, a good school at which to be taught. The reports of the school's governors are always warm in praise of teachers and pupils alike, and you sense that they are responding to a place where the children are valued not merely for their academic and sporting achievements, but as Blake, whose poetry I don't suppose my grandfather knew, valued that proper innocence he celebrates in his great "Holy Thursday", of "Thousands of little boys & girls raising their innocent hands."

To say this isn't, however, to minimise the privations more or less habitual to many of those who attended St. Stephen's. Poverty, malnourishment, inadequate housing and clothing: Hod and his fellow teachers were faced with these and their consequences every schoolday. And the war made matters worse, not because the times were harder – between 1914-18 the poor had the sufferings to which they were fairly accustomed – but because among the many who died were, inevitably, fathers of my grandfather's pupils.

But then few if any families escaped untouched. Hod's neice Doris, daughter of his favourite sister, Polly, and a strikingly handsome young woman, was twice engaged during the Great War. Both her fiancés were killed in action and she never married. After her second fiancé died, I think at Passchendaele, The Imperial War Office sent her the trunk that had gone with him to France. Among his effects was a bugle, which much later she passed onto me. On special occasions – this was during the Second World War – I was allowed to take this bugle, which smelled of copper coins, to school, and, come playtime, I'd loop its green lanyard ending in a tassel over my neck and strut round the schoolyard at the head of a ragged procession of small boys and girls, playing the one tune I could get out of the instrument, a watery version of "Reveille".

Of the Old Exonian Cricket Club members who went to war, the only one I know about is "curly" Powe, who survived but who was deeply scarred by his experience, so much so that he seems to have suffered an irreversible breakdown and ended his days in an asylum, as of course did many who survived physically. Others, badly wounded, rejoined civilian life as long-term unemployed, in Ivor Gurney's words:

> on state-doles, or showing shop patterns,
> Or walking town to town in borrowed tatterns
> Or begged....

Marches of the unemployed became a feature of English life throughout the 1920s, as did the sight of wounded war veterans hunched at street corners over trays of match-boxes, bootlaces, *anything* that might earn them a penny or two. A Labour Party poster of 1920 shows a young soldier ready to go over the top above the caption YESTERDAY THE TRENCHES. Set next to that image the same young man, now with wife and baby, trudges through a rainswept industrial landscape, under which is written TO-DAY - UNEMPLOYED. In the immediate post-war years over 11% of the population was officially without work, although the true figure must have been higher as many were not registered at all. Moreover, other workers, the miners among them, suffered wage cuts which dropped them into poverty.

Returning teachers were luckier than most, at least in the sense that they were guaranteed employment. And as I've earlier noted, their salaries were also a good deal improved. Early in 1919 two teachers re-joined the staff at St. Stephen's. The Log Book records "Mr. Cook (since 1917) and Mr. Wardman ('15) resumed school services". Oswald "Ossie" Wardman was to become a close friend of Hod's and on more than once occasion he and his family holidayed with the Kellys. A tall, rather gangling-looking man, lean to the point of gauntness, Ossie Wardman was a classicist with a Ph.D. to his credit, and my grandfather was inordinately proud of having him on the

135

staff. Not that Wardman made anything of his academic qualifications. When not teaching, however, he was usually deep in a book. There's a photograph of the Wardmans, Kellys and Stephens (Ernie and Polly – of Doris there's no sign) taken on the beach at Southsea in the early '20s. Ossie wears a black homburg, has one child balanced unhappily in his lap and another squatting beside him. If ever a man looked out of place as a paterfamilias, let alone as someone relaxing on holiday, it's Oswald Wardman. My mother recalls the occasion of that photograph. "Oh, Ossie," his wife said, her voice hovering between exasperation and affectionate wonder, "he's nothing for children." But he must have been a good teacher.

Hod and Wardman enjoyed each other's company, I suspect, because the latter fed my grandfather's appetite for literature and because they could spend days at a time tramping the countryside, exchanging ideas, keeping up a lively conversation on topics of the day, including no doubt Hod's views on education and, a very different matter, his judgement on horses. For by now, having given up playing cricket, he enjoyed going to the races, and he dearly loved a flutter – especially on the Derby. In addition to holidays for Empire Day and other "specials", such as the Duke of York's wedding (April 26th, 1923), every head teacher was allowed to nominate his own once-a-year day's holiday. Somehow St. Stephen's "Head's Day" always fell on Derby Day.

In the early 1920s Hod's interest in horse-racing was comparatively new. But walking had always been a passion. I imagine that, whenever possible, he and Ossie would take a train or bus out of London and simply strike out for open country. Two companion photographs of the time show them outside a country pub, whose sign, looming over a hedge, declares it to be the BARLEY MOW. A gate in the hedge has over it a rusticated porch on which is written "Teas Provided." Ossie leans against the gate, cigarette in mouth, his unusually dapper dress including a grey homburg, bow-tie and a striped, perhaps fair-isle pullover under his sports coat. Hod, also leaning against the gate, wears raincoat and flat cap – a sign, I take it, that he's away from official duties, because on more formal occasions his usual headgear is bowler and, later in life, homburg or trilby. A third, unidentified man is with them, rather more formally dressed in suit and tie. He looks less at ease than either Hod or Ossie, as though he's an interloper which, for all I know to the contrary, may well be the case.

Given his love of walking, Hod must have rejoiced when, early in the 1920s, his brother became headmaster of the village school at Sawtry. Once Harry and Ella Kelly, with son Jack and daughter Margaret, were installed in the delightful school house, my grandparents and their daughter became regular visitors to what was then a small village set remotely in the wide and level Hungtingdon countryside. Cissie enjoyed Sawtry every bit as much as her husband, although she suffered inevitable mishaps. Unlike his brother, Harry still played cricket. There is a photograph of Sawtry's cricket team, taken in 1925, far less carefully posed than that of the Old Exonians, in which Harry Kelly stands at the far right of the second, back row, in his whites. The photograph may have been taken on the day of the match which has passed into family history, because of one moment. It came as the team's supporters rose in applause from the bench on which they had been sitting – a catch, a well-struck four maybe – and the bench inevitably tipped up. Inevitably, because my grandmother had been perched on one end. Now, as the other end rose, she was flipped into the tea-hamper where she lay undisturbed for some moments, a gentle shock of mild surprise carrying far into her heart while all about were prostrate with laughter.

On another occasion she accompanied the team to an away match, going with other women in a horse-drawn van. The road they took tilted steeply uphill, and the bench on which the party sat began to slide out of the van. Everyone except my grandmother stood up. She alone clung onto the bench as it shot out into the dusty road. And was it then, or a later time, that she was told a road near Sawtry – along which she was travelling – Watling Street I think it was – had originally been built by the Romans, and she gazed at it with mild approbation before remarking, "well, I must say it's worn *very well*"?

Being headmaster in such a small community gave Harry Kelly considerable cachet. He's prominently placed, wearing it has to be said a rather crumpled suit and tie, in a photograph taken in April,

1925, of Sawtry United's football team. I don't know that he had any great love for soccer. Rugger was his game, and his enthusiasm for it survived the broken nose he suffered in his second year at college. But Sawtry United clearly felt that the dignity of the team's photograph would be compromised without the headmaster being included, and so there he stands, beneath the far from straight crossbar, arms behind his back and surrounded by what was probably the entirety of the village's male population. As well as those in football kit, some in striped jerseys, others wearing broad-banded hoops, there are men, young and old, in their everyday clothes. Village dignatories, no doubt.

"Sawtry United" v "The Hut"   Apr. 10th 1925.

Harry and Ella were also in attendance at most of the village's social functions, and whenever Hod, Cissie and their daughter stayed at Sawtry, they went with them. Among the chief delights were dances at the village hall, music for which was provided by a one-eyed violinist of almost heroic incompetence, who accompanied his fiddle-work by whistling. As his whistling was even more off key than his instrument, nobody had the faintest idea what tune he was supposed to be playing and it's entirely possible that he himself didn't know.

Such ignorance proved even more blissful on those occasions when the village Dramatic Society mounted a production. Few of the cast had more than a nodding acquaintance with their lines, although the village baker always mastered his speeches and whenever there was an unscripted pause would fill in with whichever words seemed to him most appropriate to the moment and whether or not he happened to be on stage at the time. In a production of, I suppose, a romantic comedy, he played a gardener and, during what was intended to be a tenderly witty love scene between the two juvenile leads, filled an awkward silence by sticking his head round the door and addressing the audience on the subject of the seven-year weevil. And one year in the village pantomime, assuming that Prince Charming had forgotten her cue, or so he afterwards claimed, he suddenly re-appeared on stage in his role as Baron Hardup and recited the whole of "The Green Eye of the Little Yellow God" to an understandedly distraught Cinderella.

The schoolhouse at Sawtry had few amenities. No electricity, no hot running water, no inside lavatory. But it was a charming house, so memory tells me, and in addition to the garden orchard at the bottom of the playground, there were open fields stretching away on the other side of the road. Since their marriage in 1905 Hod and Cissie had lived in the one small house at Fulham. It was by no means cramped and Harbord Street was a pleasant enough, tree-lined avenue. But still, the place wasn't theirs. True, many, indeed most, people still rented accommodation – and this was so no matter the social class. Perhaps the finest achievement of the first, short-lived Labour government of 1924 was its Housing Act, which increased the state's subsidy to £9 annually for 40 years for houses built to rent at controlled rents. Nine years later the Act was repealed, but not before over half-a-million such houses had been built.

But Hod and Cissie, perhaps envious of Harry and Ella's greater freedom and – who knows? – energised by the arrival of a Labour government and the possibilities of new directions it brought with it, now wanted a place of their own. And circumstances made it easier for them to enter into home ownership. On May 31ˢᵗ 1924 the Log Book of St. Stephen's records that the headmaster was "at Everington Street." Two months later, on July 23ʳᵈ, Hod writes, "I have today relinquished the post of Headmaster of this school, having been appointed Headmaster of Everington St. L.C.C. Fulham, S.W.6."

At virtually the same moment the Kellys move from Harbord Street, Fulham, to the greener spaces of Wimbledon.

6. CHANGES

42 Melrose Avenue, Wimbledon Park, is a substantial house, one of a row in a street that was developed in the very early years of the twentieth century. Such developments, common at the time, were made possible by the extension of suburban railways – in this case, the District Line, electrification of which was completed in 1906. As one commentator has it, suburbia was really "a railway state....a state of existence within a few minutes walk of the railway station." From 42 Melrose Avenue to Wimbledon Park Station is a matter of three minutes' walk.

It's customary to describe these states as soulless, anonymous and deadly dull, made up of streets, roads and avenues which, despite their occasional exotic-sounding names, are essentially the same, and inhabited by people who are also essentially the same. In Arnold Bennett's *A Man from the North* (1898) a young woman, Adeline, speaks you feel for many when she says that although she knows precious little of London she thinks the suburbs are horrid and dull. "And the people! They seem so uninteresting, to have no character!" As with the people, so with the houses: they, too, it's implied, are without character.

But the houses along Melrose Avenue *do* have character. This is partly achieved by the builder's quirk – his signature – of introducing a pattern, as attractive as it's unusual, of imbricated red tiles between ground floor and upper storey. Besides, the houses have a reassuring, comfortable and, yes, welcoming solidity about them, a feeling that within there's plenty of scope for individuality. In which case it's worth noting that Richard Aked, the man from the North, rebukes Adeline for not knowing that "the suburbs, even Walham Green and Fulham, are full of interest, for those who can see it .... beneath [their roofs] is character, individuality, enough to make the greatest book ever written." Walham Green and Fulham. Where the Kellys lived before they moved to Wimbledon Park.

Turn in at the gate of no. 42 Melrose Avenue, set between low-brick walls, and a mere stride will bring you to the porch and front door set to one side. Inside the house, a hallway leads through to a large

141

kitchen with scullery beyond. Off to the left is a dining-room and, at the back, lounge with, an unusual feature this, French-windows giving onto a verandah some three feet above ground level. This proved a favourite setting for photographs and among the many I have of the Kellys at Melrose Avenue is one of my grandmother, leaning casually over the verandah's wooden balustrade, wide-open windows behind her. You can just make out some of the latticing – still there – which was fixed atop the brick wall surrounding the three sides of the square back garden.

Although of the four bedrooms one was little larger than a box-room, the Kellys now had space to invite guests – friends, relatives, others – to stay. There was also space to accommodate a grandfather clock as well as a cuckoo-clock, both of which Hod's mother had left to him but neither of which could be housed at Harbord Street. Now they made the journey from Torquay to Wimbledon Park.

There was another sign of – not increased affluence, exactly, but readiness to make use of what a later generation would call household amenities. To go with their new house, the Kellys became one of the million households in the UK which at that time owned a private telephone. (By 1938 the figure had trebled.) This soon turned out to be of practical importance. For some years Hod had given up one evening a week to teach the practice of writing to prisoners at Pentonville. In true Tawney fashion he also encouraged his class there to read, and was more than willing to discuss with inmates "the classics", above all, of course, Dickens. There was no money in this. He was paid his expenses, and that was it. But he enjoyed the work, demanding though it must have been after a full day at school, and he regarded one prisoner in particular as a man of outstanding intelligence with whom he was more than happy to discuss literature. I don't know whether it was this man who one evening, at the beginning of class, asked Hod whether he could borrow his pen-knife in order to sharpen his pencil. It wasn't until Hod was back home, at Wimbledon Park, that he realised the pen-knife hadn't been returned. In understandable panic he 'phoned the prison. Nobody, he was relieved to learn, had been knifed, no warder had been taken hostage, there had been no break-out.

Once installed in their new home the Kellys became regular attenders at the parish church of St. Luke's, a plain, red-brick building of very little charm. They also set about getting to know and befriend their neighbours, among them A. D. Peters, who lived next door and, as assistant secretary to Arsenal Football Club, then the most successful and famous club in the land, had a certain glamour attached to him. And they revelled in their surroundings. There was a decent variety of shops nearby, including a cockney greengrocer of whom my grandfather was especially fond. Sadly, he went bust, one of countless victims of those who practised living on nothing a year. Grand people in the posh houses on Wimbledon Hill ordered from him without bothering to do anything so vulgar as pay their bills, and he was eventually forced out of business because he couldn't pay *his*. It seems his native wit wasn't sharp enough to save him from that Meagles-and-Plornish-like propensity to look up to the nobs. "'Ah! And there's manners. There's polish .... Why, perhaps you are not aware,' said Plornish .... 'that Miss Dorrit and her sister dursn't let [their father] know that they work for a living.'" No doubt some, if not all, of those who wrecked the greengrocer's livelihood would have thought it beneath their dignity to do any work.

The Kellys still took the District Line back to old stamping grounds for visits to the variety shows which had evolved out of music hall – Wimbledon had no such theatres. But Hod's chief delight was now sauntering out onto Wimbledon Common. There, he and wife and daughter could and did watch tennis, though it never held the appeal for him that cricket, horse-racing and walking undoubtedly did. So while the women watched the likes of the French Susanne Lenglen and Jean Borotra, singles champions for 1924, Hod was heading across the common, with the family dog of the moment beside him. For like many families, the Kellys kept a dog, which I suspect was at least as much for their daughter's sake as for their own. In photographs of the time Joan Kelly regularly appears beside a vaguely mongrel-looking animal, whose coat looks to be a blotchy white-and-black. And there's a lovely one of her at Sawtry, with her cousin Margaret, Harry and Ella's daughter, the school in the background, wearing a no-doubt fashionable fur-trimmed coat as she holds onto the collar of an airedale. Looking at it I'm reminded how often at that time dogs were treated as fashion accessories or used to hint at out-of-doors activities. Hence, those advertisements for pipe-tobacco which feature lean-jawed young men in check caps or trilbies, straight pipe clamped between teeth, accompanied by a small, wiry dog as they make to tramp across open land. Women, by contrast, are typically shown indoors, and now the dog is draped over a seat or, more often, sofa, on which the women pose, head tilted in profile, cigarette holder posed wand-like in front of them. Or, no doubt in imitation of film stars of the period – Clara Bow?, Claudette Colbert? – they gaze dewy-eyed at the camera, inviting the onlooker to love me, love my dog, which in this instance tends to be smaller though perky. Lively but safe to handle, is how we are no doubt meant to read the message. McIntosh, that Aberdeen terrier of Aunt Agatha's which so terrifies Bertie Wooster, is an exception to the rule. But then so is Aunt Agatha.

The photograph of Joan and Margaret Kelly at Sawtry is dated 1927 and must therefore have been taken at the time Hod and Cissie's daughter left school and started work. Every weekday she now walked the short distance up Melrose Avenue, turned right at the top,

coming out at a parade of shops, and within fifty yards was at Wimbledon Park station. From there, she took the District Line to Earl's Court before changing to the Piccadilly Line, bound for Green Park. A short step away was Dover Street, where she was employed in an American-owned company specialising in high-class chocolate. (It went broke at the time of the Wall Street Crash.) The job had come about through an assistant teacher at St. Stephen's with whom Hod stayed on good terms after his move to Everington Street. The teacher's own daughter, who worked for the company, apparently told her father of a vacancy there, and the news was passed onto Hod. This hardly seems worth recording until we note that the teacher in question was that Mr. Fryer whom Hod had warned for dealing out "irregular corporal punishment." Obviously, neither harboured a grudge against the other.

So the Kelly's only daughter was now out in the world. Not so, the daughter of their friends, the Reynolds. In that same year, 1927, Hilda, Joan's great friend, suddenly caught pneumonia. Within a week she was dead.

Joan Kelly inherited the autograph album she'd given Hilda two years previously, and which is inscribed "To Hilda with love from Joan. 13-10-25". Inside are drawings – tracings, more like – of puppies, more puppies and still more puppies, of poems by Ella Wheeler Wilcox and others, including, and the poignancy is great, Keats's "When I have dreams that I may cease to be". There are "wise words", *bon-mots*, a crayon sketch of madonna and child, even a pen-drawing of a cigarette underneath which is written "The only thing I can draw, Sincerely Yours, M. J. Jarvis". Flicking through the autograph album and then through a photograph album of the time, "Property of Joan Kelly", I come across two photographs of Hilda Reynolds' elaborate grave, massed flowers overflowing the marble surround, at its head a plain white cross, the world HILDA carved at the grave's marble foot. The sadness of the seventeen-year old's death still rises from the albums I hold in my hands.

* * *

Trying to decide how my grandfather would have made the daily journey to his new school, I took the train from Wimbledon Park, changed at Earls Court to the Richmond branch of the District Line, got off at Barons Court, and then had in front of me a twenty minute walk in steady rain through dingy streets down to the school itself. What is left of Everington Street School faces out onto Lillie Road, a major connection running from the Fulham Palace Road to the Brompton Road, which it joins below Earls Court. On such an ill-chosen spot the school must have been constantly harassed by the sounds of traffic skirling past its front door.

The walk wouldn't have taken Hod twenty minutes, however. He'd have been able to cut down streets which are now dead ends. In the post-war period buildings went up which blocked off former through-roads, presumably flattened by Hitler's bombs. Where once were back-to-backs, so old photographs of the area reveal, are now rows of featureless council houses; and the school itself can't have escaped the Luftwaffe's raids. There must have been more to it than the one delapidated building I came upon that wet, twilit November afternoon.

For the Everington School in front of which I was standing couldn't have held more than a hundred pupils at most. Yet according to the Log-Book there were in 1924 nine full-time members of staff, including Hod; and the eight classes, of between 42 and 50 pupils each, amounted to a total of 364. Everington Street was, in other

words, twice the pupil size of St. Stephen's, and this may explain why
the L.C.C. Minutes record Hod being offered a commencement salary
of £535. Nor was this all. The Minutes also note that "as from and
including 1ˢᵗ April, 1925, Mr. Kelly be paid a salary in accordance
with the scale to be determined hereafter...." Teachers' salaries,
headteacher's salaries among them, were still rising.

But they were hard earned. Reading through the Everington Street
Log Book, I began to sense that my grandfather had a far harder time
of it here than at St. Stephen's. At first, he is all energetic resolve. The
entry for the 15ᵗʰ of September records, "A new timetable and scheme
of work were commenced today. New T.T. a month on trial." Hod
at his task! Four days later he notes that at a Staff Meeting, "The
Headmaster called attention of the staff particularly to: 1) Corporal
Punishment, 2) Sending Children Out of School, 3) Marching
Through Corridor." Whatever that last refers to – teachers getting
kids to tramp through the school as a quasi-military punishment,
perhaps? – Hod is making clear that, as at St. Stephen's, he won't
stand for physical intimidation of the pupils under his care.

But it also becomes clear that Everington Street must have been a
badly demoralised school. The warning signs are there from the
beginning. Hod assumed duties on the 26ᵗʰ August. On the 12ᵗʰ
September, he notes "Attendance poor – Several children hopping &
on holiday." A week later he writes merely "As above", and the
following week, "Attendance slightly improved. The children who
have been hopping are supposed to return next week." It isn't,
however, until the 10ᵗʰ of October that he can report, "The attendance
this week has improved; most of the boys having returned from
hopping." Most! Even now the register is incomplete. Meanwhile,
"I have been responsible for a class for the whole of this week, Miss
Boyes being still absent." That entry is dated the 5ᵗʰ of September.
Three days later "Mr Walton and Miss Boyes are still absent and no
supply has been sent."

Staff absenteeism continues to be a problem throughout Hod's time
at Everington Street, a sure sign of low morale. Poor Miss Boyes,
whoever she was, eventually resigned because of "ill-health" in
November, 1929, and her resignation comes after repeated absences,

for some of which she supplied doctor's certificates, all scrupulously noted in the Log Book, for others of which no explanation is offered, although on one occasion, dated 9/6/27, Hod remarks that Miss Boyes was "taken ill on way to school." On another, earlier, occasion in the spring of 1926, when she is away a full week, the Log Book entry against her absence reads "said to be with diarrhoea but no Dr's. certificate."

Easy enough to sense Hod's exasperation, but his recording Miss Boyes' failure to produce a certificate isn't a matter of petulance nor of him being prissily concerned with the letter of the law. The LCC Education Board clearly stated at the front of each Log Book that every Cause of Absence of a staff member is to be fully entered. "The reason must be stated in detail. It is not sufficient to state 'leave.' If the excuse is illness, the particular complaint or disease must be stated, and a medical certificate must be forwarded (in the case of a teacher absent for more than three working days), to the head office in accordance with the regulations. Date of any medical certificate submitted should be entered against the nature of the illness." During Hod's years at Everington Street, he had to state the particular complaint or disease of many an absent teacher, increasingly so in later years, although the complaints were frequently no more specific than "bad cold" or "headache."

All members of staff were, however, present on the 16th Sept. 1924, when the Log Book entry reads:

> "Mr. Coles H.M.I. visited the school to-day. He held a conference with the staff after the afternoon session on the teaching of Reading.
>
> He agreed that the majority of boys in class VIII would require a great deal of mechanical work in reading, as a large percentage of the boys on promotion from the Infants Dept. did not know the letters of the alphabet.
>
> His suggestions were most helpful & much appreciated by myself & the staff."

Class VIII contained 45 boys, whose average age Hod records as being 8.7 years. The Log Book further records that few of them were truly literate. I've no means of knowing whether Everington Street School was exceptional in this respect. It may well have been so. The area it drew on for its pupils was by and large one of very great poverty. Not surprisingly, boys were often away from school, helping their parents to bring in whatever money they could. Hence, their absence during the first month and a half of the autumn term, in the hopfields of Kent. Given such poverty, not to mention that taken-for-granted assumption among the working class that children could be put under "industrial pressure", as H.A.L. Fisher had remarked, it's easy enough to understand why teachers in inner-city schools especially must sometimes have felt that they were up against it. Grub first, ethics later, Brecht famously remarked. In common with many inner-city schools of the time, up and down the country, Hod, his teachers and his pupils might well have said amen to that, though perhaps amending it to "Grub first, education later."

Nor was it merely illiteracy Hod had to contend against. The first autumn of his new headship he insisted on holding maths. tests throughout the entire school, and the results were, he noted, "uniformly poor." Something has to be done. Hod re-jigs the classes. In the first place he makes them more uniform in size. (Even so, classes 5 and 6 still have 50 pupils each.) Secondly, he takes some boys from classes which are too low for their age, and re-allocates them to classes of their own age group, and to objections that their spelling and arithmetic aren't up to higher standard he says "well, then, make sure they *are*."

Behind this exhortation is Hod's strong belief that children of least ability will be able to feel better about themselves – will even become better – if they are put with their exact contemporaries, rather than being kept down among classes of more junior pupils. This being so, it's heartening that as I write these words in the last days of the 20th century, recent research has shown – and I quote: "children aged 11-14 made just as much progress in English and science if the most and least able were taught together .... The cleverest were not held back .... But the least able did worse in tests ... if put in a low ability set." Moreover, "mixed ability classes achieved equally good results [as classes separated by tested ability] and were better for pupils' morale." Yes, he'd have known *that*, alright.

Hod's determination to do the best for his pupils, no matter how little gifted they may seem, animates a staff meeting held on April 2nd, 1925, the Minutes of which, not in my grandfather's hand, he's pasted into the Log Book. From these it's apparent how strong was his desire to change the school's ethos, to redeem it from what nowadays would be called its acceptance of failure. Here, then, are his Tables of the Law.

1) 5 minutes of each arith. lesson to be taken for mental arithmetic.
2) One lesson per week in Arithmetic to be devoted entirely to back work.
3) Frequent practice to be given in written answers to questions in History, Geography and Science.
4) Every encouragement to be given to boys for private reading. In lower classes especially, store children's minds with stories of all kinds.
5) Particular attention must be paid to punctuation, exclamation marks, quotation marks, etc. – also to Direct and Indirect Speech.
6) Each child should learn two or three pieces of poetry of his own choosing.

In other words, his boys are to be literate, numerate, informed about the natural and human worlds, encouraged to use their memories and to feed their imaginations. "Store children's minds with stories of all kinds." How Dickens would have loved that. Add Hod's insistence on a due measure of out-of-doors' activity – sports and gardening – and we arrive at what seems to me an ideal education, especially if we allow for music, classes of which my grandfather regularly took, and occasional visits to the theatre. On 15th of Feb. '25 "Mr. Graham took a party of 20 boys to Kings Theatre this afternoon to witness a performance of 'As You Like It'", and the Log Book shows that throughout Hod's years at Everington Street there were to be other theatre visits, as well as outings to museums and exhibitions.

Such trips were, of course, a part of the life of all schools, but to repeat a point made earlier, there's no doubt that the schools where my grandfather was headmaster went more often to theatres and other places of cultural resource than most whose Log Books I've consulted. Cultural resource is, I know, an awkward phrase. I've coined it because I want to indicate how a good man's refusal to accept that the children he taught were meant for the scrap heap prompted his commitment to them as full human beings – and that included, as it ought always to include, a passionate belief that if those things which lie beyond the merely material matter at all, they matter *for* all. "So right, yer buggers, then! We'll occupy / your lousy leasehold Poetry." Tony Harrison's understandable belligerence wasn't my grandfather's way. Belief that art was freehold, and ought to be common property, certainly was.

Consider the Log Book entry at close of the Spring Term, 1925. Hod has once again reverted to the matter of poor spelling and arithmetic. He writes:

"This may probably [then he crosses out 'probably' and replaces it by 'in some measure'] be due to the type of children in attendance & the homes from which they come but a great deal of improvement is necessary. These matters have been discussed at various staff meetings & we are hopeful of an improvement all the way round during the next six months."

Probably / in some measure. A stern judge might convict him of a measure of class complacency, even of a gut social Darwinism. But he surely doesn't mean "type" in any determinist sense. He's merely acknowledging a truth: that many of the boys who attended Everington Street School were under-nourished, poorly dressed and, no doubt, suffering from, among much else, rickets, ring-worm, poor eyesight, and all the other ills resulting from poverty.

A decade after Hod wrote those words, George Orwell (in)famously remarked in *The Road to Wigan Pier* that the reason why even a communist can't think of a working man as his equal is "summed up in four frightful words which people nowadays are chary of uttering, but which were bandied about quite freely in my childhood. The words were: *The lower classes smell.*" (Orwell's italics). And, he goes on, "Everyone who has grown up pronouncing his aitches and in a house with a bathroom and one servant is likely to have grown up with these feelings; hence the chasmic, impassable quality of class-distinctions in the West." The Kellys no doubt pronounced their aitches, and although they lacked a servant they had a bathroom, both at Fulham and Wimbledon Park. I'm quite certain, however, that my grandfather didn't think there was an impassable quality between himself and his pupils, no matter how poor, dirty or smelly some of them were.

In a word, he didn't keep his distance. He must therefore have smiled wryly at an advertisement for Lifebuoy Soap that was everywhere in the 1920s: on hoardings, the sides of buses, and featured in such magazines as the *Illustrated London News*, where I came across it. Under the headline CROWDS ARE DANGEROUS comes an eye-catching invocation to mothers to watch out for grime. "Mothers will not tolerate dirty streets, dirty schools, dirty homes or dirty children." But grime is about! It is "a product of city congestion – containing millions of invisible enemies to health." As Orwell said, "Very early in life you acquired the idea that there was something subtly repulsive about a working-class body; you would not get nearer to it than you could." Unfortunately, city congestion means you have to get near to that dirty body. Dirty streets, dirty schools aren't to be avoided. Thank goodness for Lifebuoy, otherwise you'd drown in a sea of grime!

Fear of "grime" must lie behind the setting up in London of the Health and Cleanliness Council, which in the latter half of the 1920s claimed "great credit for the strides that have been made in the teaching of the first law of health – cleanliness – in many schools." So at least a newspaper cutting among my grandfather's effects tells me, and the same cutting reveals that he won third prize – £3 – in a competition to submit "badge schemes" for awards to "scholars under suitable conditions." No doubt the Council thought suitable conditions applied to schoolchildren from slums for whom cleanliness wasn't so much next to godliness as dependent on most of the things they lacked: clean air, decent housing and, therefore, sanitation, a regular change of clothes, fresh food.

The poverty of the children whom Hod taught was real enough. On 10th December, 1926, he reports tersely "Attendance poor. Several boys absent through illness & others through 'no boots'". The 10th December was a Friday and Hod's entry almost certainly indicates that the last school day of the week was as much honoured in the breach by some of his pupils as "Saint Monday" was by their working fathers. The weekend started on Thursday night. In other words, not all who stayed away from school on Friday went without boots for that day. On the other hand, they could only risk coming up with the excuse because they knew others for whom the plea of "no boots" was the truth. Among the poorest were those who came from families where a new baby each year was the norm. My grandfather took for granted the need to organise collections of baby clothes for mothers of a number of his pupils. At least one of those mothers had no fewer than thirteen children. Given this, the intervention of Marie Stopes at that time must seem not only entirely proper but long overdue.

In recent years there have been some revisionist biographies of Stopes which between them have managed to present her as a deeply-flawed woman: loveless, domineering, a crank. As evidence of her crankiness, we're told of her claim that the message about the "art of contraception" was revealed to her beneath the old yews at her house at Leatherhead. I don't see what's so very cranky about that. And even though she had her foibles, the fact remains that in 1922, when she organized her famous public meeting at the Queen's Hall, London, to advocate the use of birth-control, she was coming to the help of thousands, probably millions, of put-upon women who were struggling to raise families far too large for either their income or living space. Naturally her campaign met with opposition. And her book, *Married Love*, which eventually went into ten editions – the sales paid for the clinic she opened to advise women on contraception – triggered even more hostility. According to the Bishop of Woolwich, "the purpose of contraceptives is to make possible the exercise of a spiritual faculty for the satisfaction of a physical desire only, and to prevent the spiritual consequences for which the faculty was given by God." Try telling that to a drunken docker on a Friday night. Even more, try telling his wife to tell him. Alternatively, you could support the Bishop of Exeter, for whom contraception was anti-patriotic. The French practised it and look at them! Besides, their population was on the decline to such a degree that they had to make use of Italian and Polish workmen.

Of course, Marie Stopes' clinic was unable to help many of those who most needed its advice. Hence, those families Hod found himself helping out. I know about the collections of baby clothes, and I don't think it wildly fanciful to imagine him assisting in more material ways still, with gifts of food and money when the means permitted. He wanted to make the home life of his pupils as bearable as possible. And he wanted, oh, how he wanted them to do well at school. One way, perhaps the most likely, was through sport. On 25th of March, 1925, he records with evident pride that "Eric Nilson has been chosen as centre-forward for Middlesex v Brighton and for London v Birmingham." Then, April 24th: "Nilson has been selected to play as outside left for England v Wales at Swansea on May 9th." Nilson must have played well on that occasion, because two days later Hod records that the same boy "has been selected to play as outside left for England against Scotland."

Academically, though, matters don't greatly improve. On the 20th October of that same year Hod notes, "Poor results to maths. test. No better in English. Faulty punctuation, omission of cap. letters, quotation marks etc. were the most general adverse criticisms." Faulty punctuation! If this is the worst Hod can find to complain of, then I'd say he and his staff had done a pretty good job. The fact he has nothing to say about spelling and grammar suggests that his pupils have at least a reasonable grasp of both, as well as of numbers. And indeed in March, 1927, after he has tested the whole school in mental arithmetic, he reports the results as "satisfactory", although honesty compels him to admit that in Class VIII there are "8 boys who are very dull & who do not seem to be able to grasp anything."

* * *

The year before Hod made that entry in his Log Book he had written this:

May 3rd. All staff present by 10 am.

May 7th. The attendance throughout the week has been excellent. The percentage for the school was 96%.

May 10th. The school was re-assembled this afternoon at 1.30 pm. & was dismissed at 3.35pm. This will continue until strike is ended.

Two days later the General Strike came to its inglorious close.

154

This is not the place to discuss an episode which, brief as it was, marked a critical turning-point in the nation's social, political, and even cultural life. A few years ago I wrote a book called *The Radical Twenties*, in which I set out my reasons for believing the Strike to have been of longer-term importance than other, seemingly crucial events of the time, such as the Wall Street Crash. Here, I need to say only that the strike's immediate effects on Hod were less important, and must have engaged him less, than another turning-point in the nation's life, which also dates from 1926.

To explain what this was, we need to go back to the Labour Government of 1924. Short-lived though that administration proved to be, it created at least two major pieces of social change. The first, mentioned in the last chapter, had to do with housing. Wheatley's Housing Act replaced the shoddily inadequate, mean-minded Tory Act of 1923 – thought up by Neville Chamberlain as the-then Minister of Health – which offered a flat subsidy of £6 a year for each house within certain dimensions built by local authorities or by private enterprise for rentable property. As the permitted dimensions were ridiculously small and, at the same time, the government proposed to decontrol rents, the result was that few working-class people could either afford or manage in the envisaged houses. Few were therefore begun before Bonar Law's government fell at the very end of 1923.

One of Ramsay MacDonald's first acts as in-coming Prime Minister was to appoint C.P.Trevelyan Minister of Education. Trevelyan, well aware of the sour response to H.A.L. Fisher's attempts at expanding the state system of education beyond the age of 14, but nevertheless determined to try again, took as his cause "secondary education for all." (The title of a pamphlet which Tawney wrote for the Labour Party.) He accordingly asked the Board of Education, whose chairman was Sir Henry Hadow, how best to implement changes for those who wanted to remain in school until 15. The Hadow Report, as it inevitably became known, appeared in 1926. Its consequences for elementary schools were to be profound.

The Report's first and perhaps most important recommendation was for what it called "the break at eleven." From now on, Hadow and his committee urged, children of that age should either go on to the existing secondary and technical schools or transfer to a new type of school, to be called a "modern school." They would then stay at their new school – this was the second recommendation – until a minimum age of 15. The committee recognised that this would mean an enormous reorganisation of the elementary schools, which would no longer see pupils through from the age of 7 until 14; but it insisted that after 11 all children should be in separate schools, or at least in entirely separate parts of a school.

And the outcome? In his masterly account, to be found in *Britain Between the Wars*, C.L. Mowat writes:

> It was no easy task for counties to reorganise their elementary schools so that the children above 11 would be taken from them and sent to other schools – either newly built or adapted from elementary schools whose younger children were now concentrated in the surviving (or 'primary') schools .... Yet reorganisation went forward. By 1931 one-third of all children over 11 in elementary schools were in reorganised departments.

This didn't however mean that the raising of the school-leaving age to 15 was also achieved, not, anyway, until much later. The Tories, in government between 1926 and 1929, did nothing about Hadow's Report in this regard, Ramsay MacDonald's second administration announced that the raising of the school-leaving age would be introduced in 1931 but chose not to vote any money for its implementation, the churches said they couldn't afford to meet the cost of reorganisation and enlargement of schools in the voluntary sector, and the Lords rejected the bill altogether. Now there's a surprise.

As far as Everington Street was concerned, reorganisation must have meant the school merging with the far larger and newly-built St. Dunstan's. I say "must have" because although I can't find the records of this plan it's what eventually happened. That, however, didn't come about until 1931. In the meantime, Hod had to do his best to maintain the morale of Everington Street. How hard a task he found this becomes blackly apparent from a long letter he sent to all members of staff in November, 1929. The letter, in which exasperation mingles with the idealism of a dedicated, enlightened and loving teacher, deserves to be quoted in its entirety.

Hod begins, tellingly, by complaining that "In some classes very little poetry has been committed to memory, and still less has been studied." Then he goes on:

> *Recreation*: The boys should be in school and at work by 10.40 a.m. in the morning, and in the afternoon by 3.30 pm.
> *Arithmetic*: There is a general lack of knowledge of tables. The four simple and compound rules, particularly in the lower classes, were very imperfectly known. It is absolutely useless to mark page after page of sums wrong, and to let that be the end of it. The boys must be *taught*; they must be shown their mistakes, and must be made to get the sums right. It is far better to get one sum right than to do fifty and get them wrong.
> *Composition*. Only subjects that are really well known should be given. Imaginary subjects are totally unsuitable for little boys. To realise a picture of what they have never seen is most difficult. Suitable subjects for London boys are: Hoardings, trains, buses, barges, the Thames, postmen, policemen, cinema, etc – *in fact anything they are familiar with*. Stories from the Bible may also be used.
> Please familiarise yourself with the address of Dr. Spencer:
> "Every child, under any scheme of education, should leave school able to work any simple rule in Arithmetic, to write a good legible hand-writing, and to use effectively ordinary King's English in written work such as letters and plain statements; and "fancy" subjects are not wanted in default of these main essentials."
> *Finally*: Please do not visit other classrooms during working hours unless it is absolutely necessary. It means that two classes are wasting time.

This is not the letter of a contented man. It is, however, a model of good sense, and through its implicit reprimands to members of staff can be felt Hod's determination that the boys at Everington Street ought to be offered far better teaching than that which they have to endure. Poor and disadvantaged as they undoubtedly are, they nevertheless deserve a decent education. In fact, it's precisely *because* they're disadvantaged that Hod wants them to be well taught. And he'll do his damnedest to make sure that they are.

* * *

Brooding over this letter, I find myself wondering whether its energy of resolve, its intensity, almost its suppressed anguish, mightn't in some way be connected with current events. In June of 1929 Ramsay MacDonald's second Labour administration had taken office. Hod would have approved of that, but he'd have been dismayed by the fact that, as in 1924, Labour formed a minority government, although for the first time it was the largest party in the commons, with 287 seats. The Conservatives had 261 seats and the Liberals 59. Between them, the opposition parties could therefore bring the government down at any time they might choose to do so. In consequence, Ramsay MacDonald was likely to proceed cautiously, which he was anyway inclined to do; he was careful to choose the bulk of his cabinet from the right wing of the party. And in his contribution to the debate that followed the King's speech, MacDonald went out of his way to appeal to the other major parties for support, while implying that they needn't fear he was about to succumb to socialistic tendencies. "I wonder," he mused aloud, "how far it is possible, without in any way abandoning our party positions ... to consider ourselves more as a Council of State and less as arrayed regiments facing each other in battle."

Not at all, as it turned out. The new government had taken office at the very moment when, as all commentators agree, the British economy, which since the war had been at best convalescent, became sicker by the day – partly infected by illness elsewhere, of which the Wall Street Crash in the autumn of 1929 was the most spectacular symptom – partly due to its own indecisions. MacDonald's characteristic hesitancy was from the first a serious problem and must have disheartened many who sympathised with the Labour cause. In his summing up of the failure and eventual fall of the second Labour government, Mowat speaks with keen regret of how in 1929 a great opportunity was lost: "the last one offered for the building of a better nation out of the calamaties and transformations of war." He means the last opportunity before 1945.

Nobody in 1929 could have known it would take *that* long before there would come another chance to try to build a better society. But I think of my grandfather as one of thousands, no, *millions*, who in the post-war years yearned for new styles of architecture, a change of heart, only to discover that the government they'd helped to elect was unwilling or unable to bring these things about, was, perhaps, not even interested in trying to do so. And over them all hovered the spectre of future war. They sensed that, too.

It's still customary to suggest that fears of a second world war only took root after Hitler's rise to power. Such fears undoubtedly came more swiftly to the surface after 1933, and in the late years of the decade they flowered as never before. But they didn't spring up overnight. Nor was it merely a prescient few whose forebodings told them that the settlement at Versailles had in fact settled nothing and that "we must suffer it all again." In 1926 the Earl of Halsbury published a clumsy but interesting novel called *1944*, in which he prophesies a future war in which Germany and Russia join forces to subdue the rest of the world. They plan a campaign of aerial bombardment, using incendiary and gas bombs to devastate cities across the globe. An Englishman learns of the scheme and passes the information on to a friendly MP, who attempts to raise the issue in the House.

'Mr. Speaker, sir, [Sir John Blundell] began, "you have heard me on many occasions declare that at some time London and other great cities in this kingdom will be attacked by aeroplanes, that they will be obliterated, and that we can do little to stop such a catastrophe."

And so it proves. A few hours later the air raids begin and London is reduced to smouldering ruins.

1944 is clearly intended as a warning. Act now before it's too late. Whether many people read the novel I don't know, but I rather doubt it. I've never come across a review or so much as a mention of it elsewhere. Yet Halsbury must have been speaking for others. On August 18, 1928, the *Illustrated London News* carried an article on "The Dramatic Side of London's 'Air-Raids'", together with several photographs. 23 TONS OF BOMBS ASSUMED IN ONE DAY ALONE a headline explained. The following week the *News* returned to the subject. On its cover was a photograph of a simulated air raid above the caption "The Air Menace to Great Cities in a Future War: Bombers Attacked by Fighters." Inside were more photographs, together with a double-page spread showing how a city could deal with the threat of air bombardment by literally going underground. Readers were given an artist's impression of the imagined city in cross-section, including a "Proposed Underground Dwelling House", a "Business Office", power station and, it almost goes without saying, underground railway. Covering the whole caboodle was a "Gas-Proof Concrete Roof."

I don't suppose such cities got beyond the early-planning stages, although provision was later made for the government to go underground in the event of a Nazi invasion; and years later still the threat of nuclear war led to further underground installations. When I went on the first Aldermaston march in 1958, several marchers broke away to converge on a spot in woods just outside Reading where there was rumoured to be the entrance to an underground "regional government shelter." Not far into the woods we came on what looked like a freshly-raised burial mound – a long barrow – with, at one end, a large – can it have been wooden? – door, outside which a policeman stood impassively, arms folded, "not at liberty" to explain what he was guarding.

PROPOSED UNDERGROUND WORKS

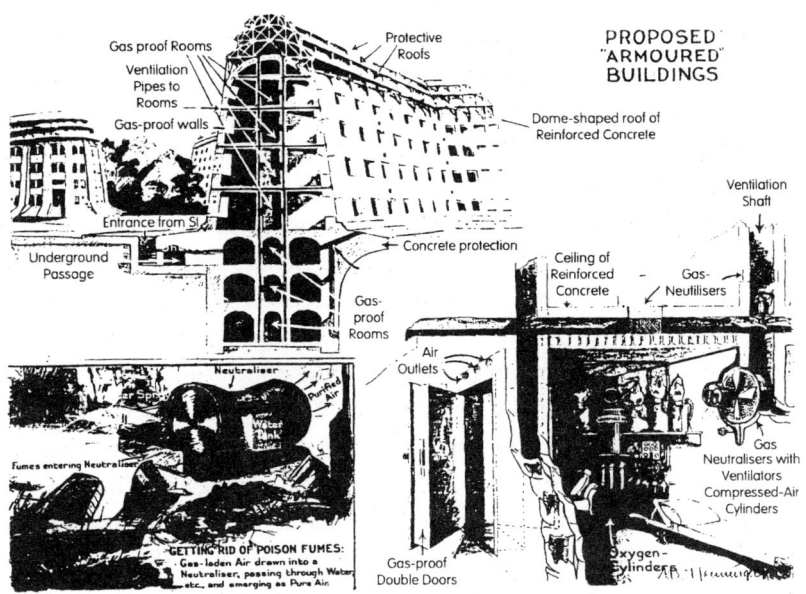

PROPOSED "ARMOURED" BUILDINGS

Gas proof Rooms
Ventilation Pipes to Rooms
Gas-proof walls
Protective Roofs
Dome-shaped roof of Reinforced Concrete
Ventilation Shaft
Entrance from St.
Underground Passage
Concrete protection
Ceiling of Reinforced Concrete
Gas-Neutilisers
Gas-proof Rooms
Air Outlets
Neutraliser
Purified Air
Water Tank
Fumes entering Neutraliser
Gas Neutralisers with Ventilators
Compressed-Air Cylinders
"GETTING RID OF POISON FUMES: Gas-laden Air drawn into a Neutraliser, passing through Water etc. and emerging as Pure Air
Gas-proof Double Doors
Oxygen-Cylinders

People of my age think of ourselves as "the war generation," in two senses. We began to grow up during the second world war – I was two when it started, eight when it came to an end; and post-45 we learned to live with the constant threat of a third world war. But my grandfather's generation was also a war generation, and the 1920s never ceased to remind them of the fact. I've seen scarcely a single issue of the *Illustrated London News* during that decade which is without allusion to the Great War, as it came increasingly to be called. There are features on war art, on the funerals of military top-brass, there are visits to battle-fields, coverage of the building and erection of new war memorials, photographs of "Cenotaph Day", of naval exercises, of troops on parade, and of simulated air raids. These last must have brought the fear of future war especially close to anyone who lived in London and watched the planes circling overhead or occasionally falling out of the sky, as at least one did in the exercises of August, 1928. (A single-seater Simkin fighter. The pilot, Flying Officer Leslie C Bennett, parachuted to the safety of a roof in Richmond. His plane burnt out on the nearby tow-path.)

I say all this, not by way of implying that Hod spent the 1920s oppressed by anxieties for the future, but to suggest that as the decade came to an end he would have shared the forebodings of many who felt deep in their bones that the war to end all wars had achieved nothing of the kind.

He also had anxieties nearer to home, although these were of a far more conventional variety and I don't for a minute suggest they weighed all that heavily on him. Now that his daughter was out at work she was liable to meet young men. Joan Kelly had grown into a petite young woman, with an attractive, wide-boned face and engaging smile. Hod assumed the role of paterfamilias. Whenever she went out of an evening, she had to promise to return by 10.30 pm. He'd be there to greet her, fob watch in hand, when she came through the door.

Among Joan's boyfriends was the son of old Torquay acquaintances. An album of photographs, most of which date from 1928, includes one of a middle-aged man standing beside a rocky wall. The photograph, one of three companion pieces, was almost certainly taken at Torquay. Still, it isn't the background of promenade and sea which draws my attention. It's the man himself. He is laughing that lovely, untroubled, guileless laugh which I always associate with his memory. His name is William, "Bill" or "Billy", Lucas. My paternal grandfather.

7. HOD'S FRIEND

If you come out of Baron's Court station to walk to Everington Street School, your likely route will take you right along Margravine Road before you fork left onto St. Dunstan's Road. To the left of this road Hammersmith Cemetery spreads south and west, and the road itself eventually comes out on the Fulham Palace Road. Before that, however, on the right-hand side, you see a wide-fronted, three-storey educational establishment, set well back behind high walls. "Those old London three-deckers loomed over the area like Bastilles, designed to resist the barbarian natives who surrounded them," Harold Rosen writes, by way of recalling his school in the 1930s, but the school I stood outside one afternoon in the autumn of 1999 didn't strike me as Bastille-like. Signboards identified it as the William Morris Academy. Given that Morris's house, Kelmscott, on the banks of the Thames just past Hammersmith Bridge, is no more than a short walk away, this makes good sense. But in 1931 the school was more predictably, if less interestingly, called St. Dunstan's. On 26th February of that year, the Log Book records that Mr. H.W.S. Kelly visited, and that the purpose of his visit was "reorganisation." Just over a month later, Hod himself makes his first entry in the St. Dunstan Log Book. "I have today commenced duty as Headmaster of this School."

He took with him four teachers from Everington Street: Arthur Downer, A.J. Moore, Miss H. Crust and Mr. G.J. Woodman. The last of these retired two years later and Moore, Hod's deputy, followed in 1935. At the same time the total number of pupils registered at the school gradually dwindled, from 304 in early 1932 to scarcely more than 150 by the end of the decade. "Reorganisation" was clearly an unceasing process.

Hod was 49 when he took command at St. Dunstan's Junior School. The Kellys were by and large a vigorous, long-lived family, and all of Hod's siblings were still fit and, with the exception of idle Jack, active. As for Jack himself, re-installed at Barnshill and in receipt of his monthly hand-outs, life meant a steady progress from breakfast to lunch to tea to pub to bed – a daily round sufficiently

163

congenial to ensure that, delicate of heart though he was, he would outlive the lot of them and die a tranquil death at the age of 85. Not many of his generation could have aspired to live that long, but in 1931 Hod must have reckoned on many more years of headmasterly work before retirement forced him out of office. Certainly, the opening pages of his Log Book show him setting about his task with all his customary energy and commitment. A new time-table is to be tried out (of course); classes are re-arranged so as to even up numbers. There will be at best no fewer than 42, but no more than 44 at worst. Moreover, the entire school is tested with on the whole encouraging results, although Hod notes faults in composition. "Capital letters omitted; done for did; were for where; misuse of relative." And some compositions show "but few original thoughts".

However, his most striking and, I suspect, innovative decision was to follow his practice at Everington Street by putting together boys of similar age groups, irrespective of their achievements. Hod believed that to force those of lower ability to remain in classes below their natural age groups is doubly bad. It lowers their self-esteem, which is inhumane, and it almost certainly means that they won't bother to improve. Instead, they'll settle into duncehood. And to the argument that if they are placed in classes of their own age they will hinder the progress of others, Hod would have said, "show me the evidence." A challenge he could rightly put, given the comparative success of boys of his in transferring to further education – despite class sizes which, normal then, would nowadays cause educationalists to throw up their hands in horror. Throughout the years he was at St. Dunstan's, Hod was able to report that an appreciable number of boys were awarded county junior scholarships and as a result had gone on to, among other schools, Latymer and Sloane.

Reading through the records of my grandfather's early years at St. Dunstan's, I'm struck by the buoyancy of his tone. He clearly enjoyed being at this school as he equally clearly hadn't much enjoyed Everington Street. No mistaking, for example, the pleasure he took from the series of Lantern Lectures he organized in the autumn of 1932. Their subjects ranged from "Alice's Adventures", "Pied Piper of Hamelin", "Robinson Crusoe", to "Merchant of Venice." Various members of staff were roped in to give these lectures, but Hod reserved one for himself. "Marley's Ghost – to be given by Mr. H.W.S. Kelly". Who else?

A year later, on Nov. 7th, 1933, he sends a circular letter to the parents of all the boys then at St. Dunstan's.

> Dear Mr and Mrs....
> Knowing the interest you take in the education of your child, I should be very pleased if you would call at the school to see me at any time convenient to you.
> You would see for yourselves what your boy is doing and an exchange of views would undoubtedly be of benefit.
> There are many points we could discuss in relation to your child – health, games, special aptitude, behaviour at home, in the school etc.
> Yours sincerely

Underneath the copy of this letter, which is pasted into the Log Book, Hod has written: "As a result of this letter more than 50 parents visited the school & had informal chats with the Headmaster & Staff."

Given that in 1933 the total number of boys registered for the seven classes at St. Dunstan's was 304, the number of parents who took up the Headmaster's invitation may at first look disappointingly low. But Hod didn't see it that way, and nor do I. There were after all still many parents who regarded their children's attendance at school as an interference with their more proper task of making money. At the beginning of the term in which he sent out his circular letter, Hod noted "Attendance rather poor owing to some boys being still on holiday and others hopping." And elsewhere in the Log Book there are the familiar entries, "Some boys absent through 'no boots'", or "Attendance poor: 'no boots'". As always, the worst attendances usually coincided with Fridays.

Hod also records one visit to the school by an uninvited parent. "June 14th, 1934. A complaint was received by a parent re her boy's head. She said she thought he had caught 'them' from another boy – I sent for the nurse who examined all the boys' heads & found them all clear." Bad housing conditions – slums – made body and hairlice a near certainty among many of the boys who attended St. Dunstan's. The wonder is not that one boy might have had them but that the nurse Hod sent for couldn't find any on the boys she examined.

For as with all Hod's schools, most of the boys of St. Dunstan's came from desperately poor families. Two pieces of evidence make this abundantly clear. On May 10th, '35, Hod records that "35 children whose fathers are unemployed will be entertained to tea at Everington St. School & afterwards to an entertainment at Fulham Town Hall." There's no indication as to who organised this occasion, but I'd stake a good deal that it was Hod himself. He'd have had ready access to his previous school, which was now used as a recreation hall; besides, had others than himself been responsible for the arrangements he'd almost certainly have named them. That 35 children were entertained doesn't of course mean that only 35 were eligible. But even this number suggests that getting on for a sixth of the by then 235 boys registered at St. Dunstan's came from homes where there was either no or precious little work.

Some of those boys must have been involved in a sporting triumph of which my grandfather was plainly very proud. His own Log-Book entry is brief enough. Towards the end of the autumn term, 1934, he notes: "On Saturday the school football team were taken to see the Arsenal play Wolves. The school team has a wonderful record having scored 67 goals for 0 against." Not much to go on there. Fortunately, the clipping from a local newspaper, which he pasted into the Log-book, tells the story in some detail. This is what it says.

> The small boys at St. Dunstan's-road L.C.C. J.B. School evidently know quite a lot about soccer. In the Juvenile League of the Fulham Schools F.A. they have won nine matches without having a goal scored against them. On two occasions they have scored 13 goals to nil, a rather unlucky score for the losers, St. John's and Fulham Palace-road schools. The other day, directly after beating St. John's (Waltham Green) by 7 – 0, their headmaster, Mr. H.W.S. Kelly, a Devonian like Mr. John Peters, Arsenal assistant secretary, took his boys to Highbury at the invitation of Arsenal F.C. to see a first league match.
>
> After the match there was tea on the ground with James and Bastin, and a visit to the Finsbury Park Empire as guest of the manager. This was a wonderful day out for the kiddies who are so poor that Mr. Kelly provides bovril and milk for all of them on match days.

Interesting, that even in this write-up, which would have been the work of not very-well paid hack, the proprieties have to be observed. As professionals, those great footballers Alex James and Cliff Bastin aren't permitted the dignity of their christian names. (I have a special reason to remember Bastin's name, because when my father, himself no mean footballer, was playing occasional games for Fulham in the early 30s, he found himself up against the Arsenal man in a reserve match and early rounded him on the way to a goal he didn't score. "Don't try that again, son" the England wing-half growled in his ear. But my father was young and eager, no use to talk to him. He did try again and this time ended up on the cinder track which surrounded the touch-line.) How typical of Hod that he should take the boys to what must have been a variety show at one of the music halls he'd frequented as a young man. Perhaps Max Miller was featured that evening? In my grandfather's *Commonplace Book* are cuttings from the *Sunday Dispatch* for which Miller wrote during the 30s, by arrangement, the paper tells its readers, with "Warner Bros. First National Productions Ltd." Unlike his stage act, the jokes are innocent enough. They are also very unfunny. "The missus and I went to see some neighbours the other day, and as soon as we got inside the door the lady of the house rushed up and said, 'What'll I do? Baby has swallowed the matches!' 'Here!' I said. 'use my cigarette lighter.'" It must be how you tell 'em.

The following season was almost as successful. Hod records late in 1935 that his boys have scored 102 goals and conceded only 4, that of their 16 matches one was lost and one drawn, and that they were equally successful in their challenge matches, drawing 2 – 2 with St. Margaret's Gravesend, beating Hammersmith Old Oak, champions of their league, 6 – 1, and finally defeating Adderson Gardens 2 – 1. Whether Hod's Wimbledon neighbour, John Peters, again arranged for the boys to visit Highbury, isn't recorded; but his being a Devonian must have helped cement the friendship between the two men.

Hod was proud of his Devon origins. In the opening chapter of this book I've imagined him hearing about those events, such as the great pudding battle and the storm of 1865, which went on being talked about in South Devon for years afterwards; and it seems equally likely that he'd have heard about the Torquay bread riot of the 1860s. Pride in Devon included pride in those Devonians who fought against social injustice. Such pride must have played its part in another friendship which developed in these years. Maddeningly, I know little about it and what I do comes from my mother. It was in fact a casual remark she let drop about her father which rooted itself in my memory and eventually grew into this book. We were discussing the hardships that so many people endured in the 1930s, including no doubt her parents. Yes, she said, her father's salary had been reduced by the national government which, needless to say, didn't pay itself or its civil servants any less. He'd been outraged by that, though not more angered than he was by the poverty so many of his pupils had to endure. And she recalled the grandee who had one day visited the school in his capacity as a governor and who'd complained that the work of some of the boys wasn't up to standard. Hod later recounted the man's comments to his wife and daughter. How, he wondered, would the titled gent. have fared if day after day *he'd* had to go to school on an empty stomach? I don't know who this version of Jack Maldon was, but it may have well been the Lord Haddo who is recorded as visiting St. Dunstan's on January 31st, 1933. "He heard classes I & II sing songs under the direction of Mr. Moore. He also saw class II (Mr. Lyons) and class III (Mr. Anthony)." That's all Hod says, but as he always records complimentary remarks made by visitors to his school it's entirely possible that to Haddo, who clearly said nothing Hod felt he could report, belongs the infamy of statements as viciously stupid as they are ignorant.

My mother finished her story about this unwelcome visitor to St. Dunstan's. Then she said, "of course, your grandfather was friendly with Ernie Bevin." "But you've never mentioned that before," I said, amazed. And then, "how, when, why?" "Well," she said, "I think they were at school together and I suppose they kept in touch over the years. I know your grandfather used to visit Bevin at Westminster and they sometimes had dinner together."

As soon as I could, I got hold of Alan Bullock's excellent two-volume biography of Bevin. I was in for a disappointment. Bevin was a close contemporary of my grandfather's and he was certainly a

Devonian. But his birth on March 7th 1881 – he was the youngest child of seven – took place in the village of Winsford where his father had been an agricultural labourer, although by the time of Ernest's birth Bevin senior had gone to South Wales looking for work. He never returned, and after his mother's early death Ernest moved to be with his half-sister at Morchard Bishop Church School. From there, in 1890, he went for a brief spell to Haywood Boys' School in Credition. By the spring of 1892 he was out of school and at work on a farm, first at Chaffcombe and then, later that year, at Beere, a village on the Okehampton Road. Two years later, in 1894, he was off to Bristol, where he worked at a succession of trades, baker, tram conductor, driver for a firm of mineral-water manufacturers, before, crucially, finding work at Bristol docks. At the time he was increasingly involved in trade union affairs. Then, in 1920, this committed socialist moved to London, where he was soon established as a figure of national importance, the powerful and influential leader of what was to become the Transport and General Workers Union.

He didn't however enter parliament until 1940, when he joined Churchill's war cabinet. I doubt therefore that he and my grandfather dined at Westminster. More likely Hod went to call on Bevin at Transport House. Age and Devon connections apart, they had much in common. In a number of speeches at TUC congresses and elsewhere, Bevin argued in favour of free nursery schools for all, for raising the school-leaving age to fifteen, and for free secondary and university education. In 1918, H.A.L. Fisher addressed a Union conference at which Bevin was present, and where he had to reply to Fisher's words. Thanking him for his championing the cause of better education for all, Bevin said, "The desire that the children shall have a better chance than their parents is inherent in the working class. The bolder the Minister of Education is in his proposals, the bigger the response he will get from the people. The working class will only be able to emancipate itself when it has the power of knowledge." Reading these words it's easy to understand why Bevin and my grandfather would have got on, but as to how and when they met – these questions remain unanswered.

They clearly didn't go to the same schools, nor is it likely they met socially. None of the Devon places associated with Bevin has any connection to the Kellys. Moreover, Bevin was off and away to Bristol at the age of 13 and there's no reason to believe that Hod could have come across him there. He would, however, certainly have known of Bevin's part in what was called "The Shaw Enquiry", because it was this, widely reported in the press, which brought Bevin to national prominence and earned him his soubriquet, "The Dockers' K.C." And as it is an inspiring story, one that explains why my mother could tell me that her father thought Bevin "a great man", it deserves to be recounted here.

The enquiry was set up in 1920 to look into dock labour. Dock work was then, as it had always been, casual work. When ships had to be loaded or unloaded, men were taken on and paid by the day. When there was no work the same men were left "standing on the stones." Foremen could pick and choose which men they wanted, and many workers were left in enforced idleness, especially those who complained of harsh working conditions. Deaths, for example, were frequent because there were minimal safety precautions. Only the mines had a worse accident rate than the docks. But protest and you'd be a marked man. Your work was also at risk from those who weren't regular dockers but who would drift down to the docks when all other employment failed, understandably keen to pick up whatever scraps of labour they could. Registration of dockers was needed and eventually, in 1919, it was achieved, at all events for the port of London. But it hardly brought comfort to the dockers. An estimated 34,000 would be at work in these docks during a normal day. Yet 61,000 men registered. Bevin, as a leader of what was then the National Transport Workers' Federation, argued that what was now needed was a reduction of the numbers registered, to a figure approaching the actual needs of the port. There should also be far more efficient means to move labour from one dock to another. But above all, dock work must be decasualised and there must be a guaranteed minimum wage for all registered dockers.

Bevin had first put these two proposals to the Ministry of Labour in April, 1918, and they'd been promptly turned down. At the end of 1919 he tried again, this time sending his proposals, made on behalf of all the dockers employed throughout the UK, to every employer and port authority in the land. Their response was to suggest a public court of enquiry appointed by the Minister of Labour. Far from being a generous a suggestion, this was a shrewd tactic, a way of calling the dockers' bluff, as the employers no doubt saw it. By offering to go before a court of enquiry they would appear to be open-minded, keen to let others decide the validity or otherwise of their employees' case. They could, after all, afford the most expensive barristers in the land to present their side of the argument. Who had the dockers got? The answer was, Ernest Bevin, a man of minimal formal education and no legal experience whatsoever. Moreover, he had very little time to prepare for the enquiry. In Allan Bullock's compelling words:

> The first sitting of the court was fixed for 3rd February [1920] and before that he had to master the detailed methods of recruitment, work and pay, varying from dock to dock and cargo to cargo, for a substantial proportion of the three hundred ports of the country. Since so much turned upon the ability of the industry to pay higher wages, he had also to discover and familiarise himself with the financial arrangements of the dock undertakings and shipping firms and to have the detailed trade returns for several years at his fingertips. At the same time, he had to organise and rehearse witnesses who could testify to the conditions of the docker's life, his family budget and earnings, what he paid for rent, food and clothing. It was a formidable task, the more so as the employers promptly briefed Sir Lyndon Macassey, K.C., who was acknowledged to be the most experienced counsel then practising in industrial cases, and prepared to bring up expert witnesses to overawe their working-class opponents.

The chairman of the enquiry was Lord Shaw of Dunfermline, a Law Lord who had at one time been a Radical member of parliament, and agreed by all to be a shrewd and fair-minded judge. It was to him, at a packed Law Court in the Strand, that Bevin made his opening speech. It lasted for the whole of the first two days and for part of the third. "He spoke", Bullock says, "for eleven hours in all without ever losing the thread of his argument or repeating himself."

Bevin's argument was based on two major considerations. One was that dockers' wages, inadequate even when they were fixed after the Dock Strike of 1889, had fallen behind the rising cost of living to such an extent that now, with the casual nature of dock work taken into account, they were simply too low to maintain life and health. The other was that the dock employers, ship owners and principal industries using the docks, could easily afford to pay higher wages out of the vast profits they had made during and since the war. The argument was a strong one; what made it iron-clad was the evidence Bevin marshalled to support it. He mentioned the high death rate among dockers and the uselessness of protesting against working conditions that were little better than slave labour; and he tellingly contrasted the fact that dockers were told during the war not to exploit the economic difficulties of the country with the equal fact that employers were given permission to fix the rates they would charge the state. Bevin then quoted Bonar Law's acknowledgement to the House of Commons that in the last year he had made a profit "on shipping shares of 47 per cent, after the excess profits tax had been paid." Bonar Law was at that time Lord Privy Seal and leader of the House. In view of such profits, Bevin suggested, the docker's request for a minimum payment of 16 shillings a day or £6 per week was perhaps not excessive. He was, however, aware that such a request had met with the accusation of self-interest by no less a person than Lord Devonport. This was a serious matter, Bevin said.

> "I am glad to have found a super-man who can abstract himself from his 280,000 shares in Kearley & Tonge and the Independent Tea Stores and all that means in money and goods going to these firms through these ports – who can abstract himself from any of these influences and look after the interests of the great public, while we who have not a penny invested in the world, nothing but an investment in the well-being of the great human element which we represent, are described as looking out in the main for ourselves and for our interests. I leave it at that."

Bevin's words were widely and fully reported in the newspapers. I can well imagine my grandfather not merely nodding in agreement with the sardonic power of Bevin's remarks about Devonport but thrilling to their eloquence. But he'd have been most especially impressed by his closing words. If the court is to refuse our claims, Bevin said, I suggest it adopt an alternative.

> "You must go to the Prime Minister, you must go to the Minister of Education and tell him to close our schools, tell him that the industry can only be run by artisan labour on the pure fodder or

animal basis, teach us nothing, let us learn nothing, because to create aspirations in our minds, to create the love of the beautiful and then at the same time to deny us the wherewithal to obtain it, is a false policy and a wrong method to adopt. Better keep us in dark ignorance, never to know anything, if you are going to refuse us the wherewithal to give expression to those aspirations which have thus been created. "

Reading this across a gap of eighty years I'm moved to a fierce joy by the impassioned dignity of Bevin's words. They come out of that Morrisian, Tawney-inspired socialism which in the first part of the twentieth-century was energised not merely by the demand for better wages and living conditions, but by a deep, unshakeable belief in the right of all to a decent education, and an equal belief in education's transforming power as an agent for good. My grandfather, who shared these beliefs, wouldn't have had any trouble in deciding whose side he was on when he read the reports of the Shaw Enquiry.

And his conviction would doubtless have been strengthened by the employers' counter arguments. Suppose the dockers' request for a guaranteed minimum wage were met, Sir Lyndon Macassey said, why, that would disturb the wage structure of the whole country. (Sir Lyndon plainly did not think that this might be a good thing.) Besides, Mr Bevin had exaggerated the amount dockers needed to live on. He proposed to call a witness who would show that a family of five could get by very nicely on £3. 13. 6 a week. And bringing up the profits made by employers during the war was irrelevant. Macassey neglected to explain why this was so. Perhaps he meant that it was somehow ungentlemanly of Bevin to draw the court's attention to just how fat certain profiteers, including titled men, had grown on the sufferings of others. One of them was Sir Alfred Booth, a leading Liverpool shipowner and chairman of the Cunard Line. In giving evidence to the court, Booth maintained that the most he or anyone could afford to pay a Liverpool docker would be £3. 4. 2. Bevin cross-examined.

"Do you seriously suggest that is a living wage? – I do.
"I put it to you very straight. Could you maintain your family on it? – No. I could not.

173

> "Then are you more to the community than the docker who handles your ship? – That is a matter of opinion. As an individual, certainly not.
>
> "Do you think it right to ask a man to live and maintain himself on what you would not dream of asking your own family to live upon? – It is not a question of what I ask him to live upon; it is what the economic conditions render possible.

Then came Professor Bowley, who held the chair of Statistics at London University, and who had very precisely calculated that £3. 13. 6 was a proper living wage for dock workers. After Bowley had finished, Bevin and his secretary, Mae Forcey, went down to a street market in Canning Town and bought exactly the amount of cheese and vegetables specified in Bowley's budget. The following morning Bevin produced these in court, divided into five portions. Then he asked his witness, a docker from Birkenhead, "If you went home from the dock to a meal like that and you were told by your wife that Counsel said there was sufficient calorific value in it to maintain you ... What would be the result" "I think the dockers would emigrate in a body."

Bevin turned to Bowley. Placing the scraps of food in front of him, he asked whether this was what a man educated at Cambridge thought was a sufficient breakfast for a man who had to carry heavy weights on his back during a long working day. Bowley protested at the question, so Bevin produced a menu of the Savoy Hotel restaurant.

> "This is the menu which an ordinary shipowner, whom we are asking for a living wage, would go to the Savoy and have today at 7/-. You allow for five persons 40/- a week for food, and that is 7/- for one person for lunch. What is the calorific value of that when he has eaten it?
>
> "As a scientist have you entered into a careful diagnosis of what the rich live on compared with the poor; have you worked out a budget for them? Do you live on 40/- of food?
>
> "Have you ever carried 5 cwt. bags on your back for eight hours continuously? – No."

Having demolished Bowley, Bevin made his closing speech. If something is right, he said, then the structures to implement its being put into practice must follow. "Parliament declared that it was essential that children should be educated and then proceeded to build the structure. I want the same principle adopted here." And so, "I appeal to you. Whatever the economic consequences may be – surely, my Lord, justice cannot be dependent on consequences. If the claim I have made is just, then the consequences of its granting must follow and be met."

When Bevin sat down, Lord Shaw addressed him and through him the court: "Be assured that, whatever the result be, the Court will be unanimous in this: that you shall get justice, nothing more nor less than justice, in this case. We congratulate you on the cogent and impressive address which you have now delivered."

On 10ᵗʰ May, 1920, new rates of pay came into operation in every port in the country.

It's immensely heartening, this story of how Bevin took on the employers and their star Counsel, and won. For the dockers themselves, their leader was quite rightly a hero, and across the Labour movement as a whole he earned huge respect in which my grandfather shared. But I've no reason to think Hod came to know Bevin then, whereas there are grounds for believing that their meetings may well have begun in the very early 'thirties. For after the defeat of the second Labour Government Bevin went into opposition, in the sense that he recognised the need to rebuild the party and that the principal building blocks would have to be supplied by education. True, it was political education he had chiefly in mind, but he didn't neglect education in its wider aspects. In August, 1931, Ramsay MacDonald, having dissolved parliament, became head of the first National Government. That lasted precisely three months before it was in its turn dissolved. In November of the same year, the second National Government was returned to office, again with Ramsay MacDonald as prime minister. Bevin stood for Labour at Gateshead, but so great was the disillusionment with the second Labour administration that, despite rising unemployment, the previous Labour majority of 16,700 was wiped out. Instead, Gateshead voted by a majority of 12,938 in favour of the National Liberal candidate. Overall, the 289 Labour MPs of 1929 were reduced to a pitiful 46, and Ramsay MacDonald's administration had an overall majority of 500.

Hugh Dalton records in his diary at this time an occasion when MacDonald said to members of his Economic Advisory Council, "you must remember the low mental calibre of those I have to deal with", to which Bevin replied, "Mr. Prime Minister, you shouldn't say that sort of thing in front of me." Distrust of those with little formal education or, more frequently, those whose way of speaking is held to imply lack of education (and therefore intelligence), has always plagued the English Labour movement. It still does. But what depressed Bevin during the time he spent in Gateshead was his recognition that the Labour government's betrayal of those whose interests it existed to represent had resulted in its natural supporters rejecting politics altogether. And so, as is repeatedly the case, the party had to be re-built. In a letter of 1931, Bevin told his correspondent, J.R. Bellerby, that he was joining the newly-formed Society for Socialist Information and Propaganda because "it is an attempt to work out problems and to give the new generation something to grip. A good many of us feel that the younger people are just drifting; there is a kind of apathy which is appalling."

* * *

It doesn't seem wildly speculative to imagine that in this state of mind Bevin should wish to make contact with teachers who might themselves be pleased to help with the task of giving the new generation something to grip. Not that my grandfather could be expected to use the classroom for overt political education. He'd have had to step very carefully to avoid any show of party colours. But it was at this time that he came, briefly, to something like public attention. An illustrated London magazine ran a short series on "Popular London Headteachers", and Hod was one of the teachers chosen. The magazine sent him to a photographic studio and the picture taken on that occasion has survived. He's in left profile, in a dark grey suit jacket, with rounded collar and tie. Already very nearly bald on top, though his neatly-trimmed side hair is still plentiful, he looks impeccably "well-groomed" as the phrase used to go. But what holds my attention is his eye. Bird bright, gleaming with what might almost be withheld laughter, it's the eye of someone most intensely

alive. If Bevin saw that picture, as he well might have, I'm not at all surprised he wanted to make contact with Mr. H.W.S. Kelly, headteacher of St. Dunstan's School, Hammersmith.

8. "SUMMER IS ENDING"

On February 28, 1935, my grandfather noted in his Log Book, "I have today returned to duty after an absence of five weeks with a ruptured calf muscle." He may have provoked this rupture on one of the walks which he still regularly took with companions, either across Wimbledon Common or further afield. But in the light of his later medical history it's possible the "rupture" was a mis-diagnosis. No matter, he was back in charge of St. Dunstan's on the occasion of a royal parade though local streets, part of the celebrations for George V's twenty-five years on the throne. The parade took place on June 8th and boys from the school were permitted to line the route, although Hod had to explain in a cover note to parents that there were to be "no drinks, no bottles, no parents to accompany boys – flags but not on poles (or red, white & blue handkerchiefs.)" This was to be a very English celebration.

It's therefore good to know that the Transport Workers Union made a charming, amateur and silent film called "Busman's Holiday", about a group of London bus-drivers and conductors who used the day of the King's progress to take their buses, chockfull of school kids, to Brighton for their own celebrations. Looking at that jumping, scratchy black-and-white film, the children scampering across the beach, doing their mostly unsuccessful best to hang onto the backs of shambling donkeys, splashing in the shallows, occasionally risking deeper waters, I'm reminded of one of Phiz's great illustrations to *Dombey and Son*, "Dr. Blimber's Young Gentlemen as They Appeared when Enjoying Themselves." A line of schoolboys, in top-hats and eton suits, winds its doleful way along a cliff walk at Brighton, their every move watched over by the intolerably smug headmaster, while small urchins make acrobatic use of the iron hand-rail behind which Dr. Blimber's "young gentlemen" seem to be caged, or tumble on the grass in derisive glee. Hablot Brown has perfectly caught Dickens's Blakeian delight in spontaneous joy, the sounds of the echoing green. All the more remarkable then that the illustration doesn't in fact refer to any episode in the book itself, as my grandfather, that keen student of

Dickens, would have known, just as he'd have warmed to Phiz's comic celebration of childhood's unbraced actions.

The month following George V's jubilee, Hod had his own reason to celebrate. As I've already mentioned, from the early 30s, Joan Kelly had been seeing a good deal of the younger son of Hod and Cissie's Torquay friends, Billy and Matt Lucas. (Matt being the family name for Billy's wife, Anita Annie.) Len Lucas had come up to London to work for an Insurance company and lodged nearby. In mid-June 1935, family and friends of the young couple received a printed invitation, picked out in silver, from Mr and Mrs Horace W.S. Kelly, "on the occasion of the marriage of their daughter Joan with Mr. Leonard T. Townsend at St. Mary's Church, Wimbledon, on Saturday, July 20th, 1935, at 12.30 pm. and afterwards at the Wimbledon Hall Hotel." St Mary's, across the park, had been chosen because Joan Kelly found St Luke's, the Kelly's parish church, gloomily unattractive, as indeed it is. Her preferred church was older, stone-built, and that was where her father accompanied her down the aisle on the morning of July 20th. Among photographs of the wedding party is one showing him in fine fettle, dapper in his smart suit and positively beaming at the camera. Cissie looks placidly content. She is wearing, so the local newspaper is able to report, "a midnight blue georgette gown and coatee to match, with white hat and gloves," while Matt Lucas, the same paper reveals, is decked out in "a wine coloured lace gown, with georgette coatee to match, and hat." Queen Mary occasionally wore Georgette coatees. If not obviously fashionable they were at least beyond reproach.

Looking at those wedding photographs, faithful as no art is, it's easy to sense the unfeigned delight my grandfather took in his daughter's marriage. What can't be guessed from them is the near agony an ulcerous leg was causing him. But by the middle of 1935 he was in almost constant pain, and from this time on his health begins a remorseless downwards curve. Merely to look at his Log Book is to see this. On Feb. 27th, 1936, he notes: "After consultation with the Chairman of the Managers I have left school occasionally soon after 4 pm. when my leg and foot have been particularly painful, in order to avoid the rush hour, as I have a long journey by train and bus." The walk to school from Baron's Court now becomes a thing of the past. He takes the train to Putney Bridge and from there catches a bus which drops him outside St. Dunstan's.

Hod was suffering from diabetes miletus, to give the illness its full name, and his leg ulcers, as well as an excruciatingly painful one on his heel, were among the effects of his condition, which had been diagnosed late in the previous year. Hence, the need for constant monitoring of his health, as recorded in the Log Book. "30/4/36: To attend Hospital for Med. Exam." "21/10/36: To attend Hospital for Med. Exam." "4/6/37: Attend Hospital." "5/10/38: Hospital for Exam." Not many years before his condition became known, insulin was discovered to be an effective means of treating both forms of the disease, although it worked better for what was called Diabetes A, which affected younger people, than Diabetes B, which it seems clear is what my grandfather suffered from. The insulin, which at that time was extracted from pigs – Danish pigs were apparently much favoured as having better (and, who knows? cleaner) supplies – was doled out in fortnightly batches to registered diabetics who had to administer their own daily injections. Over the years my grandfather found this an increasingly difficult and painful task as he struggled to locate a vein that hadn't already been perforated and was within his reach.

Diabetics had to take precautions with their diet. My grandfather cut down on beer – not that he'd ever been more than a social drinker – but probably consumed more fatty foods than were good for him; and he continued to smoke the cigarettes which he rolled himself. (Though he occasionally treated himself to a packet of Capstan.) He also from time to time struggled out on weekend walks with friends, coping with the pain as best as he could. "Nobody wants your tears", he once told his daughter after he'd come in from a tormenting slog across Wimbledon common and sat exhausted in his easy chair.

* * *

That remark must have been made sometime late in 1938. Joan Lucas was by then back at Melrose Avenue, expecting her second child. On her marriage, she and her husband had gone to live in Exeter, where, after the failure of the London insurance company for which he'd originally worked, he'd joined another such company. This greatly cheered my grandparents, who were beginning to consider their retirement years. For some time Hod had been considering a move back to Devon. Now that his daughter and son-in-law were, it seemed, settled in the city where he'd been at College, he decided to take out a mortgage on a small cottage there. He would be able to live out his last years in his beloved native country and at the same time be near his son-in-law, daughter, and, now, grandson. For on 26ᵗʰ June, 1937, Joan gave birth to a boy.

But then came black news. The company which employed their daughter's husband had for some time been struggling to survive. In the middle of 1938 it finally closed down and Len Lucas was left without work. There was nothing for it but to sell up. While his pregnant wife and small son moved in with Hod and Cissie, the young man went looking for alternative employment. The dream of Exeter was abandoned. The cottage was first let, then sold off. With it went most of the money Hod had paid towards a mortgage.

Anxieties at home were made darker by what was happening in Europe. Some time before his marriage, my father offered to show a young German woman around London. She was the daughter of a friend of a friend of Hod's. Dr. Bruchner, a German educationalist, had come over to England in the early 1930s. He'd been sent to study and report back on the theory and practice of what went on in English schools. Somehow he and Hod met and struck up an acquaintanceship that quickly warmed into friendship. I have a photograph of the two men standing shoulder to shoulder in the back garden at Melrose Avenue, Hod smiling, affable, Dr. Bruchner all walrus moustache, gravid stomach buttoned into his waistcoat, a grin surrounding his ample pipe. He looks a good man, and I gather he was one.

The same can't be said of the young woman. She arrived in London, eager to be shown all the sights – Covent Garden, Piccadilly Circus, Trafalgar Square, the Mall – and my father did his best to oblige. He didn't greatly mind her inexhaustible determination to go everywhere, or so he later said, but he was first alarmed and then embarrassed by the ostentatious way in which she greeted fellow Germans, and indeed others to whom she was introduced, by snapping her heels while raising her right arm in a fascist salute. Hitler, she explained ardently to anyone who would listen, was not only her hero, he would soon be a hero to the entire civilised world.

By no means all who witnessed this behaviour would have been embarrassed by it. Sir Oswald Mosley had formed his British Union of Fascists in 1932, and it soon gained the backing of a number of prominent men and women, among them Lord Rothermere, who owned the *Daily Mail*, the *Evening News* and the *Sunday Dispatch*. The last of these announced "five £1 prizes to readers who send in postcards on "Why I like the Blackshirts." It was this newspaper for whom Max Miller provided his regular diet of jokes, and which my grandfather must therefore have bought. This seems decidedly odd until we remember that there are many reasons for buying a particular newspaper. When I was a student I worked during summer holidays with two brickies who were ardent socialists and who always bought the *Daily Express*. Why on earth did they do that? Because it had the best racing column, they told me. For all I know the *Sunday Dispatch* also had a reliable tipster. If so, my grandfather would have had a further reason for buying Rothermere's rag. He'd not, however, have sympathised with its enthusiastic reporting of Mosley's monster meeting at Olympia on 7th June, 1934, at which Mosley gave a passable imitation of Hitler and his methods. According to Margot Heinemann and Noreen Branson, in their *Britain in the Nineteen Thirties*, the leader of the British Union of fascists "spoke with the aid of twenty-four amplifiers and a spotlight. Some interrupter would shout an objection .... At once Sir Oswald would pause, the spotlight would be swung onto the interrupter, a posse of blackshirts would seize him, punch him, kick him, carry him struggling from the hall, beat him up in the corridor, perhaps throw him down the stairs, and finally eject him."

Hitler had come to power in 1933. He may have been a hero to young Germans and to the Mosleyites, but to others his emergence seemed the grim fulfilment of that prophecy which J.L. Garvin had uttered in an editorial for the *Observer* of May 11th, 1919, following the signing of the Versailles Treaty. "All the Treaty," Garvin wrote, "apart from the incorporated and saving Covenant of the League [of Nations] – scatters Dragon's teeth across the soil of Europe. They will spring up as armed men unless the mischief is eradicated .... For civilisation there is now one hope, and no other. That hope lies in the development of the League of Nations by the more united democracies of the world." Garvin's hope for the always frail League was shattered by a crisis of 1935 which, though some tried to pass it off as a local squabble, was in fact of international significance.

In the late summer, Fascist Italy declared its intention of invading Abyssinia. The T.U.C. annual congress, held that year at Margate, voted to condemn Italy's promised invasion and to support the government in any action it took to uphold the League of Nations. After Congress came the Labour party annual meeting at Brighton. In the debate held in the Dome on October 1st, a resolution in line with the T.U.C. position was put, urging the government to use "all the necessary measures provided by the Covenant" to support the League of Nations in preventing Italy's "rapacious attack." The resolution was opposed by George Lansbury, still leader of the parliamentary party at the age of 76, and, as he had always been, a pacifist. If mine was the only voice at this Conference urging peace, he told the delegates, "I would say in the name of the faith I hold, the belief I have that God intended us to live peacably and quietly with one another, if some people do not allow us to do so, I am ready to stand as the early Christians did, and say, 'This is our faith, this is where we stand, and, if necessary, this is where we will die.'" Lansbury, a much-loved man, received a heart-felt, lengthy ovation.

Then came Bevin. He spoke on this occasion, one commentator tells us, "with the weight and warmth and rough directness which held and quelled his audience even when they disliked his words." He was profoundly vexed by Lansbury's pacifism, which, as he saw it, allowed free rein to fascists and Nazis, whom he hated "as murderers of working men and women and wreckers of the free trade unions." His attack on Lansbury amounted to the cut direct. "I hope this Conference will not be influenced by either sentiment or personal attachment," Bevin said. "It is placing the Executive and the

Movement in an absolutely wrong position to be taking your conscience round from body to body asking to be told what you ought to do with it." Hard words, but they had their effect. Conference voted for the Resolution and almost immediately afterwards Lansbury resigned the party leadership. I can imagine that Hod would have had some sympathy with Lansbury. But he'd have shared Bevin's conviction that fascism had to be resisted.

Before the end of the month the government, too, had resigned. Baldwin called a general election for November 14th. The National Government, as it continued to call itself, was in truth a Conservative administration with a rump of Liberal Nationals and National Labour members. Baldwin made foreign policy the dominant issue of the campaign. The League of Nations, he promised electors, would "remain, as heretofore, the keystone of British foreign policy," and the government would "do all in our power to uphold the Covenant and to maintain and increase the efficiency of the League." As regards Abyssina, therefore, "there will be no wavering in the policy we have hitherto pursued." The result was a foregone conclusion. The Conservatives, vowing to maintain a strong foreign policy, won 387 seats, the Liberal Nationals 33, and there were in addition 8 National Labour members in the new parliament. Labour elected 154 members, the Liberals a mere 17, 4 I.L.P. members were returned, the same number as for those who declared themselves Independent Opposition members, and there was 1 Communist. (William Gallagher.) With the exception of a tiny handful, the whole House was united in its determination to uphold the League and to prevent Italy's aggression against Abyssinia.

And in the event Baldwin twisted and slid away from the commitments he had given. By May the following year Mussolini's annexation of Abyssinia had been completed, at which moment he proclaimed the Italian King an emperor. "Italy has her empire at last: a fascist empire", il Duce announced. He was following the lead given by Nazi Germany, for in early March Hitler had jackbooted his way into the Rhineland with no opposition from the League. The way was now open for other fascists to do as they pleased: overthrow democratically elected governments, ignore the rights of sovereign states, spread the foul contagion of racist *Übermenschen.* In July, Franco began a war to bring the Spanish Republic under his fascist control, and despite the *New Statesman's* gloomy warning that without opposition to the fascist advances "there can be no peace in Europe, but only a terrified waiting for war", neither the French nor British Governments did anything to help the Republic's cause. On the contrary, the farce of non-intervention ensured that while Germany and Italy were free to supply Franco's forces with military aid (non-intervention saw to that), no arms could get through to the Republic. Non-intervention meant that UK and French-registered ships, on their urgent, voluntary errands of providing arms for the legitimate government, were turned back by the French and British navies.

Of course, there were the International Brigades, mostly untrained volunteers from all parts of the world, who converged on that table-land scored by rivers, come there to present their lives. But though their actions shamed the hapless inactivity of Western governments, the fact remained that the swelling tide of Fascism how held sudden death before the eyes of dazed Europeans. There was the *Anschluss,* there was *Kristallnacht,* and, in the autumn of 1938, Hitler's invasion of the Sudetenland, and still Chamberlain, who had succeeded Baldwin as prime minister, could announce on his return from Munich that there would be "peace in our time." But the *Statesman* was right. Terrified or not, people were now waiting for war.

Meanwhile, Hod had to keep his school running. Numbers diminished. The roll call for 1936 was 222, the following year it went down to 207, and there was a further drop the year after that to 192. But there were the customary tests, visits to theatres, and, for 34 lucky pupils, a fortnight's trip to the Kent coast, an event written up for a local newspaper by Mr. A.E. Worrall, one of the teachers who went with the boys. "The hedgerows and streams provided material enough to fascinate us all .... [we] discovered the secret haunts of the heron and the buzzard, and were impressed by the flight of the sea-birds and the dragon-fly."

Early in 1936, George V died. "The King's life is moving peacefully to its close" was how Stuart Hibbard, a senior BBC announcer, conveyed the news to the nation. The words had been drafted for him by Lord Dawson, the royal physician, who chose not to reveal the patient's retort to his suggestion that Bognor might provide a welcome change of air from Sandringham where he lay. "Bugger Bognor" his majesty growled, human at last.

Hod's Log Book records merely:

"Jan. 28th '36: The school was closed today on the occasion of the funeral of Geo. V. A short memorial service was held in the Hall on Monday morning." A new king replaced him, abdicated, was replaced.

There was a death closer to home, which must have brought with it a shiver of mortality. "25/2/37. Funeral of father-in-law." After his first wife's death Cissie's father had remarried. Family rumour has it that the new wife took him because she thought he was a wealthy widower, and he married her because he expected her to look after him. Both were to be disappointed. Still, a photograph of the early 30s, taken in the garden at Melrose Avenue, shows a sturdy-looking, jovial man with white spade beard, sitting at ease in a canvas chair. Cissie and Hod stand either side of him, smiling benignly. He was 85 when he came in from gardening one afternoon, sat down and died instantly. A good ending, I think. After so much of life, so little death.

* * *

22nd Sept. '38: A staff meeting was held today to consider the letter from the E.O. re air-raids. It was decided that three-fourths of the staff should make for the nearest G.W.R. station – Ealing Broadway – this being the most likely station from which the children will be evacuated.

The address & phone numbers of the staff have been given to each member & to the Schoolkeeper.

Mr. Catalani is to consult the Head Masters of the contributory schools as to the best method to deal with the boys attending Handicraft.

There obviously weren't handicraft facilities in all schools, which meant that, in the event of air-raids or indeed war itself commencing during school hours, Mr. Catalani would be held responsible for deciding how best to round up such boys as were scattered about at handicraft classes in order to get them to Ealing Broadway.

My grandfather hasn't included the Education Office letter in the Log Book, so I can't know what it said. I have, however, consulted the Minutes of the L.C.C. Education Sub-Committee meetings, and fascinating reading they make, too. They reveal that evacuation plans were being considered from the early summer of 1938. At the meeting of 4th May, the committee for the first time insists on Minuting its belief that plans to close the schools and evacuate the pupils in event of war are "essential". It will also be essential to train teachers in the techniques of first-aid and "gas cases and anti-gas precautions generally." The committee rejects a proposal that schools might be kept open in order to prevent children from the "serious and far-reaching psychological consequences" of seeing wounded people in the streets. Once war has begun, the chairman reasonably notes, it will be impossible to expect children to attend school.

On the other hand, at a meeting of 6th July, the same committee members recommend that although schools should be closed as far as teaching is concerned, a room in each school should remain open "for the purposes of a respirator distributing depot in connection with air-raid precautions." And at the final meeting of the year, held on 7th December, the committee receives and approves a Report submitted by the London Teachers Association which recommends widespread civilian evacuation but urges that the need for children's evacuation be especially pressed. The Association further recommends the setting up of a committee to oversee plans for evacuation, and suggests that such a committee should consist of representatives from local borough councils, the London authority, and teachers. "Everything is going to plan," Louis MacNeice noted sardonically in his great *Autumn Journal*, about the closing months of 1938: "They want the crest of this hill for anti-aircraft, / The guns will take the view/And searchlights probe the heavens for bacilli / With narrow wands of blue."

But not all was going to plan. Early in January 1939 Hod entered St. Thomas's Hospital for an operation on his throat. For some time he had been experiencing a growing discomfort whenever he swallowed food or drink, and the pain and, indeed, blockage in his throat had now become so acute that he feared that, like his father before him, he was suffering from throat cancer. In fact, examination showed that he had a particularly virulent throat ulcer, brought on by his diabetic condition. He was hospitalised for nine days while the ulcer was dealt with by surgical means, and two pencilled letters that survive from that episode make plain that he didn't at all enjoy his enforced idleness. In the first, he tells his wife that "the days & nights are so long. The nurses are wonderful & do everything in their power to make one happy & comfortable, but it's difficult to know what to do to pass the time. I hope you are keeping fit & also Joan & Bill [his name for his grandson] and Jillian. [His granddaughter, who had been born on 6th November, 1938]." He feeds his wife further scraps of information, before adding "Had the T.T. yesterday." I assume this is to be a reference to a tracheotomy, or some similar operation to clear the blockage in his throat and treat the ulcer.

The operation couldn't have been a complete success because a few days later he writes to tell Cissie that "I am feeling pretty fit, but I believe that (drs.) are to do something more to my neck as they have altered the treatment somewhat. Chief surgeon was here yesterday morning & they are going to take the pimple off too." Then, amazingly, he implores her, "Don't forget the *Blue Rizlas*." (His underlining.) And so anxious is he for a supply of cigarette papers that later in the same letter he remarks "if you get this in time you might slip a Blue Rizla in an envelope, then I should get it in the morning. Don't forget to bring along 2 or 3 boxes of matches on Sunday. Best love to yourself & all at Melrose, Your affectionate Orris." I'm staggered that even if he'd been freed from the dread of cancer he could bear to smoke, knowing the pain the throat ulcer caused him. I'm even more amazed that the hospital permitted it.

But I'm simply astonished that he was so soon back at his desk. Yet nine days after entering hospital he returned to St. Dunstan's. Soon afterwards, his son-in-law found work in Coventry and sent for his wife and children. I was then not quite two years old, and after we left Wimbledon in the early summer of 1939 I never again saw my grandfather. One fragmented image remains from those months, at least I think it does. I am sitting at a scrubbed wooden table, surrounded by adults, and someone offers me a slice of tomato. That's all. When I once, many years later, told my mother of this, she confirmed that there was such a table in the kitchen at Melrose Avenue. That image must, then, be the meagre remains of the months I spent at Wimbledon. I've run the image over, again and again, and once or twice think I've caught sight of a man's head coming into view round a door to the right of the table where I sit. But there is no definition to it, nothing that lets me know for sure that the head, supposing it to be part of the original memory, is indeed that of a man. And when did you last see your grandfather? The honest answer is, I don't *know* that I ever saw him.

* * *

In May Hod was again in hospital for what the Log Book records as "Operation on Face". Face? Does he mean that, or for "face" should we read "throat", and assume that the ulcer needed further attention. I don't know. I do know however that his health was now in serious decline. Not that he says anything about it, but from my mother I learn that his diabetic condition had worsened and that he was in constant pain from ulcers. This must have been deeply depressing for them all, as depressing as the certainty of a coming war. Dismissed from St. Thomas's Hospital, Hod was at once back at school, worrying over evacuation and related plans. At its meeting on 8th Feb. 1939, the L.C.C. Education Sub-Committee had minuted an item on "Air-raid precautions – Training of Teachers."

> We are of the opinion that it is an essential part of any evacuation scheme that the teachers should be able to render first-aid, and we are advised that a suitable course would consist of twelve lectures of two hours each, two of which would deal especially with gas.

The Minute goes on to stipulate that "two volunteers from each Dept. of all elementary schools" are to be trained. This would produce "about 4,560 teachers from the 2,280 departments or schools concerned."

Another Minute insists that the schools must also have an Air-Raid Evacuation Scheme in place, although for this only one member of staff per school be appointed. And one further Minute recommends that the existing rule concerning married women be suspended, "to enable a married woman to be employed to fill a temporary vacancy for an assistant organizor of children's care work." Easy to mock this reluctant admission that even married women may have a part to play in the event of Britain at War, but reading through these Reports is a salutory experience. Never mind the excessively sobersides prose, the occasional stuffed-shirt observation, the needless huffing and puffing over minutiae. Between them, these may suggest a committee of self-important small-time bureaucrats, fiddling with inessential details while the world prepares to burn. In fact, it's impossible not to be deeply impressed by the care which the Education sub-Committee brings to what are wholly responsible deliberations over the schoolchildren it recognises as its concern. Those ageing men in their heavy suits and with their ponderous talk, really do want to do the considered and considerable best they can for thousands upon thousands of London schoolchildren.

So, it goes without saying, do the teachers. All of them, like the population at large, knew deep in their bones that a major war couldn't long be postponed. Events now move fast. On July 19th, Hod calls a staff meeting "to consider the details of the Evacuation scheme." A week later, "the boys were instructed this morning in gas-mask drill by the Schoolkeeper who is a qualified air-raid warden." Meanwhile, a circular, a copy of which is pasted into the Log Book, is sent to all parents.

EVACUATION
If Evacuation should prove necessary during the holidays, wireless announcements will be broadcast.
In this case your children who are going away with the school party

MUST BE AT SCHOOL AT 7 A.M.

on that morning with the necessary clothing and food as set out in a previous notice.

H.W.S. Kelly,
Headmaster

KEEP THIS NOTICE

What caused this surge in preparation for war was the nation's realisation that Chamberlain's paper promise of peace in our time was about to be shredded. The policy of appeasement associated with Munich had perhaps seemed worthwhile when it was announced in the autumn of 1938. But at best it was a means of buying time. After Hitler's demands in the spring of 1939 for the return of the free city of Danzig from League of Nations to German control, few doubted that war could be averted. For Hitler was now demanding extra-territorial rights of way across the Polish corridor where Danzig was situated. In other words, he was going to extend his control to Polish territory. Perhaps the liberal democracies believed or hoped that Russia, which also thought of Poland as somehow its "natural" territory, would rebuff this demand. If so, hopes were crushed like a hollow egg when, to their horrified amazement, on August 28th came the announcement of the Russo-German Treaty (the Molotov-Ribbentrop Pact), which guaranteed non-aggression between the two nations for ten years and at the same time carried an acceptance by Germany that Finland, Latvia and Estonia were legitimately within Russia's sphere of influence. Lord Halsbury's worst fears looked as though they were about to be realised.

I have read accounts of this period which suggest that even at this desperate time Chamberlain hoped to keep the peace. Perhaps he did, but if so he was one of a minority which had shrunk almost to vanishing point. Which isn't to say there was nobody left who thought a deal could be done with Hitler. The Astors, for example, considered him an honourable man of principle whom they were

191

happy to support. So, it was rumoured with good reason, did the Duke and Duchess of Windsor. So did other nobs. But for most people, war against Nazi Germany was now inevitable. It is no surprise to find the Log Book for St. Dunstan's, August 26th – 29th recording that "The Staff were recalled & were in attendance at school on Saturday, Sunday & Monday for the purpose of evacuation." But nothing happened. Accordingly, "the schools assembled at the usual hours on Tuesday & Weds. but registers were not called. We await further instruction. Aug. 30th. The total number of children prepared for evacuation in the 3 Depts. is 150."

These words mark Hod's last entry in the official Log Book.

* * *

On August 24th, 1939, six days before my grandfather wrote those words, the British government met and passed the Emergency Powers bill which affirmed, *inter alia*, that the nation stood united and prepared to fight, not so much for Poland as for the freedom and security of the peoples of the world. The affirmation was echoed by the French, and the Polish government, no doubt strengthened by the noises coming out of London and Paris, refused to accept the insulting terms Hilter offered them for a guarantee of non-intervention. Anyway, what were his guarantees worth? On 1st September Germany invaded Poland and two days later, on Sunday, September 3rd, after the British ultimatum to Hitler demanding the withdrawal of his troops from Polish territory had met with silence, Chamberlain broadcast to the nation. The Second World War had finally begun.

9. GOING OUT WITH THE TIDE

Sept. 1ˢᵗ 1939

> Arrived at Longwick about 10.30 am.
>
> Detrained at Risborough Station. Children given 48 hrs. rations & then taken on motor coaches to their destinations. The Infs. To Monks Risborough. 34 boys with myself & wife & Messrs Rothen & Jenkins to Longwick & the remainder with Messrs Lyons, Showan, Catalani, Pearce & Mr & Mrs Buxton were billeted in Princes Risborough.
>
> The girls were taken to another village. (Butler's Cross.)
>
> On arrival at the village hall the children were allocated billets & I sent wire to Schoolkeeper. This work completed they were taken to their billets by the billeting committee.
>
> I cannot speak too highly of the arrangements made & of the wonderful reception given to us.
>
> The billeting officer Mr Walker with his band of helpers, Mrs Walker, Mrs Williams (head Mistress) & Miss Wootton (asst) & other ladies, worked untiringly to get the children settled.
>
> In the afternoon Messrs Rothen and Jenkins & myself visited all the homes where the children were billeted & found everything quite all right & the children happy.
>
> Most of the children – in fact all except 2 – had already informed their parents of their address.

Thus Hod's first entry in his new "Log Book." It wasn't however standard issue. No folio-size, stiff bound volume with printed subheadings – ABSENCES, VISITS etc – and indexed sheets. This is small, saddle-stitched, bearing on its buff-coloured paper cover the legend LONDON COUNTY COUNCIL and below it, in larger bold pointing, NATURE NOTE BOOK No.2. I assume my grandfather had chosen the notebook because it was easy to slip into his pocket and could be written in, whatever the circumstances. It's one of two, a third having been lost. Note Book No.1 ends with an entry for October 1ˢᵗ, the other (made from an L.C.C. Exercise Book which has been cut in half length-ways), commences with an entry for November 16ᵗʰ. On its cover, Hod has written *No.3 Diary*.

Presumably all headteachers had been enjoined to keep records of their schools during evacuation, although as the Metropolitan Archives are bound by a 60 Year Rule – goodness only knows why

194

– I'm unable to discover whether the records of other evacuated schools do in fact exist. They may be in the Archives, they may not. My grandfather's two Log Books / Note Books certainly aren't. I have them beside me as I write. The reason is simple. After he died none of his family thought to hand them over to the relevant authority. This is as understandable as the LCC's failure to ask for them. In the confusion of war-time England – even in the "bore war" period as it was known at the time (the "phoney war" was a phrase adopted later) – it isn't surprising that the whereabouts of a junior school's Log Books should have been overlooked.

By the time he began his records of St. Dunstan's in evacuation my grandfather was seriously ill. His diabetic condition had become acute, and his ulcerated leg made not merely walking but standing for any length of time agony. Yet the Note-books of this period, (they can't really be thought of as Log-Books) are more detailed, and even, more vivacious than most of the Log-Book entries of his earlier, happier and fitter years. It's as though the war has released a new surge of energy in him and with it a determination to record as fully as he can all that's happening to his school at this momentous time. These note-books are his modest contribution to the history of the second world war as it affected ordinary people, at least in its early days.

That there was a degree of self-consciousness about this is evident from the very beginning. Throughout, my grandfather writes all his entries in ink. The only exception is the opening date: Sept. 1st. It's in red pencil. Not so much a Red Letter Day as an indication of that Friday's absolute significance. Careless historians have written that evacuation plans were put into operation at the outbreak of war. Wrong. Two days before Chamberlain addressed the nation, the evacuation of over a million children and, in some cases, mothers, from what were called "vulnerable areas" began. It may be that even after Germany's invasion of Poland in the early hours of the 1st, Chamberlain still hoped to strike some sort of a deal with Hitler. Mussolini, perhaps alarmed by the turn of events and fearing all-out war, proposed a form of mediation, but as the British and French were insisting Hitler must withdraw his troops from Poland before a meeting between the interested parties could occur, a condition Hitler certainly wasn't going to meet, it seems that even Chamberlain had finally woken up to the fact that there was no alternative to war.

There was a general expectation that as soon as hostilities began, Britain would be subjected to aerial bombardment. Chamberlain broadcast his announcement of war at 11.15 a.m. on Sunday 3rd September. He had, he told the nation, asked Hitler to undertake to withdraw his troops from Poland. "I have to tell you that no such undertaking has been received and consequently this country is at war with Germany." Five minutes later the first air-raid siren was sounded. A false alarm, as it happened. So were many subsequent warnings across the U.K in those first few weeks of war. My grandfather records for the following Thursday, 7th September, "There was an air-raid warning about 11.30 a.m. at Longwick. This was not given at Risboro. It proved to be a false alarm."

Not surprisingly, however, Hod made sure that all the children under his care were, as he says in another note of the time, given "instructions as to air-raid precautions." This will have included practice in the handling of gas-masks and, even, how to cope with the effect of gas. One of the most widely-disseminated of war posters to appear in the early days was put out by the Ministry of Home Security. Under the title *GAS ATTACK*, the poster gives visual and annotated instructions about HOW TO PUT ON YOUR GAS MASK and what to do IF YOU GET GASSED. If the gas is *vapour gas* "Keep your gas mask on even if you feel discomfort. If discomfort continues go to First Aid Post." If on the other hand the gas is *liquid or blister gas*, you must "1) Dab, but *don't rub* the splash with handkerchief. Then destroy handkerchief. 2) Rub No. 2 Ointment well into place. (*Buy a 6d. jar now from any chemist.*) In emergency chemists supply Bleach Cream free. 3) If you can't get Ointment or Cream within 5 minutes wash place with soap and warm water. 4) Take off at once any garments splashed with gas." Above all, the poster urges people, "Always keep your gas mask with you – day and night. Learn to put it on quickly. Practise wearing it."

Two years later, by which time we had moved from Coventry to a small rural village in Leicestershire, I was kitted out with a gas mask which I had to practise putting on in front of the postmaster, a Mr.

Goodwin, whose bulbous nose sprouted thistle heads of hair as gingery as his sports coat. I didn't like him, although I envied the row of pencils stylishly lined up in his breast pocket. Looking at the Ministry's poster now, I can hear again the postmaster's voice as he barked at me "Hold your breath. Do NOT breathe. Make QUITE sure your chin goes into the mask first, NOT your forehead." With the rubber-smelling mask clamped round my head, I stared at him through glass now rapidly misting over. Then, just in time, I clawed the contraption off and gulped air into my lungs. "I did NOT tell you to remove your gas mask." "I couldn't breathe", I said. "Foolish boy. You breathe once you have the mask secure about your head." Well, why hadn't he told me.

The gas mask came with a cardboard box complete with shoulder strap. I don't recall carrying it to and from school or when I went out to play, but perhaps by then we'd become *blasé* about the likelihood of gas attacks, especially in the rural Midlands. In September 1939, it was, however, a different matter. At any moment gas bombs might fall from the air. So might German invaders, either in force or singly.

Many years later, my father told me of the heart-stopping occasion when he and another man from Burbage, both of them at that time in the Home Guard while they waited for their call-up papers, were sent out to fight off an invasion of the village. That at least was how the matter was put to them. They were on night duty when a call came through on the field telephone to say that a villager had witnessed dark objects falling from the sky above Farmer Record's fields. German parachutists! Never mind there had been no reports, let alone sounds, of enemy aeroplanes over the night skies of the Midlands, it was apparent that Hitler had now decided to begin his master plan of subjugating the entire United Kingdom, and where better to start than Burbage? Standing alone against his dastardly ambition were messers. Dick Powers and Len Lucas. The nation's future depended on them.

The two young men, grasping rifles nobody had taught them how to fire, crept into Farmer Record's bottom field and took up position behind a haystack. Soon enough they heard, coming steadily towards

197

them, a rhythmic tramp of feet. Then a deep, hoarse cough, which froze the sweat on my father's forehead. More sounds, this time from the other side of the haystack, and then, nearer still, moving round to where the young men crouched, rifles raised in what they hoped was the correct position. Finally, after what seemed an endless moment, a large head and shoulders came slowly into view. "Moo", the cow said.

Afterwards, the men heard that a barrage balloon, which had punctured and slowly subsided from its sky-mooring, had been mistaken for German parachutists. Such mistakes felt natural in the atmosphere of late 1939. If you met a stranger, you had to keep quiet about the war. *CARELESS TALK COSTS LIVES* was another, widely-distributed poster-campaign of the time. And if you thought it necessary to put the stranger to the test, you could try him on a pass-word – presumably to be used only in extreme circumstances, such as his asking to see around your school or to be taken into your house, or to your leader. My grandfather was issued with the pass-word "Pied Piper", although I've no idea by whom nor how widely this was spread among other teachers or those who lived in the vicinity of Princes Risborough. Certainly, the opportunities for misunderstanding, comic or otherwise, must have been abundant.

They were increased by the immediate adoption of black-out. Show a light after dark and you were aiding and abetting the enemy. Almost as immediate was conscription for all men between the ages of 18 and 41. Then in September came the first war budget, which raised income tax from 5/6 d to 7/6 d in the pound. My grandfather was responsible for handing out the new tax demands to members of his staff, as a Note Book entry for Dec. 15th reveals. Rationing of food didn't, however, begin before January, 1940. (Butter, bacon and sugar were first on the list.) Though the bore war or, as Chamberlain called it, "twilight war", didn't bring the sudden aerial battering of Britain which had been so generally expected, there were, even in September, disasters aplenty. On the very day war was declared the steam ship *Athenia*, bound for Canada, was sunk by a U-boat and a hundred and twenty people drowned. According to Mowat, "survivors related that passengers awaiting death [sang] the then popular song 'Roll out the Barrel', which shocked some moralists but reassured others of the courage of ordinary people." On the 17th of September the aircraft carrier *Courageous* was torpedoed and sunk with the loss of half its crew. Before the end of the month Poland had been overrun by a combination of Hitler and Stalin's forces.

* * *

None of these events is so much as mentioned in my grandfather's Note Books. Princes Risborough and still more Longwick must have felt a long way from the grimmer actualities of war. In 1939 the former was a small market town, while Longwick, almost hidden away on the road to Thame, qualified as at most a village. In many ways reminiscent of Sawtry, its chief attraction lay in the rich farming country that stretched all around. For boys from the back streets of Fulham and Hammersmith, the contrast between their London and this rural England could hardly have been greater. My grandfather's Note Books record that on the whole they took to their new circumstances with delighted ease.

Which isn't to say there were no problems. Hod records at least a few cases of impetigo, and he notes some bed-wetting – probably the result of emotional insecurity, especially among boys billeted on unsympathetic foster-parents. There are accidents (one boy is hospitalised with an arm injury, another requires several stitches in his hand after cutting it with a sharp implement); and finally my grandfather has to deal with the occasional charge of theft ("I found the story greatly exaggerated"), of general misbehaviour ("I have given [the boys concerned] a good talking to & warned them as to their conduct in the future"), and of one boy accused of "interfering" with the foster-parent's daughter.

Against these matters, however, is the fact that country living was on the whole wonderfully good for the boys. September 1939 was a particularly fine one. The first Note Book is full of such entries as "It was very hot indeed this afternoon", "this afternoon Mr. Jenkins has taken some of the children for a country ramble while others are helping on the farm" (Sept. 5th) – Mr. Jenkins, I should note in passing, is credited with starting the school garden on Sept. 19th, "some boys helped to pick plums", "saw several boys this morning & took them gathering nuts" (the experience of hop-picking no doubt came in useful), "Mr. Jenkins took some of the boys for a ramble", and, most spectacularly, "Geo. Owen and Hy Bousfield brought a grass-snake – 3 ft. long – to school & Mr. Jenkins gave a talk on its life & habits. He was particular to point out the danger of adders & how to distinguish them." Later that term, the same two boys were "given permission to be absent tomorrow in order to attend a meet of the hounds at Ilmer. They will go with their foster-parent Mr Brown."

The result of all this is that Hod is able to report that parents visiting their children generally find them in excellent health and spirits. "Wed. Sept. 20th. Mr Rockel of 66 St. Dunstan's Rd. called at the school. He told me he was delighted with David's appearance. He had called to see the foster-parent & expressed his thanks for what had been done for his son." "Sept. 25th: Several of the boys' parents came to see them on Sunday and, in response to Mrs Kelly's letters, brought the boys clothing. The parents were very pleased with the well-being of the boys." And, much later, on Dec. 16th: "Saw Mrs. Payne & Mrs Keefe this morning. Both expressed their pleasure at the way their boys were looking & thanked me for what was being done for their boys."

For all this, some boys opted to return home. My grandfather records that in all cases he wrote to parents telling them how unwise he thought this to be. But as Marion Yass remarks in *This is Your War: Home Front Propaganda in the Second World War*, (1983) the problem was that during the first months of the war "apathy, not panic, was in the air. It particularly affected both the evacuees and their hosts." Evacuation had initially been undertaken to save children from a bombing campaign which in the event failed to materialise. There now seemed precious little point to all those posters showing terrified children huddled together as the bombs fell. A new poster was therefore hurried out, this time showing a ghostly Hitler whispering in a mother's ear "Take them back! Take them back!..." The scene is a rural one, and small, healthy-looking children play contentedly in the foreground above the message *DON'T DO IT,*

MOTHER – LEAVE YOUR CHILDREN IN THE SAFER AREAS.
Judging from the numbers who were nevertheless back in London and other cities by Christmas, the poster campaign didn't have much success. According to some estimates, by the end of the year as many as 50% of children and 84% of adults had abandoned evacuation, and while those figures are probably an exaggeration there's no doubt that, in the absence of bombing, many went back to the cities. It therefore says much for my grandfather that the vast majority of children in his care chose to stay at Longwick and the surrounding villages.

Because they were so dependent on him, he had to look after both their education and their day-to-day concerns. He and the other teachers took with them from St. Dunstan's supplies of books and paper. I can't imagine, however, that much other equipment was on the train which pulled into Princes Risborough station on that momentous morning of Sept. 1st. So Hod simply set to and devised a programme for the children which would keep them occupied and, as far as possible, happy. There were two immediate problems. The first was that nobody knew when the school year was supposed to start. Eventually, on Sept. 9th, Hod was informed that "schools would re-open on Tuesday Sept. 12th." Before then, he organized rambles, games, reading sessions, church and Sunday School attendance, and a health inspection at which all the boys were weighed.

The second problem was more acute. Where exactly were the boys to be taught? At first Hod and the head teacher of the village school at Longwick, Mrs Williams, agree "(subject to the approval of the Bucks Ed Authority) for Mrs Williams to use the school from 9 am to 1 pm and St. Dunstan's to use it from 1 to 5 pm." The Authority must have refused permission because very soon my grandfather is noting that "It is impossible for the village school & the boys of St. Dunstan's school to meet in the school at the same time, as the village school has a full roll." He therefore proposes that his school should use the village hall. Ah, but this can't be done until the Bucks Ed. Co. have given their consent. Some days elapse. Not only is the consent not forthcoming, but Mrs. Williams shows Hod a letter from the Sec. for Education instructing the two schools to work together. *"This is impossible*," is my grandfather's exasperated response. "It would mean herding into one room 84 children where there is accommodation for only 52. In addition the ventilation is very bad. The sanitary accommodation is quite inadequate. There is only 1 tap for drinking water."

I don't know when exactly the combined efforts of the two head teachers brought the Bucks. Education committee to see sense, but by the time the 3rd Note Book comes into operation, on "Weds. Nov. 16th", the boys of St. Dunstan's are installed in their new premises. Not all problems are, however, at an end. The Village hall proved ill-equipped to double as a school. On Dec. 1st. a representative of the Education Committee "called this morning and agreed that a latrine was desirable." And in cold weather, such as clamped down at the turn of the year, the hall was by modern standards uninhabitable. "Weds. Jan 17th: Very cold. Temperature of hall at 9 a.m. 29°. The boys were given P.E. & games until 11 a.m. Then stories from Robin Hood were read to them. No written work was attempted this morning. Temperature at 1.30 p.m. 46°." Presumably the boys were too cold to grip pen or pencil.

Yet despite these difficulties my grandfather ensured that lessons were properly conducted and that the boys worked at the 3 Rs. He also saw to it that somehow or other they got hold of stocks of library books, which meant at least one visit to High Wycombe for himself and another teacher, and further trips to Aylesbury. "Library books were exchanged" is a regular entry. And on one occasion Hod writes of "a school reading from 'Black Beauty'", by which I take him to mean that boys took it in turns to read from Anna Sewell's then famous children's novel. Four years later, in my first year at Grove Road Junior School, Burbage, I, too, would be reading *Black Beauty*, although not, as I recall it, aloud.

* * *

By then my grandfather was dead. Knowing now how ill he was during those final months, I find it astonishing that he managed to do so much. Quite apart from his daily teaching duties, there were trips to doctors with injured or possibly ill pupils, he had to journey to various towns in pursuit of books, and, as Christmas approached, he became increasingly involved in preparations for such festivities as could be arranged. On Nov 21ˢᵗ. he records that a Mrs Way "is very kindly coming on Friday afternoon to coach the boys for the Xmas party. She will also provide some of the costumes." Parents are persuaded to dip into their pockets and give whatever they can. "Sunday Dec. 10ᵗʰ. I saw Mrs Edgson who expressed their delight with their boys & gave me 3/6 towards the Xmas treat. I also saw Mrs. Dowse who gave me 2/-. She said she had never seen Wm. looking so well." A few days later he is able to report that the parents of other boys have agreed to send "some eatables for the Xmas party". Foster parents also chipped in, with the result that on "Sat. Dec. 16ᵗʰ Mrs Kelly & myself went to Aylesbury this afternoon to get the Xmas presents for the boys." The next day both of them are at the village hall "from 11 a.m. to 2 p.m. to welcome the parents who were visiting their children." On the 20ᵗʰ: "Finished decorating the Hall," and two days later, on Friday, 22ⁿᵈ "Saw Mrs. Williams this morning and invited her children [I take it he means the village schoolchildren] to the entertainment this evening .... Mrs. Way & Mrs Maitland provided the costumes for the play which was a great success. Many foster parents & village children came to the entertainment & a very happy evening .... Most of the foster-parents contributed something to the 'tea'".

Nor does it end there. On Tuesday 26ᵗʰ, "The boys were met at the Village Hall both morning & afternoon for games and boxing." The following day, those who chose not to go with Mr Jenkins "for a walk", again took part in games, and then, on the 28ᵗʰ, with "Severe frost last night & snow this morning", the boys were "amused in Hall morning & afternoon." Amused? I can't help hearing behind that word what Mr. Sleary of the horse-riding circus says to Mr. Gradgrind at the close of *Hard Times*. "People mutht be amuthed. They can't be alwayth a learning, nor yet they can't be alwayth a working, they ain't made for it." Hod and his staff had obviously decided they'd do all in their power to give children away from home as good a Christmas as they could possibly devise. Quite how much this ceaseless activity took out of my grandfather I can only guess, though there can't be much doubt that it hastened his death. But he wasn't going to give in. It appears that the L.C.C. belatedly sent through some money for the boys and so, on Friday 29th. Dec., at the start of what was meant to be a six-day break for him, he records that "I am going with Mrs Walker and Mrs Williams to High Wycombe on Monday to get the presents." Having got them, "went to Mrs Walker's to help to tie up & label the presents."

On Jan. 3rd "The children's tea party & entertainment went off excellently. Again Mrs Way & Mrs Maitland gave invaluable help with the play. The presents were supplied by the LCC and the tea by the Bucks authorities." There followed more days of organized games, of walks, of visiting the billeting officer, of taking the boys to Sunday School, of being present while the school nurse "examined the boys ... & found all of them clean," before finally, on Jan. 9th, he notes "I returned to duty this morning after 6 days' leave." Leave? You could have fooled me.

My grandfather took his pastoral responsibilities every bit as seriously as his educational ones. I'm not at all sure, in fact, that he'd have thought there was much distinction between the two. What *is* certain is that as soon as the evacuation party arrived at Longwick my grandmother took on many of the responsibilities for seeing the boys well and happily settled in. She must have received official approval to accompany her husband because she was paid £1 a week for her work. But knowing how ill he was, I suspect she'd have gone anyway. The house in Wimbledon Park was shut up and they took lodgings, at first over a grocer's shop, and then, from mid-November, at Rose Farm, Longwick. From there she set out, day after day, to visit foster-parents, (occasionally taking with her waterproof sheets for children who wet their beds), attend meetings of the local Women's Institute which had agreed to wash and darn and otherwise repair the children's clothes; and she also found time to write letters to parents requesting items of wear for children who needed them. These weren't always successful. On one occasion my grandfather reports that "the 2 Murtaghs are very under-nourished and Mrs Turner is doing her utmost to feed them well & provide clothing. They come from a very poor home." Some time later, my grandmother writes to the boys' mother, telling her that her sons need new shoes, but though a letter comes by return agreeing to supply them, the new shoes never arrive. Mrs Kelly, therefore, "managed to find a nice pair of shoes for each of the Murtaghs." No need to guess who provided the money.

Later, on Jan. 12th, 1940, "Mrs Kelly visited the foster parents of several boys to-day with regard to clothing needed. She saw Mrs. Walker who will probably be getting a parcel of clothing from the Canadian depot." Later still, she discovers that Ed. Bousfield needs a new pair of trousers and gets Mr. Buxton to take him to Princes Risboro, where a pair are bought for 2/11. Hod reports that "I sent the remainder [of money available] to Mrs. Brown [the foster parent] with instructions to buy Bousfield any other article of clothing he wanted." The two Note Books are full of such reports on what might, I suppose, be called my grandmother's supervisory and pastoral responsibilities, and from them it seems clear that she worked almost as hard as her husband to look after the boys of St. Dunstan's.

Certainly her care and concern for these boys rebuke my habitual memories of her. Until I read these Note Books I thought of her as someone whose mild temper seemed inseparable from a settled feeling that the world was a bewildering place and that the best way to cope with its happenstance was by means of a resigned passivity. After her husband's death, when she was living with us in wartime Burbage, she would go about the village collecting war-bonds. On one occasion she decided to visit the vicar and was no sooner in the vicarage grounds than she was set upon by his bad-tempered gander which answered to the name of Horace. In an attempt to scare the bird off she threw her handbag at it. Horace promptly grabbed the bag by the handle and retired with it to the middle of its pond, where he sat hissing over his booty.

"But you got it back, I see," my mother said, as she and my grandmother sipped tea in our parlour.

"Not quite", my grandmother said. "It was Mr. Pugh [the vicar] who rescued it. But unfortunately by then the bag had come open and," here she lowered her voice, "my spare set of false teeth had fallen out. I mentioned that to the vicar and, do you know, he offered to lend me a set of his own. But I didn't like to accept. Not from a *vicar*."

My grandmother was always keen to uphold her own and the

family's dignity. All praise to her, then, that she worked so hard for children in what must have been by her standards pretty undignified circumstances.

∗ ∗ ∗

By early January, 1940, it seems that most people around my grandfather knew how desperately ill he was, even if he wouldn't or couldn't admit this to himself. He still struggled in to teach and kept his Note Book up to date. But death was coming near. On Sat. 13th Jan, "a very cold & frosty day," he records that "as I have a bad cold have remained indoors all day," a condition which had worsened by the following Monday, when he notes "loss of voice". Nevertheless, he's back at school on the 17th, that day when the temperature barely manages to crawl above freezing point.

But the 17th is his last day in office. The next day, "My voice is gone again so I did not go to school." He is, however, determined to keep in touch. "Mr Baker, foster parent of John Coventry (8) called to see me this evening. He told me his wife had caught John Coventry interfering with his little daughter (6). I reported the matter to Mrs. Walker (billeting officer) who has promised to billet him elsewhere." The day following, "Mrs Kelly saw Mrs. Walker with regard to Coventry." And then, on Sunday 21st, he writes:

> Still freezing & snowing. Mr Buxton took the boys to Sunday School this morning. Have had to have the Dr to-day because of my legs. I am not to attend school at present.
> The Hall is so very cold. The average temperature of a morning is 30. This is undoubtedly where I have caught a chill. No oil stoves have yet been delivered. Mrs Betts who visited the Hall on Jan 10th reported on the temperature & urged the provision of extra heating.

Then comes the last entry of all.

> *Monday Jan 22nd*
> Snowing heavily
> Mrs Kelly has taken my place at school to-day.

* * *

Hod may perhaps have convinced himself that he was suffering from no more than a chill, but his wife knew otherwise. So did the doctor attending him. "We could try moving him to hospital," he told her, "but I don't think he'd stand the journey." For gangrene had now set in. His daughter was sent for. Leaving her two small children at home with her husband, who was still working in Coventry while waiting his call-up papers, she made the difficult journey by train to London, where she arrived at Euston in the black out and had then to find her way to the right platform for a train to Princes Risborough, terrified she'd miss it. When she finally arrived at her destination she was met by a kindly neighbour and driven to Rose Farm. Desperately ill though her father was, he somehow managed to greet her with a pretence of his old genial warmth. She spent hours at his bedside, went exhausted to bed for a few hours' sleep, and returned in the early hours of the morning to his room. There she sat with him for some time before having to start on her return journey. As she prepared to leave he muttered something about the strange coincidence of dying at the same time of year as his father, and when she attempted some conventionally cheerful response, he said, "No, Joano. Like Mr. Peggotty I'm going out with the tide."

He died in the early hours of Tuesday, February 6th, 1940, watched over by his brother Harry, who had come to share nursing responsibilities with my grandmother. The cause of death was given as a) Hyperglycaemic Coma. b) Diabetic Gangrene of Leg.

On Saturday 10th, at the parish church of Princes Risborough, a burial service was held for the man described in one newspaper as "Mr. H.W.S. Kelly, late head master of St. Dunstan's Road J. B. School." A notice torn from another newspaper reports that among "the principal mourners were: The widow, Mr. L.T. Lucas (son-in-law), Mr. H.P. Kelly (brother), and Mr and Mrs. A.J. Reynolds." (The parents of Hod's daughter's dead friend, Hilda.) Other mourners included Mr. John Peters (secretary, Arsenal Football Club) and members of the Exonian Lodge.

A further notice, this one from the *Torquay Times*, informed readers that "Mr. Kelly had been evacuated with his school to Bucks since September last, and had been in indifferent health for some time. He was in his 60th year and was shortly due for retirement." What this doesn't say is that, because of a quite iniquitous rule, my grandmother wasn't entitled to receive her husband's pension. He had died a few months short of his 60th birthday, when the pension was due to mature. Apart from the house at Wimbledon Park, which she was later tricked into selling for a ridiculously low price, she was therefore left with nothing.

Nothing, that is, except the loving warmth of the many letters she received as people came to hear of her husband's death. Among them was one from Dan Maskell, by then a famous tennis player. (He'd later become even more famous as a television commentator on Wimbledon Fortnight.) Maskell had been a pupil at St. Stephen's, and now wrote to tell my grandmother how deeply he revered her husband for his ceaseless care for all his pupils and his inspirational teaching, both in and out of the classroom. (I didn't know of this until recently. Had I been aware of the connection in 1982 I'd have wanted to ask Maskell what he recalled of my grandfather, for in that year he came to Loughborough University, where I was then Professor of English, to receive an honorary MA.)

There were many other such letters, but the most poignant of all was written to Hod's daughter by his sister, Polly, recovering from illness, but, as she said, testifying to one of life's ironies, in that "I, eighteen years older, should be spared, while your dear father, who loved life so, should be dead." "*Time*," she goes on, underlining the word, "is the only healer. I have discovered that by my own experience. When I lost our darling Frank I thought I should never smile again & for years felt always sad & miserable at heart – but time has softened the grief." There are other consolations, including "the devotion of the villagers some of whom walked two miles [to the burial service] who had got to know and care for him, the lovely letters your mother had from so many villagers and friends .... Better to leave this world loved and respected than for no one to care." There is no doubt, she adds, "that Horace had a wonderful gift of attraction for 'all sorts and conditions' & could make himself at home & the centre of any company he liked – with his clever gift of repartee; & his wonderful *courage* & self-control for so many years when he suffered so much & was debarred from the recreations he loved most (walking & getting about seeing folk etc.) make me feel of him as a hero." Even taking into account the partiality of a sister, and the occasion of the letter, this rings true.

* * *

I began writing this book in an attempt to find out as much as I could about the man whose glance evades the camera in that carefully-posed photograph of the Old Exonian Cricket Club taken in the summer of 1907. The last photograph I have of my grandfather comes from summer, 1939. Hod, this time taken unawares, is sitting in a garden deck-chair, his now virtually bald head bent over a colander gripped between his knees as he shells peas or beans into it. Beside him is another deck-chair on which he has thrown his sports coat so that, what with his braces and open-neck short-sleeved white shirt, the scene is one of unstudied casualness, of a held contentment. In the sunlight on this garden there is no shadow of war or death, though neither is far off. "Look up", I want to say to him, "let me *see* you." But he's concentrating on the work in front of him.

Bibliography

This isn't a scholarly book and I don't therefore propose to provide a detailed bibliographical account of all the works I consulted in the writing of it. The list that follows is, however, intended to help anyone who may wish to track down any of the books mentioned in the text.

Ian Beckett & Keith Simpson (eds), *A Nation in Arms: A Social History of the British Army in the First World War*, Manchester University Press, 1985; Arnold Bennett, *The Journals*, Vol. II, (1911-1921), Cassell, 1932; Arnold Bennett, *The Pretty Lady*, Cassell, 1918; James Bishop, *The Illustrated London News Social History of Edwardian Britain*, Angus & Robertson, 1977; Julia Briggs, *A Woman of Passion: The Life of E. Nesbit, 1858-1924*, Penguin, 1989; Allan Bullock, *Ernest Bevin*, Vol. 1 (of 2), Heinemann, 1960; Erskine Childers, *The Riddle of the Sands*, Penguin, 1975 (the novel was first published in 1903); Robert Clarke, *Hope and Glory: Britain 1900-1990*, Allen Lane 1996; David Crouch and Colin Ward, *The Allotment; Its Landscape and Culture*, Five Leaves Publications, 1996; George Dangerfield, *The Strange Death of Liberal England, 1910-1914*, Capricorn Books, 1961 (originally published by Constable in 1935); John H. Drew, *Kenilworth, A Manor of the King*, Malcolm Peters, 1971; T. Elliott-Binns, *English Thought, 1860-1900: The Theological Aspect*, Longmans, 1956; Ian Fletcher, *W.B. Yeats and His Contemporaries*, Harvester, 1987; Michael Freeman, *Railways and the Victorian Imagination*, Yale University Press, 1999; Frederick Fuller, *The History of St. Luke's College, Exeter*, 4 vols, 1970, bound, unpublished, and in possession of the chaplain at Exeter University; Robert Graves and Alan Hodge, *The Long Weekend: A Social History of Great Britain 1918-1939*, Faber, 1941; Mary Greensted, *Arts and*

Crafts in the Cotswolds, Sutton, 1993; Margot Heinemann & Noreen Branson, *Britain in the 1930s*, Weidenfeld & Nicolson, 1971; James Hepburn, *The Letters of Arnold Bennett*, vol IV, "Family Letters", Oxford, 1986; O.S. Knock, *The Railway Enthusiast's Encyclopaedia*, Hutchinson, 1968; John Lucas, *The Radical Twenties*, Five Leaves Publications, 1997 or Rutgers University Press, 1999; Helen Merrell Lynd, *England in the Eighteen-Eighties*, Frank Cass, 1968; Arthur Marwick, *The Deluge: British Society and the First World War*, Penguin, 1967; Arthur Marwick, *Women at War, 1914-18*, Fontana, 1977; C.L. Mowat, *Britain Between the Wars, 1918-1940*, Methuen, 1956; J. B. Priestley, *The Edwardians*, Heinemann, 1970; Prince Ranjitsinhji, *The Jubilee Book of Cricket*, Blackwoods, 1897; Donald Read, *Documents From Edwardian England*, Harrap, 1973; Donald Read, *Edwardian England: 1901-1915: Society and Politics*, Harrap, 1972; Donald Read, *England 1868-1914*, Longman, 1979; Harold Rosen, *Are You Still Circumcised?: East End Memories*, Five Leaves Publications, 2000; David Rubenstein, *Before the Suffragettes: Women's Emancipation in the 1890s*, Harvester Press, 1986; R. H. Tawney, *The Acquisitive Society*, Fontana, 1961, (first published 1921); R. H. Tawney, *The Radical Tradition*, Penguin, 1966; Paul Thompson, *The Edwardians: The Remaking of British Society*, Paladin, 1975; Cecil Torr, *Small Talk at Wreyland*, Forest Publishings, 1996, (first published in 3 vols. by Cambridge University Press, between 1918 and 1923); J. T. White, *The History of Torquay*, The "Directory" Offices, Torquay, 1878; Marion Yass, *This is Your War: Home Front Propaganda in the Second World War*, (Public Record Office) H. M. O. 1983.

Acknowledgements

Several people have helped me in the writing of this book. They include Barry Cole, who at my request made more than one visit to the Registry of Births, Marriages and Deaths, John H. Drew, the historian of Kenilworth, Tony Elwell, from whom I learned about headteachers' Log Books and who gave me other insights into the history of elementary schools, Mervyn Gould, who shared with me his unrivalled knowledge of the history of Music Hall, Judy Haynes, whose mental computing system allowed her to discover the date for Easter Sunday, 1905, Ben Lucas, who provided information about the outcomes of pre-great War elections for parliament in the Fulham area, and Matt Simpson, who read and valuably commented on draft chapters of the work in progress. The chief source of information for the book was, of course, my mother, *sine qua non*.

Staff at the Metropolitan Archive were invariably helpful, as were those at the newspaper archives of the British Library, Colindale, and at the *Tatler* library.

Last but not least, Carmen Glover typed the manuscript, made valiant and often successful attempts to decipher my handwriting, and came up with a number of excellent suggestions for the book's title.

To all, my grateful thanks.

GREENWICH EXCHANGE BOOKS

Student Guides

Greenwich Exchange Student Guides are critical studies of major or contemporary serious writers in English and selected European languages. The series is for the Student, the Teacher and the 'common reader' and are ideal resources for libraries. The *Times Educational Supplement (TES)* praised these books saying "The style of these guides has a pressure of meaning behind it. Students should learn from that... If art is about selection, perception and taste, then this is it."

(ISBN prefix 1-871551- applies)
The series includes:
W. H. Auden by Stephen Wade (-36-6)
William Blake by Peter Davies (-27-7)
The Brontës by Peter Davies (-24-2)
Joseph Conrad by Martin Seymour-Smith (-18-8)
William Cowper by Michael Thorn (-25-0)
Charles Dickens by Robert Giddings (-26-9)
John Donne by Sean Haldane (-23-4)
Thomas Hardy by Sean Haldane (-35-1)
Seamus Heaney by Warren Hope (-37-8)
Philip Larkin by Warren Hope (-35-8)
Tobias Smollett by Robert Giddings (-21-8)
Alfred Lord Tennyson by Michael Thorn (-20-X)
Wordsworth by Andrew Keanie (57-9)

OTHER GREENWICH EXCHANGE BOOKS

All paperbacks unless otherwise stated.

LITERATURE & BIOGRAPHY

Shakespeare's Non-Dramatic Poetry *by Martin Seymour-Smith*
In this study, completed shortly before his death in 1998, Martin Seymour-Smith sheds fresh light on two very different groups of Shakespeare's non-dramatic poems: the early and conventional *Venus and Adonis* and *The Rape of Lucrece*, and the highly personal *Sonnets*. He explains the genesis of the first two in the genre of Ovidian narrative poetry in which a young Elizabethan man of letters was expected to excel, and which was highly popular. In the *Sonnets* (his 1963 old-spelling edition of which is being reissued by Greenwich Exchange) he traces the mental journey of a man going through an acute psychological crisis as he faces up to the truth about his own unconventional sexuality.
It is a study which confronts those "disagreeables" in the *Sonnets* which most critics have ignored.
ISBN 1-871551-22-6; A5 size; 90pp

The Author, the Book & the Reader *by Robert Giddings*
This collection of Essays analyses the effects of changing technology and the attendant commercial pressures on literary styles and subject matter. Authors covered include Dickens; Smollett; Mark Twain; Dr Johnson; John Le Carré.
ISBN 1-871551-01-0; A5 size; 220pp; illus.

In Pursuit of Lewis Carroll *by Raphael Shaberman*
Sherlock Holmes and the author uncover new evidence in their investigations into the mysterious life and writing of Lewis Carroll. They examine published works by Carroll that have been overlooked by previous commentators. A newly discovered poem, almost certainly by Carroll, is published here. Amongst many aspects of Carroll's highly complex personality, this book explores his relationship with his parents, numerous child friends, and the formidable Mrs Liddell, mother of the immortal Alice.
ISBN 1-871551-13-7; 70% A4 size; 130pp; illus.

Norman Cameron *by Warren Hope*
Cameron's poetry was admired by Auden; celebrated by Dylan Thomas; valued by Robert Graves. He was described by Martin Seymour-Smith as one of "... the most rewarding and pure poets of his generation..." and is at last given a full length biography. This eminently sociable man, who had periods of darkness and despair, wrote little poetry by comparison with others of his time, but always of a high and consistent quality - imaginative and profound.
ISBN 1-871551-05-6; A5 size; 250pp; illus.

Liar! Liar!': Jack Kerouac–Novelist *by R. J. Ellis*
The fullest study of Jack Kerouac's fiction to date. It is the first book to devote an individual chapter to each and every one of his novels. *On the Road, Visions of Cody* and *The Subterraneans*, Kerouac's central masterpieces, are re-read in-depth, in a new and exciting way. The books Kerouac himself saw as major elements of his spontaneous 'bop' odyssey, *Visions of Gerard* and *Doctor Sax*, are also strikingly reinterpreted, as are other, daringly innovative writings, like 'The Railroad Earth' and his 'try at a spontaneous *Finnegans Wake*', *Old Angel Midnight*. Undeservedly neglected writings, such as *Tristessa* and *Big Sur*, are also analysed, alongside better known novels like *Dharma Bums* and *Desolation Angels*. *Liar! Liar!* takes its title for the words of *Tristessa's* narrator, Jack, referring to himself. He also warns us 'I guess, I'm a liar, watch out!'. R. J. Ellis' study provocatively proposes that we need to take this warning seriously and, rather than reading Kerouac's novels simply as fictional versions of his life, focus just as much on the way the novels stand as variations on a series of ambiguously-represented themes: explorations of class, sexual identity, the French-Canadian Catholic confessional, and

addiction in its hydra-headed modern forms. Ellis shows how Kerouac's deep anxieties in each of these arenas makes him an incisive commentator on his uncertain times and a bitingly honest self-critic, constantly attacking his narrators' 'vanities'.

R. J. Ellis is Professor of English and American Studies at the Nottingham Trent University. His commentaries on Beat writing have been frequently published, and his most recent book, a full modern edition of Harriet Wilson's *Our Nig*, the first ever novel by an African American woman, has been widely acclaimed.
ISBN 1-871551-53-6; A5 size; 300pp

PHILOSOPHY

Marx: Justice and Dialectic *by James Daly*
Department of Scholastic Philosophy, Queen's University, Belfast.
James Daly shows the humane basis of Marx's thinking, rather than the imposed "economic materialistic" views of many modem commentators. In particular he refutes the notion that for Marx, justice relates simply to the state of development of society at a particular time. Marx's views about justice and human relationships belong to the continuing traditions of moral thought in Europe.
ISBN 1-871551-28-5; A5 size; 180 pp

Questions of Platonism *by Ian Leask*
In a daring challenge to contemporary orthodoxy, Ian Leask subverts both Hegel and Heidegger by arguing for a radical re-evaluation of Platonism. Thus, while he traces a profoundly Platonic continuity between ancient Athens and 19th century Germany, the nature of this Platonism, he suggests, is neither 'totalizing' nor Hegelian but, instead, open-ended 'incomplete' and oriented towards a divine goal beyond *logos* or any metaphysical structure. Such a re-evaluation exposes the deep anti-Platonism of Hegel's absolutizing of volitional subjectivity; it also confirms Schelling as true modern heir to the 'constitutive incompletion' of Plato and Plotinus. By providing a more nuanced approach - refusing to accept either Hegel's self-serving account of 'Platonism' or the (equally totalizing) post-Heideggerian inversion of this narrative – Leask demonstrates the continued relevance of a genuine, 'finite' Platonic quest. Ian Leask teaches in the Department of Scholastic Philosophy at the Queen's University of Belfast.
ISBN 1-871551-32-3; A5 size; 154pp

The Philosophy of Whitehead *by T. E. Burke*
Department of Philosophy, University of Reading
Dr Burke explores the main achievements of this philosopher, better known in the US than Britain. Whitehead, often remembered as Russell's tutor and collaborator on *Principia Mathematica*, was one of the few who had a grasp of relativity and its possible implications. His philosophical

writings reflect his profound knowledge of mathematics and science. He was responsible for initiating process theology.
ISBN 1-871551-29-3; A5 size; 106pp

POETRY

Lines from the Stone Age *by Sean Haldane*
Reviewing Sean Haldane's 1992 volume *Desire in Belfast* Robert Nye wrote in The *Times* that 'Haldane can be sure of his place among the English poets.' The facts that his early volumes appeared in Canada and that he has earned his living by other means than literature have meant that this place is not yet a conspicuous one, although his poems have always had their circle of readers. The 60 previously unpublished poems of *Lines from the Stone Age* – 'lines of longing, terror, pride, lust and pain' – may widen this circle.
ISBN 1-871551-39-0; A5 size; 58pp

Wilderness *by Martin Seymour-Smith*
This is Seymour-Smith's first publication of his poetry for more than 20 years. This collection of 36 poems is a fearless account of an inner life of love, frustration, guilt, laughter and the celebration of others. Best known to the general public as the author of the controversial and best selling *Hardy* (1994).
ISBN 1-871551-08-0; A5 size; 64pp

Baudelaire: Les Fleurs du Mal in English Verse *translated by F. W. Leakey*
Selected poems from *Les Fleurs du Mal* are translated with parallel French texts, are designed to be read with pleasure by readers who have no French, as well as those practised in the French language.
F. W. Leakey is Emeritus Professor of French in the University of London. As a scholar, critic and teacher he has specialised in the work of Baudelaire for 50 years. He has published a number of books on Baudelaire.
ISBN 1-871551-10-2; A5 size; 140pp

FICTION

The Case of the Scarlet Woman - Sherlock Holmes and the Occult *by Watkin Jones*
A haunted house, a mysterious kidnapping and a poet's demonic visions are just the beginnings of three connected cases that lead Sherlock Holmes into confrontation with the infamous black magician Aleister Crowley and, more sinisterly, his scorned Scarlet Woman.
The fact that Dr Watson did not publish details of these investigations is perhaps testament to the unspoken fear he and Holmes harboured for the supernatural. *The Case of the Scarlet Woman* convinced them both that some things cannot be explained by cold logic.
ISBN 1-871551-14-5; A5 size; 130pp

THEATRE

Music Hall Warriors: A history of the Variety Artistes Federation *by Peter Honri*

This is an unique and fascinating history of how vaudeville artistes formed the first effective actor's trade union in 1906 and then battled with the powerful owners of music halls to obtain fairer contracts. The story continues with the VAF dealing with performing rights, radio, and the advent of television. Peter Honri is the fourth generation of a vaudeville family. The book has a foreword by the Right Honourable John Major MP when he was Prime Minister – his father was a founder member of the VAF.

ISBN 1-871551-06-4; A4 size; 140pp; illus.

MISCELLANEOUS

Musical Offering *by Yolanthe Leigh*

In a series of vivid sketches, anecdotes and reflections, Yolanthe Leigh tells the story of her growing up in the Poland of the nineteen thirties and the second world war. These are poignant episodes of a child's first encounters with both the enchantments and the cruelties of the world; and from a later time, stark memories of the brutality of the Nazi invasion, and the hardships of student life in Warsaw under the Occupation. But most of all this is a record of inward development; passages of remarkable intensity and simplicity describe the girl's response to religion, to music, and to her discovery of philosophy.

The outcome is something unique, a book that eludes classification. In its own distinctive fashion, it creates a memorable picture of a highly perceptive and sensitive individual, set against a background of national tragedy.

ISBN 1-871551-46-3; A5 size 61pp